SPOKANE

HEE

MOSES LAKE

PULLMAN

YAKIMA

RICHLAND PASCO
KENNEWICK

WALLA WALLA

Dec 18, 1978

To Mr. Shea —

Hope you enjoy
this history of the
Tri-Cities and the Tri-City
Herald.

Love,
Zelma

FRANCES TAYLOR PUGNETTI

"TIGER BY THE TAIL"

TWENTY-FIVE YEARS WITH
THE STORMY TRI-CITY HERALD

TRI-CITY HERALD
PASCO, WASHINGTON 99302
1975

To Brian, Jerry, Gene,
Mary Dawn and Lester

CONTENTS

ACKNOWLEDGEMENTS

This being my first venture into the field of literature, I would like to mention the people who assisted me along the way. I would like to express my gratitude to Paul W. Harvey, retired news editor of the *Tacoma News Tribune* and author of the book *"Tacoma Headlines,"* who took out his copy editor's pencil and carefully went through the book offering suggestions he thought I could use. There is also the late Federal Court Judge Charles Powell, who took time away from his court to take me to lunch and grant me an interview. Likewise, there is Hugh Scott, who drew on his memory of interesting little sidelights for me.

A word of thanks to Hugh Horton, Kennewick attorney, who opened his law library to me, helped me select the needed material and gave me a desk in his office on which to do my research; also to Bill Bequette, present editor of *The Herald*, for his critique in the early stages of the manuscript.

I appreciate the help of Sam Volpentest, executive secretary of the Tri-City Nuclear Industrial Council, for the use of his files, and to Mrs. Neil (Mary) Bryant for her help in typing some of the chapters. Thanks to the Mid-Columbia Library for sending to Olympia for some needed micro-film, and to Mrs. Bob (Marty) Bell, one of the World War II residents of Richland who put me in touch with the right people for information of that period.

Finally, and with special thanks, to John D. McCallum, a successful author, who took so much time from his busy schedule to assist me, because as he said, he received like assistance from veteran writers when he began his career.

THE AUTHOR

A WORD FROM EDWARD P. MORGAN

"Most of the problems besieging the United States are so big and complicated that they boggle the imagination of the average citizen and wilt his will to try to understand them. There is double trouble in such a state of mind. It not only discourages meaningful communication between Washington and the public on urgent international issues, it discourages public action on important matters at lower levels and spreads the blight of irresponsibility typified by that well-known reaction, 'Oh, what's the use?'

"Happily, an inspiring exception to that attitude comes along now and then to remind us that there really isn't much percentage to defeatism on any level. One such inspiration was given due recognition here in Washington today when Donald A. Pugnetti, managing editor of the Tri-City Herald *in the Tri-Cities, Washington, received the 1962 Stokes Award of $500 for reportorial journalistic enterprise in the conservation of energy and natural resources, a field in which Stokes excelled. What Pugnetti and his public-spirited publisher Glenn C. Lee did was to wage a long, relentless, relatively lonely but ultimately triumphant campaign to reverse an act of Congress that would have utterly wasted steam as a by-product from a new plutonium plant the Atomic Energy Commission is having built at its huge facility at Hanford, Washington, a few miles up the Columbia River from the Tri-Cities.*

"Far from being an added burden to the taxpayers, the project was to capitalize on energy that would otherwise

ix

go to waste—the conversion of which Congress had already invested $25,000,000 in—and not even to the detriment of private power companies who were to be allowed to purchase half the electricity themselves. Nor was the Federal Government to be out of pocket for construction of the generating plant. This 16 Washington State public utility districts had volunteered to do—financing it with a multi-million dollar bond issue. Finally, despite the continued strenuous efforts of big private power interests, including those in the Northwest which had denied they were working against it, the project won when the House reversed itself in September, 1962. Hopefully by the time the plutonium reactor is ready in 1965, the steam generating plant will be ready to produce electricity.

"In accepting the Stokes award today, Donald Pugnetti conceded the modest size of the Tri-City Herald, *but observed that the experience had taught him that in this land of ours, any voice, no matter how small, when raised for a righteous cause can eventually be heard.*

"This is Edward P. Morgan saying good night from Washington."

Edward P. Morgan
ABC Radio Network
Washington, D.C.
April 22, 1963

THE INSIDE STORY

It was my husband, Don, on the phone. "How," he asked, "would you like to live in Pasco?"

"PASCO!" I exclaimed.

"Yes," he said, calmly. "Over in Southeastern Washington."

The question stunned me. There was a pause. I mean, were you ever in *Pasco* 27 years ago?

"But why Pasco?" I said, finally.

"I've been offered a job."

"What kind of job?"

"Managing Editor of a new daily. The *Tri-City Herald.*"

"Oh, boy!" I said. "At what salary?"

Already I pictured castles in the sky. Even back in 1947, newspaper editors could command fairly substantial salaries.

"You're getting a big raise?"

"Well, no," he said reluctantly, "not exactly."

"Well, what?" I said.

"I think I'd better come home and we'll talk about it," the father of my four-month old son said.

That night, at the dinner table, Don told me the story. We were living in a small apartment on Seattle's Harvard north. Don had been working as a Public Relations man for the Seattle Chamber of Commerce. Even though he seldom talked about it, I knew he had been itching to return to newspaper work.

"I had lunch with Glenn Lee and Bob Philip today," he said. "They are joining forces with Hugh Scott to turn the

Pasco Herald into the *Tri-City Herald.* They need a managing editor. They want me. Starting salary is $90 a week. I asked for $100. They said they couldn't go that high."

Don looked at me, searching my face for reaction. He was making more than that in Seattle.

"Well," he said, "what do you think?"

"What did you tell them?" I wanted to know.

"I told them I wanted to first talk to you. I'm to let them know tomorrow. If you want to stay in Seattle, we'll stay."

"You are a newspaper man and not a P. R. man," I said. "I don't think you'll ever be happy spending a lifetime with the Chamber. I want you to be happy. I can adjust and make friends no matter where we live. So you'll have to make the decision."

I said it in such a way that he knew I would support his ultimate decision.

The next morning, Don phoned the *Pasco Herald* to talk to Hugh Scott. Glenn Lee was in the office at the time.

"Hugh," Don told him, "I've made my decision and I'm going to throw in with you."

Glenn then got on the phone.

"You won't be sorry," he told Don. "I like a man who can make quick decisions. We're going to build a real newspaper over here."

As Don hung up the receiver, he looked across at me and grinned. "Well, honey," he said, "a guy could lose his shirt on a proposition like this. So I'll leave a couple of fresh shirts at Mother's."

And that is how Don and I were transplanted to Southeastern Washington, on the banks of the Columbia River, and became a part of the three thriving communities of Pasco, Kennewick and Richland.

There we stayed for over a quarter of a century where our lives together became entwined with that of the fledgling newspaper which emerged that many years later as one of the finest non-metropolitan dailies published in the Northwest today.

This is the story as I remember it of the struggle of this daily to accomplish its objectives and become the newspaper it is today.

Most newspapers would have been satisfied to record history as it passed by—but the *Tri-City Herald* is unique in the fact it actually was responsible for making history. With its publisher, Glenn Clifford Lee as its ramrod, *The Herald* cut a swath through the years which followed 1947, overcoming numerous obstacles that would have buried a lesser paper with a weaker man at the helm.

The Herald, in the early days when it was newly established and under-financed, was forced to take on as its opponent, the powerful and wealthy International Typographical Union. It was a long, bitter struggle which lasted many years and plunged *The Herald* into a debt it took many years to repay.

The first round of the battle was won by the union when the presiding judge chose to side with it. But in the end, *The Herald* did win. The opposing newspaper, using the union as a tool for the purpose of chasing *The Herald* out of business and taking over the Tri-City market, closed its doors and quietly disappeared into the pages of history.

This is also the story of the people as I knew them who gave so much of themselves to make *The Herald* a paper they could be proud of.

Some of these people who were there in the very early days are still there today; others have come and gone, leaving so little of themselves that their presence is dimly remembered. Then there are those who loyally struggled and gave their staunch support for years before circumstances took them from the scene—as in the case of Jack Gillis and Mrs. Hill (Ursula) Williams who died before they could see *The Herald* reach its silver anniversary. But their contributions had a lasting effect and they are warmly remembered by those who followed *The Herald's* progress.

Those dedicated employes who came and stayed while *The Herald* rocked on the edge of disaster—not for the high salary as there couldn't be such a thing in those days, but as *The Herald's* first mechanical superintendent, Verne Husk, put it: "No salary would be large enough to induce me to take on that kind of a job. I did it because I wanted to be part of building a newspaper from scratch and that is what we did."

He and others spent sleepless nights, all caught up in a fever of being a part of something really worthwhile which at times was being assaulted from all sides—following the lead of the publisher who meant to succeed no matter what the odds.

This, then, is their story.

1   *Birth of A Newspaper*

REALLY, when you first view the Tri-Cities area of
Washington State, far off, it seems, in a remote corner of
the state, there doesn't seem to be much to recommend it.
Well, maybe as a place for a visit, but hardly as a place
to live.

I know the feeling for I have experienced it myself,
although not to the degree of my husband, Don, when we
first arrived in 1947. I happened to have had the advantage
of attending college in Pullman, Washington, about 100
miles away in the great Palouse wheat country. But Don
really knew nothing but Western Washington, with its
greenness, tall firs and, of course, the heavy rainfall that
keeps the country green and placid.

Benton and Franklin Counties, however, the home counties of the three communities, Pasco, Kennewick and Richland which make up the Tri-Cities, are arid, dry, dusty
and hot in the summer and cold in the winter. They are as
unlike Western Washington as nature could make them.
However, as the thousands of people who came to the
giant Hanford atomic facilities in World War II to make
plutonium for our nuclear weapons discovered, there is a
strange and wonderful fascination to the region, one that
can "hook" you for a lifetime.

Some people refer to the Tri-Cities as "desert country"
and it is certainly that, although you must quickly
acknowledge it is strange desert country because the mighty
Columbia River cuts right through the middle of it and the
Snake and Yakima Rivers empty into the Columbia just a

few miles from the heart of Pasco. What "desert" can claim three mighty rivers, brimming with water and the subjects of longing looks from the Southwest United States and California?

Midwesterners sometimes compare the climate with their home states but they soon discover there is no humidity with Tri-City heat and regardless of the temperature of the day, the nights are cool.

Don and I had arrived in the Tri-Cities—and that was a term virtually nobody knew in 1947—to help start a daily newspaper that would circulate in the two counties and three cities. The target date was November 13, so we had two weeks to prepare for the first edition.

If the country didn't excite us the thought of helping to create a daily newspaper did. "Anybody can work for a daily newspaper, but how many guys get to start one," Don often said, and I have always thought that is a good way to view things.

But if the Tri-Cities would support a brand new daily newspaper, something it didn't have but said it wanted, then why would the established publishers who surrounded the region and circulated their papers in the Tri-Cities, not have started one themselves? We had our own reasons for thinking we knew but now with the benefit of hindsight we were quite wrong. Dr. Robert Hutchins, the educator, has said that the trouble with experience is that it tells you what can't be done and supplies you with the reasons.

Those who started the *Tri-City Herald* acquired their experience on the job and by the time they had learned where the pitfalls to their proposition were they had, as Publisher Glenn C. Lee likes to say, "a tiger by the tail," and they didn't dare let go.

But what a wild, exhilerating ride it proved to be!

There are some marked similarities between the Tri-City region then and now, chiefly because the area was in the midst of a building boom then in which the Atomic Energy Commission was doubling the size of the Hanford plant.

Today it is Hanford again, plus agriculture, that is

2

growing and expanding and which has once more placed housing in short supply. There are differences to the two booms of course and I shall point them out for the differences are quite significant. But in 1947 the communities, particularly Pasco and Kennewick, were ill-prepared for any large expansion and their modest water and sewerage facilities were sorely overtaxed or, in Kennewick's case, it would be better described as almost hopelessly overtaxed.

People lived in tents, their cars, or rented garages. If someone said he was living in a chicken-coop very likely that is exactly what he meant. Pasco and Kennewick each had a hotel—although Kennewick's burned a few months later—but these too were of modest size and a guest's stay was limited to three days. Likewise, the few eating establishments did business of land slide proportions and lines would form extending far down the street.

World War II had caused the nation to concentrate on total war. When the war ended and the time to manufacture civilian goods was at hand industry was sorely taxed to try to fill the shelves. A severe housing shortage existed throughout the nation but American know-how in coping with it was effectively hampered by material shortages.

This situation was illustrated in the Tri-Cities. Builders had a market for whatever they could build and financing for housing projects was no problem. But construction progress went in spurts—maybe the builder would be stopped by his inability to get roofing materials, or windows, or plumbing supplies.

Don and I were fortunate because we were able to rent an upstairs room in a private residence and meet a contractor who was starting four homes nearby. The houses were only in the foundation stage but two of them had been already sold. We purchased the third after viewing a hand-drawn floor plan the contractor's wife had made.

Things were different in Richland from the standpoint that Uncle Sam was calling the shots and Hanford was still a vital government project essential to the warming Cold

War of that period. Richland was a company town, supported by the government and its population was restricted to persons either working at or in connection with Hanford. The World War II flavor persisted and security and secrecy were rigidly enforced. General Electric company was the prime contractor at Hanford under the Atomic Energy Commission. Our new newspaper would soon run headlong into what we would label the AEC-GE combine.

Hundreds of new homes were being built in Richland to house key personnel. Pasco and Kennewick on the other hand were bulging from the constant influx of people drawn to the construction jobs like moths to a porch light. The Portland *Oregonian* spelled it out very well in an editorial titled "Pasco and Kennewick Take The Rap." Said the *Oregonian:*

"Many a Western city has been left by the government to struggle with its housing, sanitation and employment problems after closing war plants and the disinclination of workers to return to their old homes. But the cities of Pasco and Kennewick in Southeastern Washington have a tougher row to hoe.

"The Atomic Energy Commission has revived operations at Richland, North Richland and Hanford, nearby war-boom cities, on a wartime scale. But the government has made no provisions for the tremendous overflow of population in Pasco and Kennewick, where housing and sanitation conditions have become the worst in the nation.

"As the *Pasco Herald* points out, editorially, the government must be made to accept its responsibility and provide emergency housing, sanitation facilities and hospital rooms throughout the area if the Hanford project, which continues on a war footing, is not to be adversely affected and the health of all citizens be threatened . . ."

Perhaps one of the best ways to illustrate the size of the problem is by relating to the comparative sizes of the communities. Richland had a 1940 population of 327. In 1947, the population was around 25,000. The 1940 census shows Kennewick with 1,918 residents. Seven years later the state census estimate was 15,000. Pasco, in the past, was the first and largest of the communities until the Atomic Energy Commission came in and rebuilt Richland. It is the county seat for Franklin County and one of the main yards on the Northern Pacific Railway (Burlington Northern) which had established the town in 1885. Pasco had a 1940 census of 3,913 and the population exceeded 16,000 in 1947.

For one living in the Tri-Cities during this and the following period, the region seemed to be involved in a series of economic booms and busts. The area, of course, was booming in the heyday years of 1947, 1948 and part of 1949. Then, beginning in the late fall of 1949, one of the meanest winters on record hit and with it a mass layoff of thousands which occurred almost overnight. It was a tragic, hectic time when the bottom literally fell out because the Atomic Energy Commission had overspent its budget.

Yet, in a manner of speaking, even the "good" year of 1948 which was wedged between the other two "boom" years was a hectic one because of the second worst flood in the recorded history of the Columbia River. This was the flood that crippled Eastern Washington, wiped out the community of Vanport near Portland, Oregon, and almost succeeded in drowning our six-month-old daily newspaper that had such a lusty birth in November, 1947.

The flood waters didn't reach the new *Tri-City Herald*. As a matter of fact they provided a lot of copy for its pages. But the economic effects of the flood were devastating as business came to a standstill, paralyzed from the enforced isolation of the three communities, each one cut off from the other except by boat, a risky way to travel, or by train, which linked Pasco and Kennewick but not Richland.

And the 1950's? Well, they began quite ominously when the *Herald's* printers and pressmen went on strike on March 3, 1950. As if that wasn't shock enough, within days they were all employed on a brand new morning newspaper, *The Columbia Basin News*, which began an immediate race to take over the territory from the *Tri-City Herald*.

"I stay around," Don told one of our Western Washington friends who had asked the question, "because I want to see what the hell can happen next."

And Publisher Lee gave each of his embattled people a little inexpensive lapel pin, on the head of which was a tiny mustard seed which was to remind them of the biblical quotation that "If ye have faith, as a grain of mustard seed, nothing will be impossible to you."*

It required a lot of faith, of course, but mostly it required long hours of hard work to keep the newspaper afloat, alert and on top of the news. Those who cut their newspaper teeth in the heat of that fierce competition were fully aware that the paper that stumbled was the paper that would die for the area could only support one. These people emerged far better newspapermen by the campaigning.

Yet the strike and the union-subsidized opposition was only one part of the equation. Another was the Atomic Energy Commission and General Electric company—AEC-GE as *The Herald* referred to them—who didn't like the free-wheeling ways of the *Tri-City Herald*, its fierce independence and its suspicion of their giant bureaucracy. They preferred earlier days with three weeklies, one in each community, each minding its own business and accepting without question the news "handouts" mailed or delivered to them. They particularly favored the weekly *Richland Villager*, a non-profit, non-taxpaying newspaper published by General Electric employes who were under their control in their well-patrolled company town.

The area was ripe for investigative reporting and that

*Matthew 17:20

The Herald plant on Fourth street in Pasco where it all began. From the weekly *Pasco Herald*, the *Tri-City Herald* emerged into a daily newspaper November 13, 1947.

The *Tri-City Herald* plant on the corner of Cascade street and Canal Drive in Kennewick, 1973.

was *The Herald's* long suit. But the aftermath of many of the investigations was a sequence of libel suits that placed new and quite ominous libel law on the state statute books. It also taxed the limited financial resources of the young newspaper and made it and its young executives almost persons non grata at newspaper meetings for many years. Eventually, the United States Supreme Court ruling in the celebrated *New York Times* case of the mid-1960's would bring some balance to the law and give newspapers a fighting chance when they undertook to defend themselves. But the libel laws of the 1950s not only ensnarled the *Tri-City Herald* but almost pulled it under financially.

More celebrated by far, however, was the spirited, lonely and legal pursuit of the International Typographical Union by Publisher Lee, his unmasking of that union and his arduous task of bringing it to trial in U.S. District Court on charges of violating the nation's anti-trust laws. It was an investigation that took six years, sent him around the United States running down evidence and witnesses, required him to spend months away from home and caused him to compile an array of testimony and evidence that was staggering.

In short, then, the Tri-Cities — "Sagebrush Flats" as Don affectionately terms it — was a very unusual community, each city separate and distinct and yet each bound to the other with a tight unity of purpose. And their newspaper, the *Tri-City Herald* is a most unusual paper which at times became as much a part of the news as the events it covered.

Yet the growth of the Tri-Cities and the *Tri-City Herald* are so closely entwined because they started together almost immediately after World War II. The decision to reactivate the Hanford plant and to double its size touched off a great building boom. It also projected Hanford and its geographical region into the limelight and held it there. But the region's great nuclear project almost became its tombstone in the 1960s when the decision was made to close its giant plutonium reactors and to lock up the huge reservation.

It was then that the *Tri-City Herald* came to the front and provided the leadership for the amazing turnaround that proved a "pilot plant" for other communities throughout the United States who were dependent upon federal payrolls. It gained the Tri-Cities national recognition and caused Richland to be dubbed in national publications as "The City That Wouldn't Die."

An entire new era was opened and private enterprise replaced or supplemented government enterprise at Hanford.

Meanwhile the long-awaited breakthrough of agriculture also occurred. Formerly parched land, suitable chiefly for sheep grazing or for growing sagebrush and Russian Thistle —Washington State's brand of tumbleweed—became rich, fertile farmland as the latest techniques of irrigation farming were applied.

Agriculture, of course, was not new to the Tri-Cities and the giant Mid-Columbia Empire that surrounds it. The first farmland of the Columbia Basin Project to be undertaken by the Bureau of Reclamation was 4,200 acres opened to settlement in 1948 a few miles north of Pasco. But it took from 10 to 15 years for the "green" of the Basin to extend south to the borders of Pasco. Then it stopped amid criticism of having caused farm crop surpluses, and because its farmers were driven from the land by uneconomical prices for their crops.

Here again the *Tri-City Herald* and Publisher Lee were key instruments in defeating an attempt to limit the amount of land to 160 acres that any single farmer could irrigate. Had this administrative order by the U.S. Department of Interior prevailed the massive private irrigation projects that have sprung up in the last few years would never have been. The land would have been effectively locked into the vise of government edict and government red tape would have tied a knot on it. Agriculturally speaking, little or nothing probably would have happened. And that truly would have been an American tragedy, when one views what has and is taking place in this portion of Washington and across the Columbia River in Northeast Oregon.

Thus the uniqueness of the region is emphasized by the fact its surging growth is based on two vastly different and virtually unrelated fields—nucleonics and agriculture. Yet, strangely enough, both of these were attracted to the region for the same reasons—an abundance of isolated land and an abundance of fresh water. And both have thrived because of these resources.

Likewise, the *Tri-City Herald* has thrived and the theory of Publisher Lee is a simple but perfectly logical one—be sure the area thrives, for when it moves ahead we'll grow with it. The late President John F. Kennedy gave his version of this theory in 1963, just two months before his assassination, when he broke ground for the giant Hanford Steam-Electric Plant. "A rising tide lifts all of the boats," he said.

But Glenn Lee's theory and unstinting effort was one thing. The manner in which he refused to spare himself in implementing it, is quite another. Nor did the mere growth of the Tri-Cities ensure with it that the *Tri-City Herald* was going to grow too. That part of the equation took work, imagination, intuitiveness and drive. There was an abundance of these qualities in *The Herald's* personnel. Those who didn't measure up to the fast pace and the intense demands found their niche elsewhere.

Don often recalls the time he was taken on a tour of McNary Dam on the Columbia River, about 25 miles south of the Tri-Cities, while the project was under construction. The Resident Engineer, who accompanied Don, was an old hand at dam-building. He pointed to the many great obstacles that were being removed to expedite the construction.

High above them on the towering basalt cliffs men dangled from ropes and jackhammered away at the rock. The structure would extend to that height.

When Don exclaimed about all the obstacles the builders faced, the Resident Engineer told him: "A few years from now some fellow will drive by with his family, look around and say, 'Now that was a logical place to build a dam.' "

Undoubtedly today, people drive through the surging Tri-Cities, witness the giant building boom, see the fantastically large nuclear facilities under construction or planned for Hanford, witness the thousands of acres of new vineyards, new orchards, the giant sprinkler-irrigation circle systems and the three thriving communities, and then think, in reference to the *Tri-City Herald*, that here was a logical place in which to build a newspaper.

But it wasn't that easy. I have often used the word "growth." A better description for *The Herald* was that it was built. Unlike Topsy, it just didn't grow.

ONE OF THE cheers I loved at college was when the cheer leader would cry out to the student section at a football game, "Give me a C!" And the crowd would answer "C!"

The cheer leader would shout, "Give men an O!" The response would be "O!"

"Give me a U" to the response of "U!"

"Give me a G!" and eventually we would spell out C-O-U-G-A-R-S for the Washington State University team.

But since 1947 every time I hear that type of yell I'm reminded of Don and Verne Husk, the *Tri-City Herald's* first mechanical superintendent, trying to put out the first issue of *The Herald.*

It was a frantic time just before deadline and they were trying to make up page 1.

"I need an E," Don yelled. Verne scrambled wildly searching for the type, opening drawers, checking letters, even looking on the floor, and finally responding, "We're all out of Es, use another word."

Later, Don cried, "Give me a T."

And again the frantic scramble by Verne and some of the other printers, followed by the response, "We can't find any more Ts. Figure out a different word."

Don was trying to put the headline on the paper's first big story. It was an *Associated Press* story about a riot in France that grew so serious the French government sent troops to control it. The headline finally read, "Troops called to Halt French Riot," and it was printed eight columns across the top of the front page of that first edition. But it was the third headline written. The other two failed for a lack of letters.

In a way, that story illustrates some of the problems that not only confronted *The Herald* on the first day of publication but were to nag it during its early years, namely a lack of facilities and a shortage of newsprint and other essentials required to publish a newspaper.

Overcoming missing letters by rewriting words is one thing. But as *The Herald* was soon to learn, how could it overcome a shortage of newsprint, the basic ingredient to putting out a newspaper?

Behind that first edition were two weeks of frantic work as the small staff burned the candle at both ends trying to fill its 22 pages.

The building that housed the *Pasco Herald* and would be the home of the *Tri-City Herald* for almost a year, was located in downtown Pasco on Fourth street between Lewis and Columbia. It was a narrow building, only about 20 feet wide, with approximately 100 feet from the front sidewalk to the back alley.

The Duplex Flatbed Goss Press was in the basement. The page forms were made up in the composing room, locked up and carried down the narrow stairway to the press. Newsprint had to be lowered to the press with a cable.

Volume I, Number 1 of the *Tri-City Herald* came off the press in mid-afternoon. The 22 pages required three press runs on the slow 8-page-capacity press. The press, heretofore, had printed the weekly *Pasco Herald* on Wednesdays. The paper was put in the mail that night and reached the subscribers on Thursday. The first *Tri-City Herald* was delivered to its readers six weeks after the decision was made to go daily.

The first editorial, titled "Volume One, Number One," was written by Hugh A. Scott, editor and publisher. It set forth the policies by which the newspaper would be guided, and they are still in effect today:

1. To provide local news concerning Richland, Kennewick and Pasco on the basis of pure news values without favor to any one community.
2. To promote the development of all three communities through sound planning, statesmanship solutions of problems and, wherever possible, unified action.
3. To recognize the needs and importance of all elements that make up our territory, including farmers, businessmen, workers, professional men and women, salesmen, housewives, school children and other groups.
4. To provide a balance and diversity in the economic background of the Pasco, Kennewick, and Richland area so that prosperity does not depend too heavily upon too few activities.
5. To underwrite the efforts of character-building organizations and institutions through publicity and editorial support in recognition of the fact that our greatest wealth is in our own progressive citizenry.

It was an excellent summation of what a newspaper must do to adequately serve such a diverse area although, granted, writing it and doing it are far different things. For example, what the newspaper regarded as "pure news values without favor to any one community" often turned out to be the opposite. There were always the chronic charges of favoritism to one city over the others, or, to two over one, or to one county over the other county.

The *Tri-City Herald* has been a unifying force for the Tri-Cities. However, in 1947, when it sought to blossom from its weekly role to a six-day-a-week daily, it found itself awkward, gangly, and somewhat like the proverbial bull in the china shop, performing before watchful but not necessarily friendly eyes.

The reactions of the three communities to the announcement of a new daily newspaper were quite different. Pasco was busting its buttons with pride; Kennewick was suspicious and somewhat alarmed that a "Pasco paper" would be planning an invasion of its boundaries. Richland was the least moved of all. It was deeply involved in organizing the big expansion just beginning. It was the most distant from Pasco—a 45-minute drive was par from Pasco to the Richland Y turnoff via a two-lane highway for what is today merely a few minutes drive.

Ironically, although Richland at first seemed aloof, the people of Richland proved to be among the most avid supporters of the free-wheeling newspaper which delighted in twisting the tail of the Atomic Energy Commission and General Electric Company. Some of the great news stories on official skullduggery were leaked by Hanford workers. They didn't dare to give vent to their feelings but *The Herald* could, and did.

Nothing illustrates the frantic rush required to make the change from weekly to daily than the fact that the Scott Publishing Company took over *The Herald* on October 1 and announced its plans for daily publication nine days later. At the same time, it also announced a contest to name the new paper.

"A daily newspaper, so far without a name, will be born in the Richland-Kennewick-Pasco area within a few weeks," *The Herald* boasted on October 9, 1947. "The name of the newspaper is to be selected through a contest announced on this page. The leading requirements of the contest is that the name of the newspaper be associated with the Tri-City area, rather than with any one of the towns in the area.

"The plan of the Scott Publishing Company, Inc. in putting out a daily newspaper is to give each of the three cities equal coverage with respect to news, circulation and advertising facilities.

"The new newspaper will appear in the afternoon, six days a week. There will be no Sunday edition. Distribution will be by carrier within the city areas of Pasco, Kennewick and Richland. Press services will bring news only two and three hours old to the residents of this area, beating outside newspapers from a few hours to half a day. Daily local news coverage will be available for the first time. Advertising and subscription rates will be reasonable and will be established in accordance with accepted newspaper practices.

"Present subscribers to the *Pasco Herald* will automatically be continued, being credited to their new account.

"The new paper will definitely be a complete newspaper, competitive with the best available anywhere in a community of similar size. This means that comic strips, editorial columns, sports, national and international news, market reports and other services will be available within the limitation of space.

"The staff of the new paper will be selected from competent, experienced people who will have the interest of this entire area at heart. On this day of writing, two excellent advertising representatives have been added.

"Office of publication will remain at the plant of the present *Pasco Herald* but branch offices will be opened in Kennewick and Richland, where news reporters, advertising salesman and circulation personnel will be located. Thus the full facilities of the newspaper will be available to every resident of the Tri-City Area."

One thing has always been true of Tri-Citians—they love a contest, particularly one with a cash prize. They responded with much enthusiasm to attempt to pick the name of the new paper. First prize was $100.

There were 302 entries and the winning name was *"Tri-City Herald."* Forty-six contestants sent in that name. Each received $5. The new name cost *The Herald* $230. But it was money well spent.

Undoubtedly the saddest contestant was Joseph A. Morath of Pasco, later to be a justice of peace. He submitted 180 different titles, all losers.

The entry judged most original was from Mrs. Hugh T. Simpson of Richland who suggested "Triumph—Tri-for

Tri-Cities, and Umph for the newspaper's star-like radiance." She received a consolation prize of $1!

Some contestants favored such names as "Atomic," "Sagebrush," "Triangle" and several "Ben-Franklin" for Benton, Franklin Counties. Mrs. M. Cooney of Pasco dug into Indian lore for "Chee-Wahna", meaning "great river."

Even the names of the three communities didn't prove too great a barrier. Entrants took Pasco, Kennewick and Richland and came up with "Pasenrick" and "Cowichland." But *"Tri-City Herald"* it was, and what a strange sounding name. Mention "Tri-Cities" in almost any section of the state today and there is instant recognition. However, in 1947 there were even many in the Tri-Cities who didn't respond to the name.

On Thanksgiving Day, Don and I were invited to have dinner with my cousin and her husband, Paul and Virginia Gast, in Richland. Among the guests were several of his associates from Hanford. Don felt somewhat left out of the conversation because it revolved around Hanford topics. Eventually one of the guests inquired:

"Where do you work, Don?"

"I'm employed by the *Tri-City Herald,"* Don answered.

"Oh," said the guest with much interest. "What is *that?*"

Within a few days the newspaper was involved in an investigation of housing conditions for Hanford construction workers who couldn't obtain housing within the city limits of Richland, and in a libel suit filed by the Franklin County Prosecuting Attorney. The newspaper with the strange-sounding name would soon be a household word.

But even on a modest scale for a beginning newspaper in the middle 1940's, the *Tri-City Herald* presented a good news package. It subscribed to the Associated Press for its national news coverage. It had an excellent comic section —too good, in fact.

The Herald was anxious to have what were considered in the trade as "blue chip" comics, these being the most popular and the best read. The leaders at that time were

17

Dick Tracy, Gasoline Alley, Little Orphan Annie, Lil' Abner and so forth.

However, syndicates have territorial agreements. Publication rights to the *Chicago Tribune* comics were held by two newspapers, the *Seattle Times* and the *Spokesman-Review* of Spokane.

Don recalled that shortly before he left Seattle to come to Pasco, Russell McGrath, managing editor of the *Seattle Times*, told him he had been queried by the *Chicago Tribune* Syndicate which wondered if the *Seattle Times* had any objections to the purchase of their comics by the soon-to-start *Tri-City Herald?* McGrath answered, "None whatever." On that basis *The Herald* was given a contract by the *Chicago Tribune*. But the contract was soon cancelled.

Presumably, what happened was that in checking a map of the state, the *Tribune* Syndicate thought the Tri-Cities was in the *Seattle Time's* territory. So *The Herald* started out blissfully unaware that it was printing comics to which it was not entitled without permission of the *Spokesman-Review*. Pasco was in Spokane's territory. This was an unexpected misfortune for the newspaper.

When the first issue of the *Tri-City Herald* rolled off the press it received considerable attention from other near-by publications, of course, because it offered competition for subscribers to newspapers in Spokane, Walla Walla and Yakima, which jealously and selfishly watched developments in the region where they had substantial circulation.

Initially it seemed strange that they were even concerned. They knew *The Herald* had little possibility of surviving, and they looked down their noses at this challenge. It was a gamble at best in view of the times. But what really upset the *Spokesman-Review* was the appearance of their comics in the *Tri-City Herald*.

The Spokane newspapers, both owned by the same publisher, considered the entire Inland Empire as their territory. They selected the features for their newspapers and only what they didn't want could be obtained by newspapers operating in their region. But what was theirs could not be used by any other newspaper, without exception.

The Herald was notified by the *Chicago Tribune* Syndicate by telegram that it would have to discontinue the comics at once. Hugh Scott protested and pleaded for time but the Syndicate was adamant.

Since that time, the *Tri-City Herald* has had enough experience with the Spokane newspapers to realize the pressure that was exerted on the Syndicate.

At any rate, *The Herald* frantically set about to get other features. They finally signed up with King Features Syndicate as their second choice. When looking back at those old newspapers, I wonder why such a fuss was even made over the matter. Comics are an important part of today's newspapers. But in the days before television and its almost daily diet of animated cartoons and wide range of dramas, comics held a tremendous grip on the public.

Most of the comics were continuity strips; that is, Rip Kirby, Buz Sawyer, Joe Palooka, Steve Canyon. The straight humor panels were Donald Duck, Bringing Up Father, Myrtle and Popeye. These were good but they didn't hold the ratings of the original comics that Spokane took away from us.

Spokane is 150 miles northeast of the Tri-Cities. At one time there was little population between the two areas. All you saw was sagebrush and dry-wheat farmland. By some standards, there isn't much more between the two regions today.

In the days before the Hanford Project, hydro-electric dams and irrigated farming brought new population and created new communities and caused small, established towns to expand, the entire region—"The heart of the Inland Empire"—was claimed by the Spokane newspapers. The start of the *Tri-City Herald* really signaled the beginning of significant changes as it threatened the territory of the Spokane papers.

No longer would they be unchallenged as the most powerful daily newspapers in the region. The *Spokesman-Review*, however, showed repeatedly that it had no intention of retiring gracefully from the territory merely because of a new newspaper. If the *Spokesman-Review* were to leave, it would have to be driven out.

Meanwhile, it redoubled its circulation efforts and boosted its local news coverage. But, as *The Herald* soon learned, the *Spokesman-Review* was no editorial threat. It was a well established newspaper in the region. Those who had been its longtime subscribers continued to read it. But they now subscribed to *The Herald* in growing numbers.

The Herald couldn't match the *Spokesman-Review* wire news reports. But the *Spokesman-Review* couldn't match *The Herald's* local news coverage either, and local news is what *The Herald* provided in growing quantities.

What *The Herald* lacked, however, was sufficient news space because it suffered from a lack of advertisements except for Thursdays.

Initially, *The Herald* published six days a week—Monday through Saturday. In 1949, it eliminated the Saturday paper and went to a Sunday morning edition.

The first edition of *The Herald* was a big occasion for the news staff of five—three men and two women—and for the communities. The birth of a daily newspaper was an exciting event and one keenly anticipated, especially so in Pasco where the people were delighted by the fact its small weekly was going to be published six times a week. It made the community leaders swell with pride.

Volume I, Number I was an instant success. The edition was a sellout. Years later, people would say, "I saved the first copy." Furthermore, the paper was filled with congratulatory advertisements.

The staff worried about the problems of producing the 22 pages on their 8-page press. It was a slow press run. The press started on Wednesday afternoon and ran into the night on the first eight pages.

Then the heavy plates were removed and carried upstairs. The second 8-page section was tediously installed on the press and the run started again.

The Herald's front office looked like a floral shop on that first day. Large displays of flowers filled the room and spilled over into the tiny editorial section, which could only accommodate three desks and a jangling teletype machine.

Don's desk was a table next to the teletype. Hugh Scott had a small walled office nearby. The days before the first edition were hectic, necessitating long hours of work, but the small staff loved every minute of it as they anticipated the first edition.

Volume I, Number 1 on November 13, 1947 would be a memorable date in their lives. But when the excitement began to wear off they were looking directly at Volume I, Number 2 on November 14, and that was something entirely different. The flowers were still there, but there were few advertisements. There was only one press run. Volume I, Number 2 was but eight pages.

And the following day—Saturday, November 15—it was only a six-page edition.

The pattern seemed to be set. A large newspaper on Thursday and small papers the rest of the week. There was a reluctance on the part of Richland merchants to advertise at all. They had their weekly newspaper, the *Villager*, with its low advertising rates, delivered free to everyone in Richland. And theirs was a captive market.

The readers' response in Kennewick to the *Herald* was somewhat better than Richland, but the advertising support was weak. In short, the cities had a daily newspaper which they wanted and their subscriptions showed that. But the merchants had a weekly habit. They wanted their newspaper six days a week but they only wanted to advertise in it once a week.

As the days wore on, and the busy Christmas season was approaching, the paper was small with only a few pages.

21

This was because business was so good. The stores were crammed with shoppers. It was a seller's market.

"I'd advertise with you," one merchant told a *Herald* salesman, "but I'm too busy to figure out an ad. Stand back and let me take care of these customers."

Probably the cruelest remark of all was by a merchant who asked, "Advertise? I don't want more business. I can't handle what I've got."

It was a busy, bustling Christmas season for businessmen in 1947. But the new *Tri-City Herald* was hurting for revenue. Its costs and losses continued to mount. It was a paradox. Business was so good that the newspaper was starving to death.

Fittingly enough, the last *Herald* of 1947 was but eight pages. Its banner headline proclaimed that the Tri-Cities would "come of age" in 1948. It was the prediction of various Tri-City leaders and *The Herald* always looked on the rosy side of predictions. It was easy to do because there was so much to be optimistic about.

Thus *The Herald* had many problems. The circulation of the newspaper was increasing but its advertising sales continued to lag. The first two months of 1948 were bad months and Glenn Lee began to spend more of his time trying to generate ideas and sales, along with efforts to borrow money and sell stock.

There is no easy way to start a newspaper. And, most assuredly, as Glenn and his staff discovered, there is no simple way to build one. But in *The Herald's* case the newspaper was started, was built and today thrives as a top-rated daily.

Yet of all the thrills connected with the paper, the greatest one was the printing of Volume I, Number 1. By today's standards it was a wide, gangly, awkward and somewhat unattractive newspaper. Looking back, however, it still glows in the eyes of those who had a hand in it.

3 *The Men Who Made It Possible*

I HAVE NEVER ceased to be amazed when I remember that the *Tri-City Herald* got its start because Glenn Lee was unable to buy a flour mill in the wheat country of Washington and Oregon.

Over the years, when I have mentioned this fact to people they invariably ask: "What in the world does a flour mill have to do with a newspaper?"

Well, obviously, a flour mill doesn't have a thing to do with a newspaper unless, of course, you have an unpredictable person like Glenn with a knack for making snap judgments, judgments based on facts but chiefly with a healthy amount of instinct involved.

But nevertheless, that is how *The Herald* eventually began — because Glenn and his partner, Bob Philip, had an export-import firm in Seattle and they were having a successful time shipping flour.

Viewed with the scanty information provided thus far it appears to have been something of a reckless decision. But to the contrary, with Glenn's and Bob's flair for quickly sizing up a situation, their willingness to take a chance, and their ability to make a decision and stick with it, the purchase of the weekly *Pasco Herald* on the spur of the moment, had a reasonably sound basis.

It also typifies why the partnership of Bob and Glenn has been a successful one, although not without its harrowing moments too. The old saying in marriage is that opposites attract. Perhaps this it true also with business partnerships. At least, it has been so in regards to Glenn Lee and Bob Philip.

They are as different as their backgrounds and there is virtually no similarity to their mode of operation. But nevertheless, if you trace the genealogy of *The Herald* it will lead you to a small Seattle export-import firm named Philip and Lee, Inc. that was started immediately after World War II by a couple of ex-Navy officers who had met in the service.

There was also a third person, Hugh A. Scott. Hugh was with the venture less than two years and the Scott Publishing Company, Inc. which publishes the *Tri-City Herald*, bears his name, as it should. Without him, Glenn and Bob wouldn't be in the newspaper business. Actually, the thing most remote from their minds was a daily newspaper.

Ironically, it was flour that also brought Glenn and Hugh Scott together. During Philip and Lee's successful ventures into the export business, Glenn on many occasions visited the Washington, D. C. office of the Seattle Chamber of Commerce for assistance with export licenses. His main contact was Hugh. Glenn was impressed with Hugh.

During one of his visits, Hugh confided that he longed to return to the Pacific Northwest. Glenn obtained a resume from Hugh and the next time they met, he said:

"Hugh, I've read your resume and it's impressive. But you are mostly newspaper oriented. Even if we had an opening, I don't see how we could use you. What are your major goals?"

"I think what I want most of all is to own a weekly newspaper," Hugh replied.

"Well, that's quite removed from my field," Glenn said. "But I move about the Northwest all the time. I'll keep my eyes open. Maybe something will turn up."

A few weeks later Glenn was seated at the lunch counter of the Crescent Drug Store at Fourth and Lewis in Pasco. He was talking to Hill Williams, manager of the Pasco Chamber of Commerce.

Williams knew of Glenn's unsuccessful attempt to purchase a flour mill. He had even supplied Glenn with a few tips. They were discussing business in Pasco when Bill Wilmot, publisher of the *Pasco Herald*, walked out of his plant across the street from where Glenn and Williams were seated.

"There," said Williams, nodding at Wilmot, "is a fellow with about the best business in town, but he wants to sell."

"Why does he want to sell?" Glenn asked.

"He doesn't care for Pasco's location. Too close to other cities. He wants something a little more remote. I think he's making a mistake. That's a good property I sold him."

Glenn looked up in surprise. "You sold it to him?" he asked.

"Yes," said Williams. "I published that paper for 20 years and if I had another 20 years left, I'd still be publishing it."

Glenn studied the front of the *Pasco Herald* for a moment, then turned back to Williams.

"Mr. Williams," he said, "tell me about that newspaper."

Because of his long and close personal relationship with Glenn and Bob, it is understandable that Don often has been asked, "How did those two fellows ever get together?" The question is usually asked as if to mean, "How could those two fellows have stayed together?"

In Don's opinion, the answer should be rather obvious. The successful partnership was joined by a common interest—to take advantage of the tremendous opportunity in the export field after World War II. It is significant that both men recognized the opportunity and quickly joined together to take advantage of it.

Their partnership has continued to exist because it has been so successful. A favorite expression of Glenn's is, "Nothing succeeds like success."

Their backgrounds, I think, explain why their manners and lifestyles are so different.

Glenn was born on a little farm near Eau Claire,

Wisconsin, the second son of Seth and Anna Lee. He had two younger brothers, Howard and Stanley, and an older brother, Leonard, and a sister, Myrtle. The family moved into Eau Claire when Glenn was young because his father was afraid the children wouldn't receive a proper education in a country school. It was a matter of great family pride years later when Glenn entered the University of North Dakota. He was the first member of the family to go to college.

Glenn's first exposure to newspapers was as a carrier for the evening Eau Claire paper. He quickly learned the necessity of promptness and dependability even when the snow was deep and the frigid Wisconsin weather dropped to 40 degrees below zero. He earned three cents a week for each subscription. When he changed to a morning newspaper route he was able to keep delivering papers through high school.

He graduated from Eau Claire High School in 1928 and then worked six months in a foundry and, for a year, at the Northern States Power Company, to earn his college tuition. During his first year in college he kept expenses down by living with an aunt in Grand Forks.

Tragedy struck his family that first year. A few weeks after registration he received word his brother, Stanley, had been in a hunting accident and was in critical condition. His friend, Vern Button, who had driven him to Grand Forks for the opening of school, drove him home where his family maintained a bedside vigil until Stanley died.

On a brighter note, Vern later married Glenn's sister, Myrtle. Glenn was best man. (In 1949, the Buttons joined *The Herald* staff.)

In May, 1930, Glenn met Elaine Greenland on a blind date. He courted her until June, 1933 when, a few days before his graduation, they were married.

Glenn had joined Beta Theta Pi fraternity at college but he was able to meet expenses by living and working in the local Dakota Hotel, first as an elevator operator, then as a bellhop. This also provided him with hotel experience, a field he didn't necessarily intend to follow, but in 1933 any job was a good job.

So from 1933 to 1935, Glenn worked as a room clerk at the Arlington Hotel in Binghampton, New York. The hotel was in bankruptcy and operated by a trustee. Glenn worked long hours, seven days a week. His pay was $23.08 a week.

One can guess with some degree of certainty that the same degree of thoroughness, energy and application that has marked Glenn's career was apparent then. One indication is that in 1935, still in the depths of the Depression, he moved to a better job as assistant manager of the Wigwam in Litchfield Park, 30 miles from Phoenix, a hotel owned by the Goodyear Tire & Rubber Company. A year later he moved to the Elms Hotel at Excelsior Springs, Missouri, in the same capacity. And in 1937, he was promoted to manager of the hotel.

Glenn stayed in Excelsior Springs until 1940, when he was recruited by the Statler Hotel chain for their 1,000-room Cleveland, Ohio, facility as assistant manager. This was followed by moves to St. Louis, Missouri, as sales manager and then back to Cleveland again, this time as executive assistant manager of the hotel operation.

In 1944, he enlisted in the Navy. By this time the Lees had become parents of Glenn C. Jr., and daughters, Terry and Vicki. Their youngest daughter, Penny, was born in 1953.

Unlike Glenn, most of Bob Philip's working experience was gained in his native state of Washington. His travelling, when it did come, was during his wartime service with the Navy, much of it in Pacific combat zones.

Bob was born in Tacoma of a pioneer family. His grandfather, Martin Ferdinand Philip, came from Germany to San Francisco and then to Tacoma at the turn of the century. He started Philip Hardware in early 1900.

Bob's father, Frank, was born in San Francisco, attended

what is today Stadium High School in Tacoma, and graduated from the University of Washington in Seattle in 1906. Bob attended Tacoma schools, graduated from Stadium High School and then entered the University of Washington where he was a member of his father's fraternity, Phi Gamma Delta. He graduated in Foreign Trade in 1940 and immediately accepted a job with Consolidated Freightways in Helena, Montana. His business sense was apparent at the University where he operated several sideline businesses. To his chagrin, he discovered he was making less money as a full time trainee executive with the freight lines than he had made as a fulltime college student!

His stay at Helena was short. The clouds of war were hanging over America and he was a member of the Navy Reserve. He returned to Seattle, expecting a call to active duty most anytime, and went to work for Dun and Bradstreet. He was summoned by the Navy on Dec. 7, 1941, served in Naval Intelligence in Seattle and then was sent to Officers Training School in Arizona.

Bob had met Mary Weatherston while at the university. They started dating in 1942 and were married a year later. But their honeymoon was cut short when he received orders assigning him to a sub chaser in the Aleutians. He later served in the South Pacific until he was mustered out in November, 1945 as a lieutenant. He then went to work for the Pacific American Trading Co. in Seattle. It was an export firm. There he met Glenn.

The Philips have two sons, James and Robert Jr. Jim is political writer for *The Herald*. Both sons, true to the Philip tradition, are graduates of University of Washington.

Probably one of Bob's proudest achievements is his service on the university's Board of Regents. He is a past chairman of the Regents and was also designated by the Regents to conduct the search for a new university president, which he successfully concluded in 1972.

It was the Navy that brought Glenn and Bob together. Glenn's duty brought him to the Sand Point Naval Station in Seattle where he was in charge of the Bachelor Officers Quarters. His duty was to provide housing and entertainment for flying officers whose planes were stationed at Sand Point while their carriers were being repaired at the Puget Sound Navy Shipyard at Bremerton.

From the officers Glenn heard of opportunities for making money if exports could be shipped to the South Pacific and the Far East, where there was an extreme shortage of civilian goods.

Glen became acquainted with a Seattle attorney, Mark Matheson, who was also in the Navy and had connections in the Philippines. Together they formed a corporation and included a third partner, Roy Martin. The firm was called the Pacific American Trading Co.

They opened an office in the White Henry Stuart Building in Seattle and, as they were still in the Navy, they hired Bob, who had just been discharged.

On the first civilian ship leaving the West Coast for Manila, their company shipped 2,000 cases of gin. Each case was purchased in Canada at $7.50 and sold in Manila for $50. But even with these large profits, internal problems developed in the firm. The contact man in the Philippines proved to be inadequate and the company suffered losses because inventories in Manila were in distress. Matheson sold his interest to Martin without offering it to Glenn.

To get out from under an awkward situation, Glenn sold his interest in the company to Martin for $5,500. Glenn figured the company had a net worth of $250,000 at the time. With the $5,500 and with $500 from Elaine to match Bob's $6,000, Glenn and Bob formed a partnership. They moved down the street and opened the export firm of Philip and Lee, Inc.

An ingenious business maneuver which helped launch the new firm began with a longshoreman's strike during which bags of flour piled up on the docks. They belonged to a number of competitive firms without export permits.

The new partners bought the flour milling orders, amounting to 80,000 bags. What remained was for them to sell the flour, get export licenses and to ship it.

Glenn hired a former business associate with the Statler Hotel chain, Bill Billow, and sent him to Washington, D. C. to sell the flour to one of the foreign delegations. Billow was successful in making a deal for shipment to Italy.

Then began a round with the banks to get a line of credit. Bank after bank advised them that Philip and Lee was too small an operation to handle the transaction alone. The bankers offered to get them private financing for a share of the profit.

Angered at this attempt to muscle in on their deal, Glenn and Bob would not accept. But how were they to get the necessary money? Together they mulled that question.

During the early days of the firm's operation, when it was decided flour was a marketable commodity, Glenn, who is a great believer in eyeball-to-eyeball business discussions, had travelled extensively, making many personal contacts with flour millers in Winnipeg, Grand Forks, Great Falls, Montana; Walla Walla, Washington; Lewiston, Idaho, and Pendleton, Oregon.

One of his contacts had been with Paul Trigg who operated the Great Falls Flour Milling Company. Most of the flour Philip and Lee had dealt in had come from Trigg's mill.

Glenn hopped a plane and sped to Great Falls. There he met with Trigg.

"I leveled with him. I explained the entire proposition fully and fairly. I didn't hold back and Mr. Trigg knew I was being completely honest with him. He also recognized our plight," Glenn recalls.

Trig looked at Glenn carefully and smiled. "Young man, I have no cause to question your personal integrity. I'll extend you the credit you need. But you'd better work fast," he said.

Glenn wrung Trigg's hand and he was on the next plane from Great Falls.

The shipments were made, totalling almost $500,000. The profits from that venture bought the *Pasco Herald* and kept the *Tri-City Herald* operating during its early days when it was not showing a profit.

Hugh Scott had entered the picture during Glenn's visits to obtain export licenses and he assisted on this one too. But Hugh's dreams of a weekly newspaper weren't really on Glenn's mind when he left Washington, D. C. that time. Glenn, instead, was thinking of the wisdom of purchasing his own flour mill. Such a mill would guarantee him a supply of flour and might enable him to shave his costs under even his most avid competitors.

As his plane winged back to Seattle, Glenn had all but forgotten Hugh Scott's resume tucked in his briefcase. Glenn was thinking flour mills.

Hugh's credentials, though, were quite impressive. He had a brilliant World War II record, participating with the Third Infantry Division during its campaigns in French Morocco, Sicily, Southern Italy, Anzio, Southern France and Alsace. He served as G-2 (Intelligence Officer) of the division during its Rhineland and Central German campaigns, rising to the rank of Lieutenant Colonel.

The Army offered him a regular Army commission but he turned it down and went instead to the University of Washington to inquire about work. He had graduated from the University of Washington in 1935 with a degree in Journalism.

Hugh was born in Ellensburg, Washington. His family lived in Montana for a short time and, when he was 10, he was a resident of Seattle where he lived until he completed college.

In his senior year of high school the family moved to Portland, where his father, Quincy Scott, became a cartoonist for *The Oregonian*. Hugh worked for a year as a reporter for *The Oregonian*. In 1936 he left to help establish the weekly *Hood River County Sun* at Hood

River, Oregon. Other positions he held prior to going into the Army included 18 months as traffic safety publicist with the Oregon Secretary of State in Salem, and as executive secretary of the City Club of Portland.

While working in Salem he met Erma Weisser. They were married Nov. 11, 1940 and their daughter Janet was born before he reported for Army duty. Their son, James, was born while Hugh was overseas. Their youngest son, David, was born in 1946.

Hugh had been an outstanding student at the U. of W. and the Dean of the School of Journalism recommended him to the Seattle Chamber of Commerce for its public relations department. Hugh accepted the job but within six weeks the Chamber transferred him to its Washington, D.C. office as assistant to Christy Thomas, former longtime manager of the Chamber. The Chamber had big things in mind for Hugh, but his Pacific Northwest roots were too deep for life in the nation's capital.

He had confided his plans to return West to Glenn in April, 1947. Now it was June and his telephone rang.

"Hugh, this is Glenn Lee," he heard the voice say. "Have you ever been to Pasco, Washington?"

"No," Hugh replied, "I've never been there. Why?"

"Well, the Pasco weekly out here is for sale and it looks like a good investment. Maybe we could work some kind of a deal. Are you interested?"

"Heck, yes, I'm interested. Tell me about it."

For some reason, Glenn found he liked the idea of being an owner of a newspaper. True, it wasn't as practical at that time in his life as a flour mill. But then, there was no flour mill to be had, either. His idea was a partnership purchase arrangement, with Scott running the newspaper and Philip and Lee continuing the export firm with the newspaper as an investment.

Things moved quickly after their conversation. In July, Hugh visited Pasco on his vacation, the Scott Publishing Co. Inc. was formed, a down payment was given to Wilmot and purchase papers arranged.

An excited Hugh returned to Washington, D. C. and gave his notice to the Chamber of Commerce. He had left his family in Portland and when he had finished his month's termination notice Hugh drove West, purchased a trailer home and towed it to Pasco to serve as temporary quarters until he could have a house built.

But right in the middle of this, the sky, literally, "fell down."

In September, 1947 the Atomic Energy Commission announced a huge expansion for Hanford that would more than double the size of the giant facility. More atomic reactors and chemical processing plants would be constructed at an estimated cost of $350,000,000, one of the largest expenditures in American peacetime history. The General Electric Company was named as the prime contractor and the work would be undertaken at once.

It was a stunning piece of news and Bill Wilmot offered the partners $10,000 to cancel the sale agreement.

"We can't do that, Bill," Glenn explained. "We've incorporated. Hugh Scott has quit his job and moved to Pasco. He's bought a trailer. It's too late."

"I understand," Wilmot said. "I was afraid it was too late."

Undoubtedly, Wilmot had other misgivings but he never mentioned the subject again. A couple of months later he purchased the weekly paper at Colfax, Washington, and he has been there ever since.

In 1971, Don and I happened to be in Colfax and by chance met Wilmot. We had a delightful visit and talked about the early days of the *Tri-City Herald*.

"It is just as well I didn't remain in Pasco," Wilmot told us. "I would have had to change the paper to a daily and I'm a weekly man. I just wouldn't care for a daily."

The Scott Publishing Co. Inc., took over the *Pasco Herald* on October 1. The purchase agreement was completed on September 27 for $80,000, with an inventory of an additional $10,519 for office supplies.

A total of $20,000 had been paid to Wilmot plus an inventory of $11,519. A chattel mortgage was given in the amount of $14,800 to be paid as follows: $5,000 on or before April 15, 1948; $5,000 on or before October 15, 1948; the balance on or before April 15, 1949. The mortgage was on the inventory, merchandise, and paper supplies held for resale.

Like most weeklies, the *Pasco Herald* enjoyed a thriving commercial printing business and carried a full complement of office supplies and some office furniture, all located in the front third of the building.

The *Pasco Herald* premises was leased from Clara E. Chute. The balance of the conditional sales contract payable to Hill Williams as of October 1, 1947 was $44,800.

The *Pasco Herald* was published weekly with about 2,000 circulation. The commercial shop also printed the weekly *Richland Villager.*

Wilmot operated *The Herald* in a manner typical of weekly newspapers and was making about $18,000 to $20,000 annually. Wilmot spent a good deal of his time in the back shop. His front office crew consisted of Bill Bates, a recent University of Washington graduate, as editor-reporter; Mrs. Hill Williams handled the social news; Chet Juvenal sold the advertising, and his sister, Ida, was married to Herb Hutchinson, the printer-pressman.

There were also two linotype operators and a bookkeeper, Erma Erickson. Edith Wilkins assisted in the job-printing shop.

But right from the start it seemed destined for the newspaper's new owners that they were never to know a dull moment. They had hardly taken possession in October when they had a visit from Jim Brown, general manager of the Boise, Idaho, *Statesman.*

"How would you fellows like to sell out?" Brown asked.

It was an odd question. Glenn and Hugh exchanged puzzled looks.

"I didn't follow you," Hugh said. "What was it you asked?

Glenn C. Lee, 1960

Robert F. Philip, 1950.

Bob Philip, 1973,
president of *The Herald*

Hugh A. Scott, 1948

Donald A. Pugnetti, 1949

"I said, 'Would you fellows like to sell out?' "

"But we just got here," Hugh answered in amazement. "We've hardly opened our doors. What made you think we'd want to sell?"

"I'm making you an offer," Brown said. "I intend to start a daily newspaper here and I realize it would be easier to buy an existing paper and convert it to a daily."

Glenn laughed and both Hugh and Brown looked at him.

"How did you hear about it, Jim?" Glenn asked. "How did the word get out?"

Now it was Brown's turn to be puzzled.

"What do you mean?" he asked.

"About the daily," Glenn said. "That's why we're here. I thought it was a secret. Who told you?"

"Nobody," Brown said honestly. "I didn't know you fellows had any idea of going daily. Are you going to circulate only in Pasco or are you going into other cities too?"

Glenn shook his head. "I'm sorry, Jim," he said. "But we shouldn't be talking about this. We may well be competitors soon."

Brown agreed and the conversation ended. When Brown had gone, Hugh quickly said to Glenn, "What is this daily newspaper talk? You sounded serious."

"I think I am," Glenn answered. "If it's good enough for Brown, it's good enough for us. What would it take to produce a daily newspaper?"

"Plenty. It would take a lot more newsprint. We'd need a wire service, comics, columnists and we'd need more staff. We could never do it with the staff we have."

"Figure it out, Hugh. Make a list of what we'd need and how to get it. We've got to move fast. If those guys are already out trying to purchase a newspaper then they've done some planning. There is no telling who else might be testing this field," Glenn said.

An so 10 days after the Scott Publishing Company took possession of the *Pasco Herald,* it announced it was going daily. And with that decision the fourth World War II veteran, Don, joined the company as managing editor.

It is interesting as one grows older to note the set of circumstances and coincidences that have manipulated your life and the lives of those around you.

Several crop up where Hugh and Don are involved. Hugh was several years ahead of Don at the university and so they had not met. But each had heard of the other through mutual friends.

When Hugh was transferred to its Washington, D. C. office, the Seattle Chamber began looking for a replacement. They again turned to the university and said, "Send us another Hugh Scott," to the dean of the School of Journalism. It was a high compliment. When the dean telephoned Don, he was flattered but was also sure he didn't want Chamber of Commerce work.

The dean persisted. He finally asked Don, "How much are you making?" When Don told him, the dean replied, "This job pays twice that." The resistance of my month-old bridegroom began to crumble!

Don was born in the little mining town of Carbonado, in the Cascade foothills above the Carbon River in Pierce County. His father, Anton Pugnetti, had immigrated from Italy at the age of 16 and at the time of Don's birth was working for the Carbon Hill Coal Company. He had met his wife, Mary, in Carbonado and they had three children; a daughter, Frances, and two sons, Lester and Donald.

Carbonado is virtually a ghost town today and the trend in that direction was started in the early 1920s when a strike closed the mines. They later were reopened by strikebreakers but Don's father, although a foreman and not a member of the union, decided against staying and moved his family to Tacoma. He died of a heart attack when Don was seven.

Don grew up in Tacoma and, like Glenn, also began his newspaper career at an early age as a newsboy. He carried papers for five years and gave up his route shortly after he graduated from Lincoln High School. Also, like Glenn, he couldn't afford to attend college at first and worked for two years to save enough money to enter the University of Washington. He worked in the lumber mills of Tacoma but he was fortunate in also obtaining work for a year as a cub reporter on the old *Tacoma Times.*

His main ambition had been to coach sports, but while at Lincoln High his journalism teacher, Homer A. Post, motivated him into newspaper work, and he decided to become a sports writer. At the University he worked for the Athletic News Service, the publicity division of the Athletic Department. Three months before he graduated he was hired to manage the department and he remained at the University until he enlisted in the Army in military intelligence at the outbreak of World War II.

Don's military time was spent in Alaska and the Aleutians. He was discharged in September, 1945, and two weeks later, his burning desire for sports now dimmed, he joined the news staff of the *Tacoma News Tribune.*

I was already working at *The News Tribune,* having joined the news staff from Washington State University while Don was in the service. Unlike most new reporters Don wasn't introduced to the staff because he knew almost everybody there. He had been the high school correspondent for the paper. He had also done some special reporting for sports editor Dan Walton, and he had earned spending money at the University by writing feature stories on Pierce County athletes participating for the Huskies.

Then, when he became sports publicity director for the University, he was really the man to know. A fair share of the staff could be found on Saturdays between the two 40-yard lines, because of the free tickets Don handed out. So no one bothered to introduce us because they figured we must have known each other. He had been there a few days when I stopped by his desk and said, "I'm Frances Taylor, what's your name?"

"Don," he replied, and with a big grin, added, "I won't tell you my last name because you'd never remember it."

And that's the truth!

We were married in August, 1946, following an office romance which the staff members all took credit for promoting. When we applied for our marriage license we took City Editor Frank Lockerby along to serve as a witness because we felt he had brought us together. He hired us both.

But now it was October and Don was in Seattle in publicity work again. The pay was good, the working conditions solid, and the Chamber personnel were friendly. But from the start Don was restless and he really missed newspaper work.

So did Hugh Scott, and Don and Hugh confided in each other their desire to return to newspapering. It was natural when Hugh became involved in his new venture and the decision was made to go daily, that he immediately thought of Don.

Don took his overseas pay which he had accumulated in the service and invested it in the *Tri-City Herald*. Which was how we happened to wind up in Pasco, Washington in the Fall of 1947. When we arrived we had a four-month-old baby named Brian and, later, Jerry, Eugene, Mary Dawn and Lester, in that order.

The turmoil of those early months of newspaper operation took its toll. Hugh left *The Herald* in the Summer of 1949 and bought a weekly newspaper in Kelso. His departure was caused by a difference of philosophy with Glenn over managerial policy. Hugh took with him Bill Bates, who had been working for the weekly and remained with the daily as the Pasco reporter; later as city editor and editor of the revived weekly *Pasco Herald*.

Today Bill is publisher of the weekly Snohomish (Wash.) *Tribune*.

Hugh remained in Kelso several years and then sold the paper and moved to Portland to work for *The Oregonian*.

The Kelso paper had two owners after Scott and then it folded. After three years in *The Oregonian's* editorial department, Hugh went to work for a publicity firm, later opening his own public relations business. One of his accounts was the Portland Rose Festival. He is now the advertising and public relations officer of the United States National Bank of Oregon.

In June of 1973, a little more than 25 years after *The Herald* went daily, Don left *The Herald*. He returned to the *Tacoma News Tribune* as its editor. Don was bac' home again.

4   *Growing Pains*

IF YOU WERE Verne Husk, first mechanical superintendent of the *Tri-City Herald,* and on your way to work in the sun's glow of those usually clear Tri-City dawns, how would you begin your day?

Well, chances are you'd swing by the Pasco police station to learn if they were holding any of your printers in their drunk tank. Then you'd go through the routine procedure of bailing them out, taking them to the Pasco Club, a cafe-tavern next door to the newspaper, and buying them a meal. Getting them to eat it was something else. But eventually, sometime during the morning, there would be a full crew in *The Herald* backshop.

So hard was it to obtain printers, or any of the other skills for that matter, that even a "hung over" printer was better than no printer.

The result, of course, was that maximum demands had to be made on the good people. They had to carry the load and anything that could be pulled from their shoulders was welcomed.

One linotype operator was the fastest Hugh Scott had ever seen. He could set a galley of type in 20 minutes but he, too, was an alcoholic. The first time he was paid he didn't show up for two days. In order to fully utilize the man and, hopefully, to keep him sober, Hugh arranged for him to be housed in a room nearby and to get his meals at the Pasco Club. It was a good arrangement but a short one. As so often happened, just about the time Husk thought he could depend on him, the printer went off on another binge and never showed up again.

One of Don's expensive headaches turned out to be a fellow he knew slightly in Tacoma where the man had worked on the *Tacoma Times* as a reporter. However, he had learned the printing trade on a weekly that his parents had owned in Oregon, and was working as a printer for *The Herald.*

It soon became a frequent habit for the desk sergeant to call and say: "Hey, Don, we've got your buddy here." Don would bail him out, always receiving a promise of payment from the printer.

But one morning when the desk sergeant called, Don growled into the telephone, "Keep him. He's all yours."

Some hours later the printer appeared at the office proceeded by a string of profanity. He berated Don for, among other things, "turning your back on a friend," and ended by shouting, "I quit!"

"But you can't quit to me," Don told him. "I'm the managing editor. You have to quit to the mechanical superintendent."

Without questioning the logic of that the printer looked up Verne and began his tirade all over again. "Look," said Husk when the printer had finally stopped for breath, "quitting's your right. But you were so broke you couldn't bail yourself out of jail. How are you going to leave town?

"I'll tell you how you're going to leave town," Verne continued, answering his own question. "Put on an apron and work the night shift. I'll pay you in cash and you can buy a bus ticket and leave town in style."

It worked. So did the printer. The next morning Don discovered a note in his typewriter from the now departed man. It scolded him, although it was somewhat conciliatory, and ended with the sentence:

"I hope this has taught you a lesson!"

Despite the fact *The Herald* placed numerous advertisements in trade publications seeking mechanical employees, the responses were few, although workers were attracted from points as far away as the Middle West.

Finding responsible men was one thing. Keeping them was quite another. The union scale was $1.60 an hour. But rent and living costs were high and there was the bugaboo of the unattractive nature of the community from the standpoint of facilities, climate, recreation and so forth. So the turnover rate was high.

By the end of 1947 the need for mechanical help was so critical and the overtime so choking that it was decided to voluntarily raise the Journeyman scale by 20 cents to $1.80 an hour. The raise was effective Jan. 4, 1948. This may seem a pittance by today's wages but in 1948 it topped the going rate for printers in the region.

Then another move was decided upon in an effort to attract and retain competent help. *The Herald* decided to purchase four new homes being completed in Kennewick. Each one cost between $9,000 and $10,000 and required $400 as a downpayment. The mortgage payments were $85 per month per house but *The Herald* subsidized $20 of the rent and it cost the employee $65 a month.

This helped in slowing the turnover rate, so in that regard it was a sound move. But housing only added to the headaches of management. Time and again when a printer would quit his job and move it would cost the financially pressed company from $400 to $500 to restore the house to good repair. Finally the company disposed of the homes.

Before the idea of purchasing homes for printers, when new employees came from out-of-town, the man would usually arrive first. A room could be rented at the Pasco Hotel for $4.50 a night but the hotel limited occupancy to three nights. Then the man would usually wind up sleeping on a cot in a basement somewhere for $2.50 a night which, back in 1947-48, was on the high side.

Verne Husk's housing problems were typical. It was a stroke of good fortune hat Glenn had found him, for he brought the experience and stability to the backshop sorely needed during those early days.

He arrived in the Tri-Cities on November 13, just in time to help put out the first edition. Behind him were 26 years with the *Daily Olympian* which he left to purchase his own commercial printing plant in Coos Bay, Oregon. He eventually sold that to become mechanical superintendent for the Vancouver (Wash.) *Sun*, but it was short-lived for the newspaper published only six months.

Glenn met Verne when he turned up at the *Sun* looking for press equipment.

"Come over and join me," Glenn urged. "We've got a good property. It's a great opportunity and you'll get in on the ground floor."

"That's what the guy said when he talked me into coming here," Verne replied.

Glenn kept talking, and Verne finally agreed. His family was raised so Verne and his wife had only themselves to care for. They lived in a one-room apartment motel on Pasco's Eastside where they stayed for four months. It cost $4.25 a day, had only a shower and bed. There were no kitchen facilities so the Husks ate their meals at Suzannes Restaurant located on the northside of Lewis street between Fourth and Fifth. The restaurant had so much business the dinner lines usually extended down the block, very much as theater lines occasionally seen these days.

It wasn't until January, 1949 that Verne was able to purchase the home he wanted.

But with rooms so limited and the rents so high, why not buy a World War II barracks and erect it in Pasco as a bachelor quarters hotel?

It was an idea of Glenn's that bore fruit and it was rooted not only in his hotel background but also in his attentiveness he had noticed officer quarters and barracks for sale in Bremerton, at the other end of the state. Glenn had checked and determined it would be relatively easy to dismantle one of the buildings and ship it to Pasco.

Two men, later to become big names in the business world, Edward Carlson and Lynn Himmelman, were induced to join with Bob and Glenn in the venture. They had met in the Navy and now Carlson and Himmelman were getting started in Western Hotels. They were refurnishing a hotel elsewhere and had extra beds, mattresses and other furnishings. So they put up the materials and Himmelman made the initial arrangements for the purchase of the surplus building.

Today, Carlson is president of United Airlines and Himmelman is president and chief executive officer of Western International Hotels.

Charles L. Powell, then a Kennewick attorney and later a U.S. District Court Judge, drew up the legal papers to form the Inland Development Corporation that would own and operate the Esquire Hotel, for men only. It was erected in 1948 near Washington street, a block from 10th street in Pasco. The two-story wooden building contained 24 rooms, with one room on each floor for showers, baths and toilets.

Occupancy, of course, was no problem but *Herald* employees had first call and special rates. About a year later when Glenn and Bob were desperately in need of cash—a never-ending problem in the early days—the hotel was sold to the Brown family who had owned the Kennewick Valley Telephone Company. The Browns had just sold their company to Interstate Telephone Company (now General Telephone) and had money to invest.

Shortly after their purchase, however, the "Big Freeze" of 1949 occured and up to 10,000 workers were laid off at Hanford in a period of days. It was a tremendous financial shock for the Tri-Cities. The new owners accused Glenn and Bob of having advance knowledge about the layoffs and "dumping" the hotel on them. The charge was based on anger, not fact, and anyway, the setback was but a temporary one. The hotel is still operating today.

So throughout those early months it was a continual, nagging problem of money, people, supplies and housing. New businesses suffer from some of these. It is just a matter of degree. In the case of *The Herald* the problems were aggravated by the region's remote location, its lack of a manpower pool and, ironically, the "boom" economy that had made living so expensive and goods so short.

Because it is off of the beaten track, manpower has essentially been a problem for *The Herald*. It has always been forced to go out and find its talent.

If that is true today, consider how magnified the problem had to be in 1947.

Glenn had located Verne Husk at the defunct *Vancouver Sun*, where he also hired *The Herald's* short-term business manager, Al Bean, and circulation manager, W. J. (Bill) Hunt. From the now defunct Hoquiam *Washingtonian* he hired advertising manager Mel Cheney. Cheney also was a short termer. One day he hopped a train out of Pasco and the next train brought in the Grays Harbor County sheriff looking for him in regards to some unfinished business he had left behind in Hoquiam. With Cheney's unexpected departure, Hunt took over the advertising department.

A large man with a pock-marked face, Hunt had a colorful personality and a flair for dramatics. At one time in his life he must have coveted being a police officer, for his spare time was spent with Pasco Police officers and Franklin County deputies. Sheriff Harvey Houston thought highly of Bill and deputized him.

Hunt left *The Herald* in 1949 and opened his own advertising and public relations firm. He later left the area and went first to Alaska and then to California where he was connected with several weekly newspapers.

The problems of news coverage leapfrogged when the decision was made to circulate in the three cities. Bill Bates was able to handle all the news duties for the weekly paper and it was decided he would continue to cover Pasco.

To supplement his work, Norman Van Brundt, just a few months out of the U of W, was hired to be Kennewick reporter, and Howard Sandsadt, a reporter on The Dalles (Ore.) *Chronicle*, was hired as Richland reporter.

For Woman's Page Editor, Glenn had hired Rovene Rhodes who had been recommended to him in Pendleton,

Oregon. Although she had no newspaper experience, Glenn was confident she could learn. Unexpectedly, Barbara Smith, an English major from the University of Nebraska, walked in to apply for work. It was a most unlikely thing to have happen but Barbara was visiting her sister and brother-in-law in Pasco. When she saw the announcement of the new daily she decided to see if she could help out. She was hired as proof reader and this completed the original editorial staff.

Although *The Herald* was branching into the other communities, its base would be Pasco, so there was naturally considerable debate on how much of the old *Pasco Herald* look and format it should have. Some of this discussion turned out as rather moot for the facilities were not available to make any great changes in the paper's appearance.

There was some feeling that stories should be datelined with the name of the city in which it originated. Hugh and Don stood firmly in opposition to this and they won. However, to prevent confusion and to quickly inform the reader as to which city was involved, writers were directed to place the name of the city in the story's first paragraph.

Likewise, Hugh and Don successfully opposed any idea of attempting to group stories of one city on one page of the paper. Barriers could best be bridged, they said, with a mixture of good stories, local and national throughout the paper.

Correspondents are the life blood of a weekly, but should they be used in a daily? Hugh and Don decided they should be used in order that too radical a change wasn't made that might alienate Franklin County readers. As a matter of fact, steps were taken to acquire correspondents in Richland and Kennewick who could keep the purely local touch in the news columns. After all, the Tri-Cities were, as Hugh often said, three small towns.

The *Pasco Herald* correspondents who continued were Gertrude Speier, who wrote a railroad column, "Switch Shanty Talk," and Edith Bergmann, who wrote social news. Edith had written for *The Herald* since high school days and she was still a correspondent in 1973, a period of 54 years.

Of course it had to come, the first discharge of an editorial department employee. Rovene Rhodes, *The Herald's* women's editor. She was an attractive young woman, eager to do her work but her lack of experience and newswriting background proved too great a barrier for her to overcome.

Ironically, the straw that did it concerned a wedding. In this day and age that doesn't seem possible but this happened to be a big wedding and one that had political significance. Alice Hogan, Democratic National Committee Woman, was marrying Roy West, an equally prominent Democrat from Ephrata. The party faithful turned out, headed by then Governor Mon C. Walgren.

The newspapers also turned out. Walla Walla and Spokane papers had made arrangements to have the event covered.

The wedding took place on a Saturday and the next day Hugh and Don discovered their women's editor had gone home to Pendleton for the weekend. *The Herald* was to have no story of the wedding in the Monday issue. I happened to be in Pasco that weekend househunting and was assigned to get the story.

I contacted Mrs. Hill (Ursula) Williams and learned she was the correspondent for the Walla Walla *Union-Bulletin*. She shared her notes with me.

"I have a maternal interest in *The Herald*," she said. "I would hate to see it get scooped."

I wrote the wedding story plus other women's page items she gave me, hung them on the hook for the Monday issue and returned to Tacoma.

Hugh and Don had decided a change in the women's page would have to come about. But who would replace Rovene? Don was impressed with Barbara Smith. He suggested that I become women's page editor long enough to set up the department and train her to take over.

Judging by Barbara's eagerness and ability she would be able to handle the position.

But that turned out to be the easy question. The hard one that remained was who would take on the unpleasant task of telling Rovene she was fired.

"As managing editor, it's your job," Hugh told Don.

"No way," Don replied. "I didn't hire her and she's a department head. You should do the honors."

"But I didn't hire her either," Hugh protested.

Finally they resolved the issue by flipping a coin. Hugh lost but he insisted Don sit in.

"It was just like shooting a wounded antelope between the eyes," Hugh recalls. "She was a lovely girl and she did have beautiful, big brown eyes!"

Surprisingly, whatever it was they expected never transpired. Rovene was very gracious and very accommodating. Some weeks later Hugh received a letter from her thanking him for sending her home and informing him she would soon be married.

The problem of finding reliable help was not the only problem *The Herald* faced in those first months of daily publication. Perhaps the most critical problem was finding an adequate supply of newsprint at a time when existing newsprint was already allocated and in short supply. A contract existed between Blake, Moffitt and Towne and *The Pasco Herald* for 40,000 pounds of newsprint (200 tons) to be withdrawn quarterly at a price of $5.25 per hundred weight. This contract was dated August 19, 1947, and was signed by Hugh. The amount would adequately serve the weekly but a daily was another matter.

Hugh wrote to the newsprint company on October 23 stating *The Herald* was planning daily publication and needed additional newsprint. In Seattle, Glenn made a personal call on Frank Carson of the newsprint company and was informed that Blake, Moffitt & Towne were "merely jobbers" who obtained all their newsprint from Powell-River Sales Co. in British Columbia. They, themselves, were on a limited budget.

On October 28, Hugh wrote to Congressman Hal Holmes stating *The Herald's* serious position with daily publication just ahead. Holmes had no solution so Hugh asked him to take up the newsprint matter with Congressman Clarence Brown of Ohio, who was assisting small newspapers in their newsprint problems.

Brown, as chairman of the Select Committee on Newsprint and Paper Supply, answered Holmes' inquiry November 8, just five days before the first daily came off the press.

"It is practically impossible," he wrote, "to find additional supplies of newsprint for any newspaper which wants considerable more newsprint than they have had in previous years, either because of increased circulation, increased advertising, or changing over from a weekly to a daily. The only hope for the average publisher in cases of this kind is to get his own supplier to furnish the paper."

When *The Herald* went daily, Glenn wrote to Holmes that, "We have literally hit a stone wall in regards to our search for additional newsprint. Two of the largest suppliers in the Pacific Northwest are Crown Zellerbach Corp. and Powell-River Sales Corp. On the weekly publication basis we have been obtaining Crown Zellerbach newsprint from Snyder-Crecelius Co. in Walla Walla. The Powell River newsprint we have been obtaining from Blake, Moffitt & Towne through the Yakima office.

"From each of these companies we have received an additional five tons for 1948 which is a drop in the bucket. We need 150 to 200 tons of newsprint for our 1948 requirements.

"As you undoubtedly know the mill price is $90 per ton. So-called black market prices are as high as $240 a ton f.o.b. New York City."

This was just the first in a long series of correspondence and personal calls in a relentless search for newsprint. The new publishers knew there was a newsprint shortage when they started but they had underestimated just how critical the shortage was. It was one of the brutal lessons they were to learn on the difficulties of operating a newspaper and, quite obviously, it was one of the reasons other publishers had decided not to start a daily in the Tri-Cities.

There was also another unexpected problem. It concerned the necessity of having a publishers' representative to assist in getting national advertising. *The Herald* quickly learned that it was not loved by neighboring publishers.

Glenn had called Charles Nicholson of West-Holiday Company in San Francisco, to make arrangements for the firm to represent *The Herald*. The company represented many other newspapers in Washington.

A letter from Nicholson followed to confirm the acceptance of the agreement. But the day the letter arrived a telegram also came from West-Holiday retracting the agreement and stating the company could not represent *The Herald*.

Glenn contacted John Kelly, publisher of the Walla Walla *Union-Bulletin,* to learn if he had objected to the arrangement. Kelly assured him the objection didn't come from Walla Walla and suggested he contact Ted Robertson, publisher of the Yakima *Herald-Republic*. Glenn did and Robertson assured him Yakima had not protested West-Holiday's representation.

A few weeks later Glenn and Don stopped in to see Cliff Kaynor, former longtime publisher of the *Ellensburg Record*. Glenn told him of his problems of national advertising representation.

"Cliff, who do you think objected to us?" Glenn asked.

"It had to be Kelly or Robertson," Kaynor said. "Why don't you ask them?"

"I have. I've asked each of them and they say it wasn't them."

Kaynor grinned and shrugged his shoulders.

"Who else would it be?"

Some years later the mystery was uncovered. Glenn learned that both Robertson and Kelly had objected.

The Walla Walla and Yakima papers would have been

adversely affected had West-Holiday represented *The Herald*. It would have cut into their national advertising lineage, as each of them claimed the Tri-Cities in their circulation area. The *Union-Bulletin* had almost 7,000 subscribers in Benton and Franklin Counties, a substantial part of its circulation.

Meanwhile, *The Herald* had obtained the firm of Lorensen and Thompson as its representative.

The small *Pasco Herald* plant became more and more cramped as the daily expanded in personnel and equipment. To obtain extra space, rooms were rented in the upstairs of a building across the street and the advertising and circulation departments moved into them. But this was most unhandy because it necessitated a constant flow of advertising copy across busy Fourth Street.

Offices were also needed in Kennewick and Richland. Space for a Kennewick office was rented on Kennewick Avenue at the northeast corner of Benton Street, in an automobile agency.

However, Richland was something else. A place could not be found because it was necessary to get permission from the Atomic Energy Commission. It seemed impossible to cut through the red tape and it was not until the *Tri-City Herald* had been operating for two years that it finally accomplished its goal of having an office in Richland. In the meantime it used the living room of the home of advertising staffer Helen Gleason.

"We can't accommodate just you," Milt Cydel, Director of Information for the AEC, told Don and Bill Bequette. "We have a responsibility to all newspapers, not just yours, and we are not in a position to provide facilities for all newspapers at this time."

It did no good to argue that no other newspapers were asking for accommodations because Cydel would say, "Can you guarantee they won't ask?"

In downtown Richland, across the street from the C. C. Anderson Department store, a shoe store was in business.

The store had a small room it was using to store brooms and other odds and ends. Glenn studied the closet and figured there was just enough room for a telephone and a typewriter but, in the emergency, it would have to do.

The shoe store's main office was in Spokane but the manager said he could see no problem. He would contact them for permission. The home office agreed but, in turn, contacted Richland AEC for permission. The AEC said no.

The Herald kept trying. Finally it managed to rent the building belonging to the Richland JayCees who used it only three nights a week. *The Herald* could use it as an office during the day. The structure was little more than a shack and had no heat. During the winter, the office girl went to work in ski pants and fur coat and used a good supply of electric heaters.

But it was, at least, a step towards gaining a foothold in Richland.

Glenn was finding that although his home was in Seattle, he was spending most of his time in the Tri-Cities. Hugh was also discovering that the job of "wearing two hats," that of editor and publisher, was involved and time-consuming. There was a myriad of financial and management decisions to be made. And the task of managing the editorial phase of the operation had grown tremendously. Don was doing both editing and writing.

It was decided that the two positions should be divided. Glenn would be publisher and Hugh editor.

Other things were changing too. Bob Philip was still in Seattle operating Philip and Lee, which was supporting *The Herald* while it was getting started.

But the export business was changing rapidly and many of Philip and Lee's good markets had either dried or were drying up. So Glenn decided to move his family to the Tri-Cities and it was agreed that Bob would remain in Seattle as long as Philip and Lee, Inc. was in business. That, as it worked out, was about another year. By 1949, the partners decided to sell their business for a nominal sum. Bob would also move to the Tri-Cities. Exporting appeared to have little future, but the newspaper appeared to be on the threshold of something big.

Glenn, the first of the partners to live permanently in the Tri-Cities, sold his home in the Magnolia district of Seattle, overlooking Puget Sound, and moved his family into a house at 916 Alder Street in Kennewick that could easily fit into the living room of his Seattle home.

When the Lee's furniture arrived in Kennewick, a third of it was put into the new home. The rest sat in the backyard to be sold through a *Herald* classified ad.

When Bob arrived he moved into Richland where a man of his temperment and ability was needed to promote good relations. He took the title of President of the Scott Publishing Company.

Money was so short Glenn was scratching all over to gain more. Even the money from the personal possessions he sold was put into *The Herald's* operating expenses.

Meanwhile, Glenn's brother-in-law, Vern Button, was operating his own business in Eau Claire. Glenn convinced Vern to sell and invest his money in *The Herald*. The Buttons came to Pasco in 1949. Glenn's brother, Howard, and his wife, Jerry, also came to Pasco.

In order to gain more operating capital, the office supply business was sold to Howard. Later, the commercial plant was sold to Verne Husk, who had decided to go into business for himself.

During the spring of 1948, Glenn and Bob had a serious discussion as to whether the newspaper could ever be made profitable. In talking to publishers around the state they learned most papers were making a profit. They knew other publishers couldn't be doing anything different from what *The Herald* was doing. But *The Herald* had an uncertain income with very high operating expenses and its owners were sorely under-capitalized.

Rather than return to weekly publication and take a serious financial loss, the partners decided on the following course:

Glenn was to spend two weeks at the *Bremerton Sun*

where, through the cooperation of the *Sun's* general manager, Alex Ottevaere, Glenn would work in the circulation,
classified and advertising departments, and also become
familiar with the other departments.

It was a "shotgun course" at best but from this experience Glenn gained considerable information in regards to
the solicitation of advertising and the management of a
newspaper. He also obtained a series of newspaper-printed
forms that were used in the various departments of the *Sun*
which would be helpful in the management of *The Herald*.
Glenn returned to the Tri-Cities to put these ideas to work.

Meanwhile, Bob was successfully selling common stock
to fraternity brothers. And Don was a unique managing
editor. He would put out the paper and then call on wheat
farmers to try and sell them *Herald* stock.

There was no humor to it then. It was deadly, serious
business. *The Herald* had shown it was a good newspaper,
but without sufficient capital the owners were going to
lose it.

5   *Vice In Pasco*

CHARLES POWELL, *The Herald's* attorney, bent slightly towards the witness chair and carefully scrutinized William J. Gaffney, Franklin County Prosecuting Attorney.

"Mr. Gaffney," said Powell in even tones, "if a woman stopped you on the street and said to you, 'Give me $5 and I'll take you up to my room and show you a good time,' would you say she was soliciting for prostitution?"

Gaffney sat upright and turned to the jury. "Why no," he answered, "she might wish to go to her room first to change so we could go out to dinner or a show. She might even want me to go to her room to play cards."

"Do you think it is likely that a woman who accosts you on the street and says that, might be talking of playing cards?" Powell wanted to know.

"It's possible," Gaffney said. "The point is, you don't know what she intends until you get to her room."

With bills due and supplies and personnel to be paid but with a limited supply of money available, the last thing in the world *The Herald* needed was a lawsuit for libel. Yet here it was in the dimly-lighted Franklin County court chamber defending itself against a $15,000 suit brought by Prosecutor Gaffney on two causes of action, both related to editorials *The Herald* had carried on his failure to prosecute and thus help in cleaning up Pasco vice and housing conditions.

It is natural to view a lawsuit by the judgement asked. But often that is the small part of the burden. There is the tremendous outlay in time and emotions preparing the case and the mounting costs in hiring attorneys and going through the legal steps necessary before trial.

Even today, in rereading the articles and editorials, if there were a way *The Herald* could have handled it differently I fail to see what it could be. The situation couldn't be ignored or, at least, *The Herald* wasn't inclined to ignore it.

As the paper said in an editorial in regards to what was required to clean up the problem:

"There is to be no temperizing with vice. The studied conclusion of social science is that the only way to control prostitution, venereal disease and gambling is to close down places that cater to such trade, arrest the practitioners for profit and generally follow a 'tough policy toward vice.' "

And vice was an agonizing thing in Pasco. The community didn't relish the title of "Sin Town" that some wags placed on it. Superior Court Judge B. B. Horrigan, a longtime resident of Pasco, gave vent to his anger one day and served up a somewhat unjudicial ultimatum that house of prostitution occupants would be prosecuted.

The judge found reports from health and police officers alarming and learned the conditions were growing worse. Capping it off, as *The Herald* reported, "the proprietor of a prospective house of ill fame in Pasco even went about the city seeking furnishings and fixtures without any attempt to conceal her purpose as though she was going into a legitimate business."

Meanwhile, the county had as a health officer an outspoken, no-nonsense physician named Charles Tudor who had declared war on unsanitary conditions in local trailer courts.

The main target of Dr. Tudor was the Connell Trailer Camp in Pasco, the same place that Hugh Scott and his family had parked their trailer in September. Dr. Tudor had ordered the proprietor of the court to "either clean up or close up."

So with a tough judge and health officer and with Pasco Police and the sheriff displaying the ability to strike out in raids, the stage was set for some real clean-up action. Unfortunately there was one part of the equation missing. They also had a prosecutor who disliked prosecuting. As a result, those arrested in police raids were soon free and busy at it again.

Prosecutor Gaffney was not corrupt. *The Herald* made it clear in an editorial one time that it had no cause to impugn his character or integrity, that they considered him honest. But his judgment and his ability as a prosecutor was something else. It was unfortunate that at this point in Pasco's history, he happened to be the prosecutor.

For instance, Dr. Tudor, at the end of his patience with the Connell Trailer Camp, requested Gaffney to maintain an action against Frank Connell, its owner, claiming it was a menace and operated in violation of the County ordinance.

A bitter dispute followed when Gaffney refused to prosecute and, as a matter of fact, also refused to take any part, maintaining that Frank Connell was endeavoring to rectify the conditions.

Gaffney told Dr. Tudor he considered Connell guiltless because no other trailer camps in the same area were in compliance with the ordinance!

The Herald made an investigation of its own. It discovered the trailer camp had only four toilets available for some 80 men and two of the four were not in operation. On the women's side there were four toilets, one of which had no door. One woman complained of carrying water for two weeks because of frozen water lines. She complained of scattered garbage and foul odors coming from the river where a drainage line emptied.

A complaint was prepared by Dr. Tudor and filed independent of the prosecutor in Justice Court. A jury trial was demanded by Connell. While the case was pending Gaffney went on radio and answered a front page *Herald* editorial titled "Gaffney Hasn't Learned."

"It was the sincere hope of this newspaper," the editorial said, "following the episode in December when a number of persons arrested for vagrancy were released without official action against them, that the Franklin County Prosecuting Attorney would make a more vigorous effort to clean up conditions of vice, gambling and health nuisances which existed and still exist in the vicinity of Pasco.

"He has not done so.

"In his latest failure . . . he has declined to prosecute Frank C. Connell . . . (he) has expressed his opinion to the effect that Connell has not violated the law in permitting about 25 of the original 60 tenants to keep their trailers in his court following (the) closure order . . .

"If Connell's court is a menace to public health, and Dr. Tudor's investigations would indicate that it is, Gaffney has a clear duty himself to close it down as a public nuisance. He has taken no steps in this direction . . ."

The editorial discussed the fears that criminal elements might obtain the impression that Pasco was a convenient place to operate. Citizens of Pasco would be justified in attempting to recall Gaffney, the editorial continued, but if they didn't surely the State Attorney General had a duty to investigate the prosecutor's performance record.

This editorial was one of Gaffney's causes of action when he sued for libel. His other cause of action was an editorial published December 26, 1947 titled "Who Fumbled The Ball?" Both editorials were written by Hugh and the December editorial was in regards to vice and gambling raids that concluded with those arrested being turned loose.

Don was an eyewitness to that raid and Gaffney almost had been except that—inadvertently or not no one would say for sure—he remained locked in a police paddy wagon when the raid was conducted.

The raid was held during the early morning hours of Sunday, December 12 and was under the supervision of Pasco Chief Alfred L. McKibbin, Sheriff Harvey Huston and W. J. O'Rourke, senior officer in charge of the State Liquor Control office. Plans for the raid had been carefully laid and when the officers assembled late Saturday night they were confined to specified areas so there would be no chance for a leak.

Ralph Smith, *The Herald's* photographer, was assigned to go along. And Don was surprised to notice that the paper's new advertising manager, Bill Hunt, although in civilian clothes, was carrying a gun and a deputy's badge.

About an hour before the raid was to commence Gaffney walked in. How he found out about it, or whether he just stumbled onto it, wasn't determined. But he was there and he insisted on accompanying the officers, much to the obvious dissatisfaction of the chief and sheriff.

Targets of the raid were two apparent rooming houses, Crescent Rooms and The Long House, the latter a small one-story structure, the former with two stories.

Don went ahead of the raiding party in his personal car and parked across the street from the two houses at a spot that provided him a good vantage position. The two buildings were located in the vicinity of Washington Street, just west of the railroad tracks between Lewis and Columbia streets. The Crescent Rooms was the first to be hit.

Don watched the police cars drive up. He blinked his eyes in disbelief as he watched Bill Hunt walk to the door and knock as any prospective customer might. A young woman opened the door. Hunt grabbed her, clapped his hand over her mouth and told her, "This is a raid!"

It was all in a moment that Hunt let out a wild yell, pulled his hand away from the woman's mouth while she screamed, "Look out everybody!" The young woman's mouth hadn't been completely closed when Hunt grabbed her. She bit down hard on his finger and the teeth marks stayed for days.

From his vantage point, Don watched men virtually ooze out through the seams of the building while law enforcement officers raced in. Don jumped from his car and ran over. As he passed one of the paddy wagons he could hear someone yelling and banging on its sides. It was too soon for any arrests to have been made.

"Who have you got in there?" he asked a deputy.

"That must be Mr. Gaffney," the deputy said tersely. "He came in that car."

Whether intentionally or unintentionally, the prosecutor was locked in the wagon while the raid was under way. Later he made his way into Crescent Rooms and Don observed him talking to the madam in the presence of one of the officers.

But if the prosecutor was the last at the raid he wasn't last in the next phase of the story which was summarized by the December 23 *Herald* headline which read:

"33 Victims of Vice Raid Released"

Excerpts from the story read:

"Hope for a grand slam play against Pasco vice was dashed last night as vagrancy charges against 33 victims of a Sunday morning police raid were dropped following an opinion by Prosecuting Attorney William J. Gaffney that available evidence was insufficient to support the charges.

"Gaffney said this morning the raid plans were drawn without his advice . . ."

The Dec. 26 editorial which followed placed the blame for the failure of the charges with the prosecutor, contending he was destroying the initiative and confidence of enforcement agencies "by turning their efforts to subjects of ridicule."

A prosecutor, the editorial said, should be taking the lead and making "constructive efforts to build cases against those persons who, in his judgment, were most liable to be found guilty of serious offenses . . ."

There was only one radio station in the Tri-Cities at that time and the prosecutor went on the air to defend himself. Next, he submitted a letter to *The Herald* that required a column and a half to print and in which he claimed the paper had attacked both his private and professional ability as a public prosecutor. He demanded a retraction.

The letter ended with the statement: "I stand for honest, decent law enforcement and I have said many times I will cooperate with all enforcement agencies to that end."

Tri-City Herald editorial staff on third anniversary, November 13, 1950; from left, Jim Grant, Jack Phillips; Ursula Williams, Womens Editor; Paul Busselle, News Editor, seated; Don Becker, Sports Editor; Ellen Turner, Photo Technician; Bill Bequette; Hill Williams, Jr.

His desire to protect the constitutional rights of his fellow men was stronger than his fear of public criticism, he wrote.

Elsewhere in the paper was an editorial stating it was not *The Herald's* intent to impugn Gaffney's character and integrity. The matter appeared to have ended and presumably would have ended there had not the Connell Trailer Camp situation arose less than two months later.

So within four months of the time it had begun daily publication, *The Herald* was a defendant in a libel suit. As it turned out, the experience was one which would not be uncommon. Within a year another libel suit would be filed and others would follow until the paper had gained the unenviable reputation of being the most sued in the history of the state. Undoubtedly that isn't true but in *The Herald's* case the suits didn't come because some reporter misread his notes or a printer created a typographical error. They came as the result of investigations, of critical editorials and probably because the area was as new as the newspaper. The Tri-Cities lacked stability in those early years and it attracted "boomers" who were after the fast bucks.

Herald attorney Powell entered a demurrer to Gaffney's suit on grounds Gaffney had not stated a cause of action. Judge Whitfield of Ellensburg sustained the demurrer.

Gaffney appealed to the State Supreme Court which ruled in his favor and the case was sent back to Superior Court for trial.

If tried today, Gaffney would not have won his case because of the U. S. Supreme Court's decision in the celebrated Sullivan vs. *New York Times* case that a person of prominence, such as a political figure, must expect criticism and can recover only if he can prove malice.

The jury trial was held in July, 1950 in Pasco before Judge Robert Hunter of Ephrata. The jury returned a verdict in favor of *The Herald* on one cause of action, and for Gaffney in the sum of $2,000 on the second cause of action.

Following the verdict, Powell advised Gaffney that he would show himself as a rather substantial individual if he would merely file a satisfaction of judgment and show he wasn't interested in the money and had sued solely for vindication.

Gaffney couldn't see it that way. "Gaffney dies hard," he told Powell.

He sought re-election that November and was overwhelmingly defeated. Gaffney moved to Moses Lake where he opened a law practice.

I sat in the court room during the trial and studied the faces of the jurors. I even sat in a car outside the Crescent Rooms waiting while Don called on the madam to gain additional evidence for our case.

Afterwards we had many discussions as to why the jury would have found against *The Herald*. Our case seemed so solid and we debated what other outside influences might have carried into the jury room.

The editorials of late 1947 and early 1948 were carried in a young, struggling Pasco newspaper. When the case was tried in 1950 we were still young and struggling but we were now printing in Kennewick and an element of bitterness persisted in Pasco because of our move across the river.

We were also controversial. Four months before the trial the printers and pressmen unions had gone on strike and the paper had continued to publish. Pasco was a strong union community.

In addition, *The Herald* had campaigned vigorously against a new housing project in Pasco that did not meet basic Federal Home Administration standards and violated city building codes. Another lawsuit—*The Herald's* second —resulted from this and although most citizens supported the paper, there were, nonetheless, many who wished it would just shut up.

Finally, there was the matter of politics. Franklin County is a Democratic stronghold, and in 1948 *The*

Herald came out in favor of the entire slate of Republicans, from President to the state legislature.

Hugh believed that every newspaper should endorse and speak out for a political party. Don didn't favor party endorsements. He also felt the paper was not on its feet yet and thus was not strong enough to get involved in something as partisan as a political campaign. But both of them were new to the Tri-Cities and didn't realize the strong undercurrent of existing political feelings. *The Herald* created much ill-will for itself when it stirred the political pot.

It was natural, of course, that the severe housing shortage in Pasco would bring in many developers and builders for the ready-made market. As a result, the landscape literally blossomed with new homes. We moved into a new house in late 1947 that was on the outskirts of Pasco. A couple of years later it was in the middle of town, so fast did the development take place.

I have remarked on how Pasco had changed in a couple of years. So had *The Herald.* Its growth had been rapid and there had been changes and additions to its staff.

Hugh Scott had left the company for Kelso and had taken with him Bill Bates and his wife, who was the Woman's Editor.

Bill Hunt also left, and the advertising manager was Jack Gillis, who took over in 1949.

Jack was a native of British Columbia. He entered the newspaper field in 1927 with the *Seattle Post-Intelligencer* circulation department. He handled specials for the *Los Angeles Times* for eight years and joined the now defunct *Bremerton News-Searchlight* in 1943. When the *News-Searchlight* consolidated with the *Bremerton Sun* in April, 1945 Jack became advertising manager. He handled this until Glenn convinced him to become advertising manager of *The Herald.*

Later Jack hired three members of the *Sun's* advertising staff, Bob Smith, Gordon Moen and John Eckert.

Al Bean was replaced as business manager by Richard Galbraith from the *Pendleton East Oregonian.* Following Galbraith from Pendleton was William Bequette, news editor of the *East Oregonian.*

A native of Montana, Bill graduated from the University of Montana and served with the 41st Division during World War II. He had been in Pendleton three years, long enough to meet and marry his wife, Neva. When they arrived in the Tri-Cities the Mid-Columbia Library was just beginning and with a background in this field, Neva was offered the position of head librarian.

B. T. Russell, from Louisiana, became mechanical superintendent when Verne Husk bought *The Herald's* commercial printing department. Ford Wiley, from the suspended *Tacoma Times,* was circulation manager. Another Tacoman, Paul Busselle, former managing editor of the *Tacoma Times,* had joined *The Herald* as news editor.

The editorial staff had expanded to nine members. In addition to Don, Busselle and Bill Bequette, there was Don Becker, sports editor; Mrs. Hill Williams, women's page editor; her son, Hill Williams Jr., reporter; and James Grant and Jack Phillips, reporters. Ellen Turner was added as a photographic technician, and Helen Jones Wheeler handled Richland women's news.

By this time the Saturday paper, never a good revenue producer, was dropped in favor of a Sunday morning paper. The first Sunday edition went to press in February, 1949.

So *The Herald* was growing rapidly. Especially heartening was the public acceptance it was receiving. It covered the news; it was aggressive; it was quick to speak its mind and it was informed. It was also controversial, but most important, *The Herald* was believed.

Were it not for the nagging financial problems the future couldn't have looked brighter. *The Herald* was demonstrating it could bring in revenue. But, unhappily, it was a costly operation, especially with three cities to serve. The paper thus was spending money faster than it was bringing it in.

Forbidden To Print

THERE was much consternation in 1971 when a federal court issued an injunction which restrained the *New York Times* from printing "The Pentagon Papers." It was announced that this marked the first time in the history of our nation that a newspaper had been restrained by court order from printing the news.

The claim was made several times and finally Bill Bequette walked over to Don with the most recent *Associated Press* story and said, "They can't really make this claim. Shouldn't we set the record straight?"

A few hours later there followed an *Associated Press* story with a Pasco dateline which corrected the error.

The dispatch said, in part:

> "The *New York Times* was not the first newspaper to be restrained by a court order from publishing an article, says the editor of a Washington newspaper which faced similar circumstances 20 years ago.

> "The *Tri-City Herald* was restrained from publication of a November, 1949, series of articles which alleged faulty construction of homes, executive editor Don Pugnetti said Wednesday.

> "Pugnetti said the *New York Times* was among papers which came to *The Herald's* support during what was a widely noted case then.

> "*The Times* has been restrained by a federal court from publication of further articles in a

series based on a secret Pentagon study of U. S.
policy in the Vietnam war."

Glenn was out of town on November 18, 1949 and Don
was in charge when a deputy sheriff entered and, in the
matter-of-fact manner he had done hundreds of times
before, served the restraining order on Don.

The order was signed by Judge Horrigan. It directed
The Herald not to publish more articles regarding shoddy
construction practices used on a group of tract houses in
Pasco, until the court could determine whether the temporary injunction should be made permanent.

It was an unprecedented action and, of course, Don was
a relatively new editor. He recognized it as an unusual
court order but at the same time he didn't know how
unusual it really was. Don and Bill Bequette carefully read
the order several times.

The fourth and final article in Bequette's series was
already in type and it was only a couple of hours before
press time.

"What are you going to do?" Bill asked.

"I'll be damned if I know," Don answered. "I don't think
the court can prevent us from publishing. The court can't
edit this paper, can it?"

"We are responsible for what we print, but I don't think
they can stop us from publishing," Bill agreed.

"What will they do if we publish anyway?" Don wondered.

"They'll probably throw you in jail."

"I'm not that sold on going to jail," Don said. "But what
I really hate to do is violate a court order, even a peculiar
one like this."

Charlie Powell's office was just a block up the street
from *The Herald* but he happened to be away. Don
presented the order to his law partner, Tom Gess. Gess
checked the law and informed Don of what his rights were
and what the circumstances could be if the order was
not obeyed.

69

But on the crucial item, to publish or not to publish, Gess backed away.

"I can't make the decision for you. The decision is yours," he said.

It was a heavy decision and Don weighed it carefully in the limited time available to him before deadline. He questioned whether a newspaper should violate a court order. Is a newspaper above the law, he wondered? He also wondered how disrespect to the court would appear to the public. Readers can respect a gutsy newspaper even though it at times may blunder into consequences of no one's choosing. But what of an *arrogant* paper?

There was also the financial consideration. One way or the other, it was obvious there would be a lawsuit. Complications could be costly.

But in the end, the decision rested on one thing only. All other considerations were placed aside. It was the question of whether a newspaper should violate a court order. Don told production manager Bernie Russell:

"Pull the story, save the type."

In place of the fourth and final article *The Herald* instead carried a notice to its readers of what had happened and the fact the last article would not be published until the restraining order was dissolved. Said the headline:

"Court Order Halts Series In Herald"

It was a somewhat subdued plant to which Glenn returned on Saturday. He was furious that such an order had been issued and Don, who was downhearted and sensitive over having pulled the story, took Glenn's reaction as criticism of what he had done.

Glenn quickly sensed this and told him, "I'm not being critical of you. I'm just mad at the whole situation."

"If you had been here, what would you have done?" Don asked.

"I'd have published the damn thing, court order or no court order," Glenn answered.

"And what would we gain by showing disrespect to the court?" Don asked. "Our argument isn't with the court."

"Pug," Glenn responded, "I always have said there is opportunity in every adversity. I think maybe we are in a better position for not having published than by publishing. What's done is done. Now let's turn this to our advantage."

Don and Glenn huddled for several hours discussing the various avenues open to the paper. Then they drafted a statement which was printed on the Sunday front page over Glenn's signature as publisher. It was a statement that was carried by the *Associated Press* and *United Press* and went around the country.

Set in two column measure and headed "A Statement" it said, in part:

> "Freedom of the Press is guaranteed by the United States Constitution and cannot be abridged by Law or the Courts.
>
> "The United States Supreme Court has repeatedly held that news cannot be restrained or enjoined before publication.
>
> "A newspaper is responsible for what it prints.
>
> "The *Tri-City Herald* is now, and always will be, responsible for what it prints.
>
> "As a point of respect and courtesy, *The Herald* complied with the court order on Friday.
>
> "*The Herald* is a newspaper by the people and for people. In the case at hand the people are deeply and vitally concerned.
>
> "*The Herald* had always printed the news and it will keep on printing the news, when and where and how it occurs.
>
> "A nation will remain a free nation only as long as we have Freedom of the Press interpreted by free newspapers.
>
> "We, and newspapers throughout the nation, await the hearing on Tuesday."

The national newspaper reaction was overwhelming. It filled the wire service reports. News reporters from distant points telephoned for details that were not contained in the wire service stories. It was the subject of much editorial discussion. Months after the matter was adjudicated, *The Herald* was receiving editorials on the subject from other newspapers that had been clipped and mailed by journeying Tri-Citians.

B. M. McKelway, executive editor of the *Washington (D.C.) Star* and president of the American Society of Newspaper Editors, said, "The case sets a highly dangerous precedent of restraint before publication."

Lew Selvidge, executive secretary of the Washington State Allied Dailies Newspaper Association, said the suit was "unprecedented in this state" and added that the Supreme Court has ruled repeatedly that such an order is in violation of the United States Constitution.

Selvidge was also shocked that Judge Horrigan had only required a $1,000 bond from the construction company.

"I would recommend that this matter be fought to the bitter end. It is in direct violation of the Constitution and rulings of the Supreme Court," he said.

The editorial comment in the newspapers was particularly rough on Judge Horrigan and it was evident Tuesday morning when the parties gathered to argue his restraining order that the judge was feeling the pressure.

His telephone had been ringing with calls from the East, South, North and West, and from news magazines like *Time* and *Newsweek* as well as the newspapers.

Time Magazine sent a correspondent to Pasco, then wrote in its December 5 Press Section:

"The construction company . . . complained to Superior Court Judge Bartholomew B. Horrigan, 69, who runs a wheat ranch on the side, that *The Herald's* series would make it impossible to get a fair trial of the Kestin suit. Headlong, Judge Horrigan promptly forbade *The Herald* to publish any more stories on the houses, forced it to yank the fourth article a half hour before press time. Last week, after rereading the Bill of

Oregon Journal editorial cartoon describing Judge Horrigan's injunction against *The Herald*. Artist Howard Fisher gave the original to Glenn.

John Cartano, Mid-Columbia Construction Co. attorney argues the injunction before Judge B. B. Horrigan. Backs to camera, from left: *Herald* attorneys Dean Loney, Mark Moulton, and Charles Powell.

Rights, Judge Horrigan decided he had gone too
far. He rescinded his injunction . . ."

Judge Horrigan held that the burden of proof in the
restraining order rested with the plaintiff.

"It is my judgement that this had not been sustained.
Therefore the restraining order must be dissolved," he said.

At the same time, Judge Horrigan also ruled that the
articles by the newspaper had made it impossible for the
Columbia Construction Co. Inc., which is no longer in
business, to try their case in Franklin County without
prejudice. He said that on this basis he would not dismiss
the suit and that the plaintiff had the right to press con-
tempt proceedings. Attorney John Cartano, who represented the construction company, indicated he would file
suit against the paper.

The fourth article in the series finally was published on
November 23. It revealed the Plumbers Union was dis-
pleased with the workmanship of the plumbing in the
houses in question. One of its members, who worked on
what the union described as a "rotten" job, was fined
$2,500 by the union.

Some of the discrepancies included the fact there were
no cleanouts in the sewage pipes, and that FHA minimum
requirement was that "cleanouts shall be provided at the
base of the main stack and at all bends in excess of 45
degrees" was violated. Cleanouts were also recommended
in the State Department of Health "basic plumbing
principles."

The article also said the union was taking issue on many
more points. The job was never "tested", as recommended
by the State Department of Health. There were "wet
vents" that shouldn't exist and wrong fittings.

The bathroom basin was wet vented by the kitchen sink.
If a stoppage occurred the sink water would come up both
in the bathtub and the bathroom basin.

Another point was that since the houses were not on the
city sewer lines, the septic tank drains were not buried

deep enough. The liquid matter was bleeding to the top of the ground in several cases.

The article also disclosed that Dr. Tudor had required that the contractor put performance bonds on the septic tanks. This was because the tanks had been covered before they were inspected. According to Dr. Tudor it seemed the only recourse short of making the contractor dig them up.

The plumber who was fined $2,500 by the union appealed to the State Board of Master Plumbers. The board, however, upheld the Pasco union's action but reduced the fine.

Columbia Construction Company houses were low-cost and built to attract veterans of World War II who could take advantage of G.I. loans at a low rate of interest. Many of the veterans were renting wartime housing units in Navy and Parkside homes, located between 4th and Court streets and the railroad yards.

One veteran who decided to purchase a home in its pre-construction state, believing it would be finished off according to specifications in the contract, was Lloyd Kestin, a young Pasco school teacher.

While waiting for his wife, Mildred, to receive her degree in Education, Kestin took a post-graduate course in industrial engineering. This helped him spot discrepancies which seemed to be cropping up in the construction.

Soon buyers got together and compared notes. In one house, it was discovered that when the pump released the water in the washing machine it would back up in the bathtub. Also, according to the contract, the houses were to be furnished with top-grade appliances. Instead they were furnished with the cheapest brands. The wall-to-wall carpeting, which was to be put down to cover the concrete floor, was supposed to have been of good quality. Instead it was an inferior brand.

Some of the more active members of the veterans group with Kestin were William Ellis, Joe Piester and Bud Markham. They made an unsatisfactory trip to Seattle to obtain help from the Veterans Administration. Finally, in desperation, the group called *The Herald* and asked for help in exposing the injustces. What resulted was a hard-hitting series of articles written by Bequette. The first article appeared November 13, 1949, *The Herald's* second birthday.

An editor's note accompanying the article said: "This is the first in a series of articles on housing conditions that exist in the Tri-Cities. This series concerns itself with housing construction that apparently does not meet minimum requirements of the Federal Housing Administration, yet these homes are approved by Tri-City area FHA inspectors and approved by the Veterans Administration. Most of the homes were sold to veterans. What they bought—with FHA approval—will be contained in the series."

Bequette wrote:

"F.H.A. stands for 'Fooled, Hoodwinked and Angry' to a score or more families who bought homes in a West Pasco housing project.

"Some of the houses, all of which were approved and insured by the Federal Housing Administration, whose stamp to most people means good construction, had cracks through which the sand—and the cold wind—whistled.

"Some had warped doors and faulty windows. Some had a heating system that easily could cause a disaster. Some had a plumbing system that apparently does not meet FHA's own minimum standards, to say nothing of State Department of Health rules and regulations.

"And some had studdings that apparently violate Pasco's building code. Some of the houses' septic tanks already are 'bleeding' through the top of the ground.

"A number of the houses in the group showed signs of poor workmanship, sloppy and, or, hasty finishing. The electric wiring in several of the houses left much to be desired. In at least two homes the light switches were cross-wired.

"Some houses, as completed, differ on several counts with the original blueprints. Yet these houses, built by

Columbia Construction Co., were approved by the FHA and by the Veterans Administration.

"Many of these homes have been sold to war veterans, who formerly lived in Parkside and Navy Homes. The contractor at present is correcting some of the faults found by this newspaper. The contractor indicates others will be corrected.

"The houses are one-story wooden frame shelters with concrete tile covered floors. They have a fairly decent sized living room, a kitchen, bathroom, and two not-too-large bedrooms. They are attractive on the outside with their pastel shades and eye-pleasing shapes . . ."

On Page 1, that day, also was a story telling of a lawsuit that was filed by the company which alleged Kestin had broken his purchase contract. It sought to collect the balance of the purchase price, about $7,500. The court had also permitted the company to garnishee Kestin's wages as a Pasco teacher and attach his bank account.

Kestin claimed he would not sign the mortgage until he was assured certain faults would be corrected. He listed these major faults as poor workmanship, a plumbing system that did not meet State Health Department regulations and an over-priced appraisal.

What resulted was an agreement to arbitrate the dispute. Both sides agreed to be bound by what the arbitrators agreed should be done. Kestin stated he felt the suit was an attempt by Columbia to coerce the other veterans into signing their mortgages. Columbia officials denied this.

The second of Bequette's articles was entitled, "They Were Burning Lots of Oil During Recent Chilly Days." This told of how the cold air seeped into the houses exceeding the ability of the space heaters to keep them warm, and how, when the wind blew, sand built up in piles on the floors.

The cracks in some of the houses were wide enough to permit a board the thickness of a lath to be shoved through. The houses were heated by small oil stoves crammed into a recess in the halls. In some houses they were set so close to the walls the fire boxes were within nine inches of the inflammable wallboard. The walls were not protected with fire-resistant material.

Some of the houses *The Herald* inspected had chimneys that appeared to have been thrown together instead of having been laid. If there was gobs of mortar on the inside comparable to what Bequette found on the outside, wasn't it reasonable to assume the flues would be clogged with soot and be difficult to clean? Yet these houses were inspected by the FHA.

High points in the third article included the fact that Pasco's building code had been violated in several instances. Some of the houses, Bequette reported, had studding that was 24 inches "on center" while Pasco's Uniform Building Code specified 16 inches. The blue prints showed 16-inch studdings.

The plans had been changed before construction started despite FHA's so-called "minimum standards," which specifically stated local regulations must be complied with "where such regulations provide for a higher standard than these requirements." Yet the houses were approved by FHA.

Bequette learned the builder had been warned by the Veterans Administration when only a few of the houses had been started, that the spacing of the studs violated the city code. The warning was only verbal and was not heeded.

When city building inspector, A. N. Haylett, discovered the violation he ordered the contractor to stop operations. Haylett then consulted the city engineer. They discussed whether they should tear down the frames and build them according to the code or allow the builder to continue on the houses already started, but make him strengthen them. They chose the latter course.

The contractor was ordered to lateral brace all houses that had "24-inch on center" studding. But after the contractor placed the lateral bracing, which should have made the houses strong enough, some of the braces were found to be cracked. It was also found that the braces had been nailed on without much care.

Irate veterans crowded the Pasco City Council Chambers and asked for a change in the building code and the dismissal of Haylett. A councilman so moved, but the motion was amended to consider the matter at a special hearing. Haylett weathered the attempt to force his resignation and the matter was conveniently placed in the hands of a committee.

In choosing arbitrators, Bert Bowell of Kennewick was appointed to represent home owners, and James Pierce of Pasco to represent the construction company. Meanwhile, other investigations of similar housing projects involving veterans took place in other cities as an outgrowth of the attention focused on Pasco. One of these cities was Spokane.

The arbitrator's report was made public on December 9. Its main points called for correction of heating systems, caulking of cracks and rough-grading of lots. In addition to general correction, the arbitrators ordered specific remedies of defects on individual houses. However, they recommended no changes in the plumbing or structure of the houses. They held that since no plumbing plan existed for the houses and since wet vents and lack of cleanouts was prohibited by any building codes applicable, the arbitrators "declined further comment."

The arbitration agreement was signed by the construction firm and about 20 of the purchasers. The court actions against Kestin were dismissed and it appeared the entire controversy had been satisfactorily ended. Perhaps it was too much to hope for. Like a forest fire that is thought under control and then flares up again, the underlying fire of this situation wasn't out, it was only simmering.

It broke into full fury again when Ray Malone, executive secretary of the Associated Plumbing and Heating Contractors of Washington, disassociated himself from that portion of the arbitration settlement on the plumbing that was based on a statement he had made.

Plumbing was one of the main points in the dispute and the arbitrators had quoted Malone as saying the lack of cleanouts would make no difference. Malone was not a plumber and he was angered that an arbitration award would be based on something he had said.

Within weeks a lawsuit was filed by the homebuyers asking the court to set aside the arbitration award which, they said, "was procured by corruption, fraud and other undue means." The lawsuit also alleged there was "evidently partiality or corruption in the arbitrators" who were "guilty of misconduct" and "misbehavior."

The Herald came out with a free-swinging editorial written by Don titled, "Veterans Are Still Fighting." It reviewed the problem and then came down hard on the Federal Housing Administration for staying aloof; it listed the obvious questions that had been repeatedly coming to the attention of the newspaper and it demanded some answers.

Shortly thereafter, on three successive mornings, Don was met at the office door by a process server. On each morning he was served with a $100,000 libel suit. The suits were based on the two news stories by Bequette and Don's editorial. The construction company sought $100,000 and so did each of the arbitrators.

The libel suit was tried in Pasco before Judge Richard B. Ott, of Ritzville. The suit alleged that the news stories and editorial "exceeded any right of fair and impartial news comment," and were motivated by spite and malice against the plaintiffs.

Charlie Powell represented *The Herald*, assisted by Theodore Peterson, a Pasco attorney. The jury panel was exhausted twice before 12 jurors and an alternate were selected. The suit quickly got down to the editorial when it was shown that the news stories had merely reported from the court pleadings.

A vice president of the construction company testified his company was "run out" of the area by the editorial. "We felt we could no longer build in this area and make sales," he said. "When a newspaper comes out and blasts you . . . brands you as the editorial of February 16, 1950, did." His company "didn't have anything left," he asserted.

But after the plaintiffs rested their case, Judge Ott dismissed the suit. He ruled the editorial was "fair comment." He observed that one in three of the Columbia-built homes had ended up in court. "If that is not a shocking development then I don't know what is," he declared. "This is not unfair comment in view of the record as it now is before the court."

While Judge Ott was reading his decision, an electrical storm raging outside knocked out the courthouse lights. Aides quickly brought in an old kerosene lantern and the judge continued his pronouncement in the flickering light that cast an eerie spell over the courtroom. Everyone sat transfixed, including me.

Powell moved for a non-suit and renewed an earlier motion for a general demurrer. Judge Ott granted the non-suit.

The plaintiff's attorney, John Cartano of Seattle, said the decision would be appealed. He also indicated he would press for a trial of another $100,000 libel suit by Columbia Construction against *The Herald*. This latter suit had been filed in November, 1949, while *The Herald* was publishing Bequette's articles, but neither of these actions ever took place.

When court was adjourned a group of home buyers, who had been present to hear the suit, swarmed around Don and warmly embraced him. It was April 19, 1951, one day after Don's birthday.

Judge Ott's decision was a day late, but it had to be the best birthday present Don has ever received.

7   *The Flood That Came To Town*

THERE was an unusually tense look on the faces of Glenn and Don when they hurried in the front door of our house on that beautiful Sunday, Memorial Day of 1948.

"Start packing your things," Don said. "You and Brian are leaving tonight, just as soon as we can get you out of here."

I was well aware, of course, that the Columbia River was flooding, but I thought it had been contained.

"Is it that bad?" I asked.

"It's not only bad, it's going to get worse," Glenn said. "Right now the city is fighting to save the sewer system. If that goes we could have a typhoid epidemic."

Just before they arrived, I had heard the fire bell pealing loudly on top of the city hall, about eight blocks away.

"That was to call for volunteers to hook up the water system to the auxiliary pump at 'Big Pasco,' " Don explained. Pasco's pump was under water.

"Big Pasco" was the name given to the huge World War II ordinance depot and reconsignment point southeast of the city. It was a complete facility with its own sewer, water, railroad sidings and gigantic warehouses. It was now in standby condition.

The Columbia River flood of 1948, the most damaging in its history, cannot be repeated because dams now regulate its flow and store its water. In 1948, the Columbia was truly a "free-flowing river," and aside from what control could be maintained by Grand Coulee, the river was king.

Stimulated by unusually heavy Spring rains and Winter snowpack, conditions spelled trouble for the four Northwest states when the weather turned unseasonably warm and the snow began to melt.

Tributaries to the Columbia swelled and eventually overran their banks. Northern Idaho and Western Montana were first to feel the force of the heavy runoffs. But Washington and Oregon residents who bordered the Columbia were anxiously watching the river gauges.

Near the end of May in Northern Idaho and Eastern Washington, the St. Joe, Snake, Clearwater and Spokane Rivers hit new peaks. These forced up the level of the mighty Columbia. As the water surged towards the Tri-Cities, floods near Ellensburg knocked out six bridges and numerous county roads.

It was only the beginning, but surprisingly in the Tri-Cities business went on as usual. No one was really prepared for what was yet to come, although Kennewick Police Chief Ward Rupp was regularly in touch with officials at Grand Coulee Dam.

By May 23, the Columbia had risen another foot at Pasco and knocked out the Sacajawea State Park water supply and threatened a few popular areas along the river banks. Dozens of picnickers were stranded without water or sanitary facilities for several hours when rising water flooded the electrical pump supplying well water. But no one could get excited about picnickers.

The next day the river reached 335.9 feet above sea level, the highest in seven years.

On May 26, a *Herald* story, written by Don, reported that Chief Rupp had been informed by Grand Coulee Dam officials the Columbia would rise another two feet within the next 48 hours. Kennewick emergency services began to gear for the trouble they belatedly realized lay directly ahead.

But nothing too serious had happened. The mooring float at Clover Island had broken away and gone sailing down the river. Owner Murl Kirk, a marina operator, rode the float downstream and finally forced it to shore. Clover Island was becoming little more than a dot in the river and some privately owned planes usually moored there had departed. Soon the water was less than a foot from their hangars.

Now things really began happening. About 2 a.m., May 27, Don received a telephone call from Chief Rupp saying that a wall of water had passed over Grand Coulee Dam and was rushing towards us. Don hurriedly dressed and dashed out the door. I didn't see him again for 22 hours.

The first alarm was sounded to trailer courts that had sprung up along the river. Frantic efforts to clear the trailer parks turned into almost near panic when some trailer owners discovered broken axles, missing wheels, and a myriad of other problems that prevented escape.

At daybreak it was learned the report was an exaggeration. But the flood did come, not as a wall of water as first feared, but in great volume.

The news story that resulted, ran that day under heavy block type an inch and a half high, which bannered the front page, "1000 Families Forced Out," and had the subheads: "General Evacuation of River Trailer Camp is Ordered"; "Columbia Due To Rise Further"; and "AEC Rushes Effort To Keep Road to 'Y' Open."

The story, written by Don, said in part:

"More than 1,000 Tri-City families fled the waters of the Columbia and Yakima Rivers this morning as county and city authorities moved to avert disaster from the impending flood. The word to evacuate the river road area from Kennewick to the Yakima River bridge was given. Immediately families began storing possessions and harnessing trailers to escape the persistent flood water.

"All trailer and cabin camps on the river side of Highway 410 were ordered evacuated. For the most part all were emptied by 5 a.m. today. However, Capt. A. E. Barron of the Richland

Patrol, said some die-hards were hanging on 'come hell or high water.'

"The Columbia, which has been threatening for the past two weeks, grew rampant yesterday when it raised an additional foot. At the same time a cloudburst north of Yakima swelled the Yakima River into a raging torrent causing authorities to estimate a high of four to six feet by sometime tomorrow."

The story also told of the strenuous effort to save a causeway which was being constructed by Wallace Bateman, owner of Bateman Island lying directly across from Island View. There were homes on the island and although much of the island was underwater it seemed that the causeway would be saved.

Pasco was not completely safe from the rising water. The Connell Trailer Camp was flooded and trailers were forced onto the road above the camp. A warning of the flood was broadcast by KPKW, the area's only radio station. The station loaned a sound truck and an announcer and they toured the flood-threatened area warning residents.

The debris-laden Columbia was now within 10 feet of the tracks on the railroad bridge, about 200-feet downriver from the State Highway 410 bridge.

As each day passed the river kept rising. The Tri-Cities resembled a scene from a modern day "Gone With The Wind." As homes were threatened, National Guard trucks carried household articles to higher ground.

Drinking water became suspect and Dr. Tudor issued a statement through *The Herald* "strongly advising" residents of the Pasco-Kennewick area to boil water for at least 10 minutes.

Tap water was so dark brown that my son Brian's diapers came out of the wash a dingy color. I wasn't ashamed to hang them on the line, however, because my neighbor's wash looked just as bad.

To take a bath in that water was a revolting experience.

It was easier to take a shower so the color of the water was less noticeable.

Typhoid shots were given free by the Health Department in the Franklin County Courthouse.

The Herald was hard hit by the sharp decline of retail business during the flood. In fact, shopping came almost to a standstill. This caused a heavy loss of advertising for the paper and, in addition, the merchants were having a hard time paying their advertising bills. This further contributed to the serious financial condition of the newspaper.

For the duration of the emergency, *The Herald* carried a box on Page One entitled, "Flood at a Glance." It contained the notation: "These are the highlights of the flood today after a thorough survey by members of *The Herald* editorial staff which is on duty 24 hours a day keeping abreast with flood information for *Herald* readers."

On Friday, May 29, for example, the feature contained the following news flashes:

"1. Young Smith, district road engineer for the State Highway Department, says the Columbia will rise another foot and four-tenths inches by noon Saturday.

"2. James Krueger, Pasco City Engineer, has been loaned to the City of Kennewick to work with the street committee in finding a solution to the increasing sewer problem.

"3. Milton Cydell, Information Control Officer for the Atomic Energy Commission, reports Richland residents do not need to boil water as the Richland Water supply has not been injured by the flood.

"4. All truck traffic has been detoured from Highway 410 through the Highlands and over Sonderman Road as water spread across Smith's Curve and 400 and 500 feet into the area west of the curve.

"5. Sections of the causeway to Clover Island have been overrun. Kennewick city engineer, Joe

Stradling, reports the north end of the causeway went out at midnight."

Another story in that issue told of *The Herald* having to fly its newspaper bundles to Richland subscribers. Two planes, chartered by *The Herald* from Washington Skyways of Pasco, took heavy bundles from the Pasco airport to the Richland Civil Air Patrol field where Richland circulation man, M. Dan Lynn, picked them up and trucked them to the carriers.

The only other possible route by land would have been by way of Benton City through the Horse Heaven Hills, and would have made the Richland papers about four hours late. By this time the approach to the Yakima River bridge was under water, despite a valiant effort by the Atomic Energy Commission to save it.

The next day, May 30, "Flood at a Glance" reported:

"1. Kennewick City Councilman, Dick Rector, said this morning the Columbia River will rise nearly two feet by noon Sunday.

"2. Mayor J. C. Pratt of Kennewick has been appointed coordinating head in the flood emergency. The Kennewick City Council declared the emergency at a special meeting last night. Pratt was given full authority to deal with the emergency in any way he deems necessary.

"3. M. M. Cydell, information control officer for the Atomic Energy Commission, said the road between the Yakima and the Richland Y is doomed. The road has been closed to traffic.

"4. Dikes are being erected in Richland on George Washington Way at the end of Haines Street; also along Ames Street because of the rise of the Columbia which is flooding back through an irrigation ditch.

"5. Traffic over Highway 410 has been detoured over the Highlands and Sonderman road. State District Road Engineer Young Smith said the roadbed has been undermined and warned drivers to heed the barricades because of the danger of the roadway giving way and throwing their machines in the river.

"6. The Benton County Sheriff's office said it was speeding help to Finley, where two families have been marooned by the flood. The Finley-Hover road is now covered by water."

Also on that Saturday was a story headlined: "Richland Free From Flood Threat." It quoted Richland Community Manager E. L. Richmond, who said, "None of the residential and business areas in Richland and North Richland are in danger as a result of the high water conditions nor will they be when the rivers reach their peak early the next week."

"Careful study of the factors that are causing the high water in the Columbia River, which measured 350.6 feet from sea level at noon yesterday, reveals that the river will rise approximately four more feet by Monday or Tuesday of next week. It is not expected that the level of the Columbia at Richland would go much above the 354.5 feet mark," the story continued.

"The water, when it reaches its highest point, is expected to remain east of George Washington Way. The lowest point on the road is the southern intersection with Gowen Avenue. At this point a levee is being constructed as added assurance that water will not proceed across George Washington Way."

But the abundant confidence of Richland officials changed as the days went by and City Manager Richmond would have to eat his words.

Memorial Day, 1948, has a special significance to *The Herald*. It marks the date of the only "Extra" the newspaper ever produced. The huge print-block letters "FLOOD EXTRA!" were two inches high and gave the page a top-heavy appearance. But the edition had the latest flood news and it was gobbled up as quickly as the sales boys could hand them out.

Regrettably, in the rush to get the paper out no one thought to save a copy of the extra. Not even the bound volumes of the paper contain a copy. The only one I know of is that which I saved and which we have framed.

Glenn and Don had plenty of reasons to be worried when they came to our house after the edition had been put to bed. The big stories in the Flood issue explain their concern—martial law had been declared and troops of the Walla Walla National Guard were enroute; Police Chief Rupp had announced he had given orders that looters were to be shot on sight; and the Kennewick water system registered such a high bacteria count it could not be used except after lengthy boiling. The approaches to the Pasco-Kennewick bridge were flooded. All traffic was stopped.

Glenn's family, Elaine and the children, left for Coeur d' Alene, Idaho, for the duration. The plan was for Glenn and his brother, Howard, to stay in our home. Don was to go to Kennewick and live in Glenn's home where both would be closer to their duties.

I was to go to Tacoma to stay with my parents. I was expecting my second child in July and Pasco was no place for me and our year-old son.

My brother, Richard Taylor, who was just out of engineering school, came to live with us a few months earlier, because of his first job, with a construction firm, Atkinson and Jones, at Hanford. Friday morning, Dick left for work. He planned to go from his job to Tacoma for the weekend. When Dick returned to Hanford the following Monday, however, there was no way for him to get to Pasco. So he moved into a barracks in North Richland used to accommodate single men.

When the Columbia receded briefly before rising again, Dick was able to drive the round-about route through Benton City, Kiona, the Horse Heaven Hills and across the bridge to Pasco to get his clothes at our home. He had never met Glenn and Howard Lee.

When Dick walked to the door he was met by a stranger. He said, "I'm Dick Taylor. I used to live here."

Glenn answered with a grin. "I'm Glenn Lee. I live here now."

But on that Memorial Day, I needed passage on Inland Airways, the only air service for the Tri-Cities. It used Vista Field in the Kennewick Highlands.

That day the river rose so high the approaches to the Pasco and Kennewick bridge, the only highway bridge across the Columbia in 1948, were under water. Only National Guard trucks were able to use the span and *The Herald's* Extra had been carried to Kennewick by this means.

My problem that Sunday was how I would get across the river to catch the Monday morning flight to Seattle. The National Guard was contacted to see if Don and I with Brian could cross the river in one of their trucks. They refused because, they said, an able bodied person could swim if the truck was stalled, but a pregnant woman with a small child was quite another matter.

Glenn called the airways headquarters, asking if their plane could land at the former Navy Air Base in Pasco. He was informed this could not be done. The only way across the river was on the Northern Pacific's Northcoast Limited scheduled to come through Pasco at 2:00 a.m. The train did not normally stop in Kennewick but because of the emergency the railroad had consented to add an extra car to accommodate passengers trapped on the Pasco side of the river.

By taking the train, Don could get to Kennewick where he would remain to cover the flood on the Benton County side.

Because of flood conditions in Montana, Idaho and North Eastern Washington, the Northcoast Limited was two hours late to Pasco.

When we arrived at the railroad station we found it bulging with weary adults, crying children, sightseers who had walked across the highway bridge that Sunday morning and then could not return when the river rose. Desperate people were walking the railroad bridge ties to get home. The railroad eventually had to post an armed guard to stop this.

We were stuffed into a railroad car so crowded it made me think of stories I had read of the Jews on their way to concentration camps in Nazi Germany. Some people, afraid there might not be room for all, pushed and shoved, their tired children dragging along, clutching frantically to their parents' hands and clothing.

Despite this, because of my condition, I was ushered to a seat where I held Brian. Hanging onto the overhead baggage rack, Don stood above me as we crawled at a snail's pace across the bridge which was sandbagged by crews working around the clock.

I'm sure that more than one of the other passengers shared my thoughts: What if at that moment a rush of current carrying huge chunks of debris should smash the foundations which held the bridge and we should all plunge into the dark depths of the Columbia? It was not a time for "happy" thoughts like that.

Once in Kennewick we stayed for what remained of the night in the Lee home on Alder street. Then Don drove Brian and me in a borrowed car to Vista Field where he put us aboard the plane for Seattle.

As we circled high over the Tri-Cities I looked down on the sun-glittered roofs of the flooded houses, looking like so many pieces of driftwood caught in the raging river. Everything looked so hopeless. The river was in control.

The Columbia was not above playing tricks and the people were at its mercy. The day after I flew from Kennewick, *The Herald* banner headline announced: "River Drops Foot, Worst Thought Past." Traffic even resumed across the Twin City Bridge. But the relief was only temporary. Within 24 hours the river was on another rampage. This time its height surpassed its previous peak by about two feet. Once again, the bridge was cut off.

Meanwhile, the momentary drop alerted Dr. Tudor to another threat—the flies and mosquitoes that would breed in the flood areas. Tudor appealed to the State Health Department for insecticide sprays.

There was another threat from the flood. Many rattlesnakes in the upper reaches of the Columbia had become isolated and clung to driftwood which deposited them along on Tri-City riverbanks. Warnings were issued to cease exploring the flood areas.

Flood or no flood, a *Herald* office romance between Bill Bates and Barbara Smith culminated in a wedding scheduled for 7:30 p.m., June 4, in the Pasco Episcopal Church of Our Saviour.

One problem was that although Bill and Barbara were in Pasco, the minister, Rev. Nelson Atkinson, and the best man, Don, were in Kennewick, and the soloist, Mrs. Malcolm (Swish) White, was in Richland.

Chief Rupp brought Rev. Atkinson and Don over the bridge in the "Paddy Wagon" and fortunately returned immediately to Kennewick. His was the last car to cross the bridge before the river covered the approaches again.

Rev. Atkinson and Don returned to Kennewick on the Northcoast Limited.

Financially *The Herald* was hurt further. The flood was a disaster. Most business had come to a standstill. People's thoughts were only on the essentials. The downtown business areas were deserted. Meanwhile the appetite for news had grown tremendously so *The Herald* was pressed to put out more news and to get it into the homes even earlier than usual. But this was impossible to do. Newspaper bundles had to be flown to distant points, or boated, or trucked over long, circuitous routes. It was tedious, slow and expensive.

Yet, now with the advantage of hindsight, the flood was also one of the great stabilizers for *Herald* readers. It emphasized the necessity of a daily newspaper. The thoroughness of *The Herald's* reporting and coverage did not go unnoticed. It was a major effort for the small staff, but an outstanding one as is apparent when one reviews the issues that involve its flood coverage.

Some magnitude of the flood was contained in a story Don did of his experience of traveling flooded Highway 410 in a National Guard jeep. The story reported in part:

"Two huge carp swimming lazily along Highway 410 were startled by our jeep exhaust as we attempted to negotiate the highway yesterday afternoon. They sped into the living room of an abandoned home.

"They were the only living things we saw after we entered the highway from Sonderman Road.

"It was strangely silent as we moved up the center of the road. Once it was considered unusual when cars weren't streaming to and from the Richland Y, bumper to bumper. Today the road—what we could see of it—was ours alone. In some high places it was possible to see the yellow dividing line. But high places on Highway 410 are scarce.

"Nearby a hood of a truck peered through the water at a crazy angle. 'Go slow,' Col. Robert Dickey, commander of the National Guard unit in the area, told the driver, 'I'll see if the highway is still here.'

"Dickey got out ahead in his hip boots to guide the jeep. Water poured over the jeep's floor boards and over the tops of his boots.

"Reports have said the water has receded somewhat. It has. But it will take a drop of over two feet before the highway is usable.

"We passed the old Christensen place. The Christensens and their neighbors had worked hard to save the house. They had bulldozed a dike and sandbagged extensively. But there was no evidence of the dike or the sandbags. Doors and windows of the house were open and the water swirled through leisurely.

"Opposite from the Park-In outdoor theater we looked at Bateman's Island. Wallace and Charles

94

Bateman had spent hundreds of dollars in a frantic attempt to save the island causeway. Trucks worked around the clock dumping dirt and rocks, building it up. Now only a ripple in the water indicated the causeway location.

"Beyond the Y the Rossi home stands alone surveying the flood scene. 'We've lived here 26 years and the water has never touched our land," Rossi's son told us early one morning some weeks before as the family was hurriedly loading its belongings in a truck to go to higher ground.

" 'I don't think it will touch us this time either.' Now, only post tops marked the Rossi vineyard; and a hay pile, representing weeks of hard labor, swirled around in the current.

"If you take a boat you can follow the road into Kingsport Landing, the once proud housing project of Bob Higgins, Spokane contractor. (Located in what is now the Yakima River delta.)

"Higgins had finished 14 homes. We rowed in among them. We couldn't locate the $1,400 well which had just been finished on the project the day before the Yakima River ran wild. Just three weeks ago Higgins had driven us over his 68-acre tract. 'Flood? What do you mean, flood?' He pointed at the nearby Yakima River. 'That river will have to come up more than 10 feet to even bother the bottom section of the property.'

" 'I've got thousands of dollars tied up here. Do you think our firm would have sunk that money here if we thought a flood could reach us?'

"Three weeks can change a lot of minds."

Merchants whose businesses along Avenue C had been flooded out, formed an association to open and operate a merchandising mart which they erected on the corner of Canal Drive and Benton Street in Kennewick. It was 250-feet long and 180-feet wide. The Kennewick Chamber of Commerce voted to donate $500 and its services toward helping the Avenue C businessmen get started at their new location. This is significant in view of competitive feelings between the two groups. The Kennewick Chamber's membership was composed largely of merchants along nearby Kennewick Avenue.

Fred Bunch, Sr., originator of the idea for the shopping center, was elected president of the new association. L. M. (Big Mike) Cronin was vice president, Mrs. Phil Grossman, secretary, and Gerald Ballaine, treasurer.

By June 7, it was estimated the river would remain high for another three weeks, so a move to open the bridge by raising Avenue B was commenced. Both cities joined in this. The plan was presented by Herschel Kidwell, chairman of the Pasco Chamber highway committee. Earlier, it had been suggested by Mayor J. C. Pratt but was dismissed when it looked like Avenue C would be open for traffic. But with more recent predictions that the high water might last another three weeks, the importance of reopening the bridge surfaced again.

The plan called for filling the flooded route from the south end of the bridge along Gum Street to Avenue B, then west along Avenue B to Washington Street.

Most of the flood prevention activity centered around Pasco and Kennewick, but what of Richland? Richland seemed to suffer the least. The reason was explained in a story written by a *Herald* advertising saleswoman-turned reporter, Helen Gleason. Her account of Richland's "Miracle Mile," won first place for news reporting in the Washington State Press Club's annual newspaper writing contest.

Her story ran June 1 under the headline, " 'Miracle Mile' Protects Richland From Columbia" and her story said in part:

> "An oasis of calm and safety in the flooding water of this national disaster, which is claiming up to $50,000,000 damages and uncounted dead, the atomic city of Richland on the banks of the

man-killing Columbia was today the four-leaf clover town of the Pacific Northwest.

"Here behind the 'Miracle Mile' which bars the river from 20,000 residents, women hung out their washing in the June sunshine and men drove to work as usual. Here, as at few other low-lying communities on the Columbia, there was safety and assurance.

"Why? Why no wrecked homes, no ruined businesses, no typhoid shots or boiling of drinking water? This four-leaf clover spot is hot with luck, blessed with perfect timing.

"At a round table sat a group of the highest caliber top drawer engineers and construction men in the country. By picking up a phone these men had at their disposal innumerable heavy duty trucks and fast operating man power.

"These are the four leaves of the lucky clover.

"1. Foresight to see the danger while there was still time to plan around and ahead of it.

"2. Experts with know how.

"3. Sufficient heavy machinery and experienced manpower to operate it.

"4. The happenstance, the quirk of fate, which has assembled this engineering talent, the equipment and this manpower in this town at this particular time. It was here not because of the river but for vital construction work on the national atomic project. It just happened to be here when the river struck.

"So the 'Miracle Mile' went up by day, by night. For five days now the town was rocked to the thunder of a continuous chain of 40-mile-an-hour trucks, some of them three abreast down a two mile speedway straight through the business section of the town. Down this blocked-off section of pavement, the trucks roared in from both ends, from a pit both north and south of the town, pits which extended several city blocks in area, as the giant equipment bit deeper and deeper to fill the endless stream of heavy duty equipment.

"The dike began with the marking of the danger spots, a culvert which had to be plugged in the central section of town, the sewage plant, electrical facilities which had to be protected.

"A curve was plotted where the dike should go. In some sections this line curved inland leaving 100 yards or so of land at the mercy of the river. This land included the public picnic park, a ball park, a Masonic building, a transportation yard, and other low-lying areas. The line was drawn where a dike could and would be held.

"The planning continued with choosing gravel pits, not just any dirt would do. There are men in this city who know dirt as a good cook knows the correct seasoning to put on turkey stuffing. The mile was made flexible. It would rise as the river rose, yet at the base, the first spread of the dike allowed for a comfortable barricade two feet above any known river height, including the infamous flood in this region in 1894.

"At present a good share of this dike is eight to ten-feet-wide at the top, slanting outward to the base, following the contour of the land around town, going as high as 10 feet.

"As this mile rose it was sandbagged. Besides those originally scheduled, 100,000 extra sandbags were flown in. As the mile lengthened it was adorned with spurs on the river side which in turn, were high, wide and sandbagged. Jutting out into the water, these broke the force of the river.

"The Columbia has not yet been able to set its current for a killing punch. The spurs keep it off balance.

"The crucial spot is the corner of the dike at the house of AEC's Carleton Shugg, the overall boss of the Atomic City. Sandbags are inside and outside of this house and literally hold up the wall of the dike at this point and the immediate vicinity.

"The mile is now solid and watched for weak spots."

By June 12, an agreement was reached between the Northern Pacific Railway and Hanford officials for a shuttle train for Hanford employees where they were engaged in the construction of Hanford reactors. The train operated between Pasco, Kennewick and Kiona, leaving Pasco in the morning and returning in the evening. Buses would meet the train at Kiona and shuttle the passengers to North Richland.

The Pasco-Kennewick bridge reopened June 11 at 3:45 p.m. and 6,500 cars rolled over it in an eight-hour period. The opening provided transportation between Pasco and Richland by the detour.

Ferry service started from Richland to Franklin County. The ferry landing on the Richland side was located east of the bus depot. The connecting road joined George Washington Way. The landing on the Pasco side was near the Franklin County Irrigation District's pumping station.

While working with city officials and businessmen in the flooded area of Kennewick, Don became acquainted with Gerald Bellaine, who operated an appliance store on Avenue C, called "Ballaine's." Jerry had been an Army flying instructor during World War II. He had purchased from Army surplus the same type of plane he had used to teach Army fliers. It had two cockpits with dual controls. He had acquired it during the flood and took Don up for aerial photos. Little could Don know how handy Jerry's plane was going to be later in the month.

While this was going on, I was in Tacoma eagerly reading the *News Tribune* and watching for stories with a Pasco, Kennewick or Richland dateline. Calls to the flooded areas were discouraged by the telephone company. So when I wished to contact Don I would call the *Associated Press* office in Seattle and one of his friends would put a message on the wire. The answer would come back the same way.

News of flooded areas in other locations seemed to take precedence over the news from our area. This was especially true when Vanport, a community in the Portland area, was overrun by water when a dike broke. Many lives were lost and many homes destroyed. This blotted out news from the Tri-Cities.

No news was good news, I kept telling myself. But as the days wore on and I had no contact with Don except through the *Associated Press*, I became more apprehensive.

"I should be at my husband's side," I reasoned. Brian was safe with my mother and I had five more weeks to go in my pregnancy.

The delivery of my first son had been difficult. In fact, had it not been for the facilities of a big Seattle hospital, I would not have had a child to bring to Pasco.

Being somewhat apprehensive about the birth of my second child I arranged with my obstetrician to return to Seattle.

There was no pediatrician in Pasco and Kennewick and only people living in Richland or who worked on the Hanford project could be treated at Richland's Kadlec Hospital. Because of possible complications the services of a pediatrician would be necessary.

Our baby was due on July 13, (my sister's birthday) and that seemed a long way off. Time enough, I thought, to go back to Pasco alone.

I flew to Kennewick and took a Greyhound bus to Pasco.

We moved back into our home and Glenn went back to Kennewick. But during the early hours of June 26 I awoke with a start. The labor pains had begun and Seattle was 256 obstructed miles away. Also, it was hours before the airlines would stop in Kennewick.

An aerial view of Kennewick flooded by the Columbia River, 1948.

The author standing beside the Army surplus trainer plane, piloted by Jerry Ballaine, which flew her and her husband to Seattle in 1948 for the birth of their second child.

The Flood That Came To Town

Don's first thought was to charter a plane. He called frantically to find a pilot but pilots were much in demand and none was available. Then Don remembered Jerry Ballaine and his army surplus plane.

Jerry's plane had only two cockpits and no room for a third person. I wouldn't go without Don, so Jerry suggested that Don ride in the baggage compartment.

In trying to start the engine Jerry discovered the battery was so low it wouldn't turn over. Don and Jerry took turns cranking the engine with what resembled a Model T hand crank. Jerry's brother and a friend, hearing of our problem, came to the airport. They also got into the act.

The engine started with a roar and billows of smoke engulfed the plane. I ran to it. In all of the excitement I forgot I was pregnant and I nearly stumbled on the hem of the long bathrobe I was wearing. Jerry and Don boosted me onto the wing and I climbed into the rear open cockpit.

Jerry boosted Don into the baggage compartment where he crouched with his knees doubled up under his chin. I could just see the top of his head.

Jerry had never flown to Seattle. In fact, he had never been there. And his lack of orientation was further complicated by the fact he had no short-wave radio to talk to airport control towers. Even worse, he had no navigation chart.

He got a highway map from the glove compartment of our car. This was his guide. Jerry was going to fly by following the highway to Seattle. We prayed that low clouds over the Cascades would not blot out the route. With confusing dual controls in front of me, Jerry's parting warning was, "Don't touch anything!"

The takeoff was surprisingly smooth; so was the flight. I could see familiar landmarks below as we climbed towards the mountains. I didn't let myself think what would happen if my baby decided to come now.

Over the Cascades Jerry was frantic. The plane was in trouble. The carburetor had started to freeze up because of the altitude required to clear the mountains. We started to lose altitude at a rate of about a hundred feet a minute.

Below us were the Cascades and ahead of us to the west, the Olympic Mountains rose stately through the mist. Jerry, unfamiliar with the country, thought the Olympics were merely a continuation of the Cascades. "Aren't we ever going to get out of these damn mountains?" he yelled.

But just when things looked darkest, the clouds parted and we could see Seattle below in the sunshine. Our destination was Boeing Field where the ambulance we had called ahead for was waiting.

At 9:30 a.m., just four hours after I awoke in Pasco, our son, Jerry, arrived, all 4 pounds, 13 ounces of him.

Across The River

"I'll miss your opening but I will be present at your funeral." Mayor Harry Custer of Pasco wrote those words across the bottom of his invitation to *The Herald's* Open House.

It wasn't the most tactful or discreet thing to do, but certainly the mayor made his point. And with just the amount of venom he wanted.

His bitterness was over the fact the Open House was in Kennewick. *The Herald* had moved across the river and now many of the Pasco leaders were crying for its scalp.

They regarded *The Herald* as their very own. Consequently they displayed a lack of sympathy toward the newspaper's problems.

It had outgrown the *Pasco Herald* facilities from the day it printed the first *Tri-City Herald*. A move elsewhere was a necessity. It was merely a matter of when or where. The sudden move to Kennewick came because a business proposition in Pasco fell through. So it was a case of having equipment and no place to put it.

Worse yet, although Pasco leaders claimed they could find suitable quarters, the point was they didn't and Glenn and Hugh couldn't find anything in Pasco.

The move to Kennewick was to accommodate a larger press that was being shipped from Saskatchewan. The Kennewick quarters were hardly lavish. The Scott Publishing Co. had purchased a bankrupt cannery. It was a matter of replacing cans and equipment with newspaper machinery.

Obviously, *The Herald* should have explained better what it was doing and why. No one could have guessed the resentment that greeted the move. Glenn was busy, deeply involved in the financial problems of the paper. His main concern was keeping the newspaper afloat, not public relations.

Getting bundles of papers across the river during the flood, and seeing that each stage of that flood was adequately covered, were not the only problems that plagued *The Herald* in the summer of 1948.

The circulation had jumped from 2,000 to 7,500 subscribers in the first 30 days of publication. The flat bed press inherited from the weekly, would only accommodate eight pages at a time. After the first two press runs, pages would have to be remade in order to redistribute the type. This was due to the shortage of type and equipment.

For the Thursday edition part of the crew went to work Wednesday morning and crews worked straight through until the paper came off the press at 5 p.m. the next day.

There were many break-downs due to the press constantly being pushed to capacity. One of these was caused by a pressman leaving a wrench on the press bed. The May 10, 1948, paper was distributed with the impression of the wrench in the middle of the Women's Page.

The day one of the biggest local stories broke, the paper didn't come out until the following morning because of so many press break-downs. The story concerned the bathtub drowning of the baby of a prominent Pasco woman who had fainted while bathing him. Shortly after the tragedy the distraught mother disappeared. It was correctly assumed she had drowned herself and a search was begun.

The day her body was found *The Herald* carried the story with a banner headline, but the readers didn't get their paper until the next day.

A better press had to be found and Glenn was on the prowl for one, which he eventually located in, of all places, Saskatoon, Saskatchewan. Glenn and Verne Husk made the trip to Canada on a Fourth of July weekend to look the press over. They purchased it on the spot.

Meanwhile, in Pasco, Verne worked day and night to get the paper out. After Friday's run he caught the plane to Seattle. He was supposed to have reservations to Vancouver, B.C., but was told his name was not listed. Verne called Glenn to ask what he should do. Glenn suggested he pick up Elaine's car, which happened to be in Seattle, and drive to Vancouver. By auto, he got there at 6 p.m., then flew the same night to Edmonton.

He could find no hotel room, and his flight to Saskatoon didn't leave until 6 a.m. With so little sleep, Verne spent the night in a chair at the airport. He finally met Glenn in Saskatoon and they immediately went to look at the press.

The business transacted, Verne and Glenn headed for home their separate ways. Verne arrived in Vancouver at noon, drove to Seattle and caught the plane back to the Tri-Cities. It took him two weeks to recover from the trip which came on the heels of all the extra work because of the flood.

The Herald required larger quarters for the new 24-page rotary Scott press being dismantled in Saskatoon.

Anticipating this, Glenn and Hugh had been in touch with a contractor named Larry Havstad, the owner of several downtown buildings in Pasco. His home was a colonial mansion on the banks of the Columbia River. The home was badly damaged by the flood.

Havstad made a verbal agreement to build a new plant for *The Herald*, on Fourth Street in Pasco, north of the Courthouse.

Plans were drawn up, the rent agreed upon and Glenn considered it safe to purchase additional mechanical equipment. The arrangements, made in good faith with Havstad, were completed before the flood hit.

The months slipped by. The new press was dismantled and was ready for shipment, but nothing had been started on the new building.

Glenn tried to contact Havstad and after much trouble,

located him in Los Angeles. Havstad said he had changed his mind. The excuse was the flood damage to his home.

The Herald was desperate to find a location for the press. None was available in Pasco. Glenn went to Pasco businessmen for their help. None had a solution.

Now an angry Glenn confronted Havstad. Without the building promised by him, *The Herald* was in real trouble, he told Havstad.

"We may have to take bankruptcy. If we do, I'm going to sue you for damages as being responsible for leading us into this embarrassing position. You promised us a building for our new press. I've got a new press now, and no place to put it."

Havstad squirmed and finally told Glenn he would help by lending him $10,000, but Glenn would have to put up stock as security. Glenn agreed and the deal was made. Glenn then borrowed $20,000 from a Kennewick friend, $10,000 from the National Bank of Commerce and paid $40,000 for the K and P Industries building in Kennewick.

K and P Industries was in bankruptcy. Officers of the firm were Julius Bahl and Lon Leeper, later the Pasco Postmaster.

K and P Industries (for Kennewick and Pasco) had a brief journey into the agricultural world in the blush of post World War II business. But it was of short duration. Local investors had financed the operation, but it didn't get off the ground.

The warehouse and canning plant is an old one, some parts of the structure going back to before 1907; at least a picture of the building appears in a brochure put out in that year by the Kennewick Commercial Club. It was structurally sound, but something less than an architectural beauty.

The warehouse had a concrete block office building facing Cascade Street on the corner of Canal Drive. Behind this was a big wooden warehouse served by a railroad spur.

The wooden structure housed the press, mechanical and

This bankrupt cannery became the home of the *Herald* in 1948.

Herald newsroom December, 1952, showing tight quarters: From left—Ursula Williams, Womens Editor; Don Pugnetti, Matt Miletich, reporter; Paul Busselle, News Editor; Charles Lamb, reporter, has back to camera.

stereotyping departments, with ample space left over for storage of newsprint. The plant also had its own well which later, because of problems with the Kennewick water system, was put into operation to supply the plant.

Maybe it wasn't much to look at, but for *The Herald* staff, jammed in the old Pasco quarters, it was a thing of beauty. They looked forward to the move with much anticipation.

The big day was October 20, a Saturday, when the staff worked all day getting the plant ready for Monday operation. The heavy equipment was in the mechanical department. It was moved with surprising ease; four Linotype machines, a Ludlow machine used for casting heads, an Elrod machine to make column rules and assorted printing accessories, and miscellaneous printing and composing room equipment.

The Herald maintained its commercial printing shop in Pasco at the original location, plus its office supply business, and office space for editorial, advertising and circulation personnel. One Linotype also remained to set Franklin County legal advertising.

Perhaps something that illustrated the necessity for the move better than anything, was contained in a story printed October 22. In the first 11 months the paper was in operation, the story said, the staff had grown from 17 full-time employees to 70.

The old eight-page flatbed press remained in Pasco. Eventually, with the approval of Mrs. Hill Williams, whose husband had died that summer, it was sold on a conditional sales contract for approximately $4,500.

There were some red faces in the new plant, however, when the new press went into operation. The reddest belonged to Hugh.

He had written an enthusiastic editorial explaining what a wonderful innovation a 24-page rotary press was for the community. It meant cleaner and clearer papers, and the end to late deliveries. He expressed *The Herald's* appreciation for the patience of the readers in putting up with late papers and assured them that now, such would not happen again.

The idea for the editorial was excellent. The timing couldn't have been worse. The new press gave its crew fits. They had trouble with the tension for the newspaper rolls which in turn, caused a lengthy sequence of break-downs, and they had trouble adjusting the press speed and its inking mechanism.

As a result, the papers were later than ever, and the printing couldn't have been worse. The new press gave a lot of trouble and in some instances, whole pages came out blank.

Everyone very generously disclaimed any responsibility for the editorial and Hugh heard about it for weeks.

When *The Herald* began daily publication the demands placed on the press and its newsprint supply caused Glenn to tell the manager of the weekly *Richland Villager*, that his paper no longer could be printed in *The Herald* plant.

This really shouldn't have come as a surprise to the Richland group, but it did. The immediate cause for concern was that they had no newsprint allocation. They tried without success to get the *Villager* printed in Walla Walla and Yakima. They finally made arrangements with the Green Hughes Printing plant in Spokane and they argued that a portion of the newsprint stored in *The Herald's* warehouse belonged to *The Villager*. Glenn took the opposite position after checking with former publisher, Bill Wilmot, and insisted the newsprint belonged to *The Herald*. Glenn's refusal to print *The Villager* and the bickering over newsprint created wounds that never healed.

Paul Nissen was the first editor and publisher of *The Villager*. It was operated by a group known as Villagers, Inc. The originator of a company-sponsored newspaper for Richland was Hayden Rector. AEC and General Electric employees were directors. The amount of newsprint that the *Villager* was arguing about was really a drop in the bucket, but *The Herald* was being forced to buy on the black market in New York for $300 a ton as opposed to the regular price of $60 per ton. The black market price was especially dear to the under-financed *Herald*.

In this instance, Glenn did not feel he could afford to tie up $10,000 in a warehouse full of newsprint although this would suffice the newspaper for a long time. So he made the logical decision to borrow and approached Bud Pearce, manager of the Pasco Branch of The Seattle-First National Bank. Glenn sought a loan on 80 percent of the newsprint value at market price, not black market price. Pearce told Glenn he would lend about 75 percent of the going price. Glenn had figured 80 percent was too low. Pearce's proposition of 75 percent wouldn't make it worth the trouble so he asked Pearce if he would try to get him a loan through the Spokane branch of the bank. Again he was turned down. But Glenn feels that it was because of this request that Wilbur Scruby, an officer in the bank in the Spokane area, learned on what a "shoestring" *The Herald* was operating and, at a later date, was one of the men who helped finance a competing newspaper.

When the Seattle-First National Bank refused to give *The Herald* its loan, the paper's account was moved to the National Bank of Commerce in Kennewick, where it is today.

The newsprint purchased in New York was of such poor quality it proved to be very costly in actual use. It would often break, causing additional delays. Yet with all its headaches, it was the difference between printing or not printing.

The year 1948 started out as a good year. The flood changed the picture. Business dropped off, advertising slumped and accounts receivable climbed. Money for *The Herald* was so short that Glenn turned to relatives for loans, and Bob began selling stock to his fraternity brothers again.

Those were times of intense emotion and intrigue, the latter triggered because *The Herald* was under-capitalized. By growing rapidly its shaky financial foundation made it vulnerable. The miscalculation, however, was that opponents neglected to take into account that it requires a lot of money to operate a newspaper. Finding vocal critics of *The Herald* was relatively easy. Finding critics who would also put up money to fight the newspaper was quite another matter.

Another point overlooked by opponents was the old adage in politics that "you can't beat somebody with nobody." Obviously you can't defeat a newspaper just by getting into the business. You have to offer the reader a product as good or better as the one he is receiving.

Glenn was never napping. The bitter campaign being waged against *The Herald* on Pasco streets greatly concerned him.

"One thing to remember," Don told him, "Pasco is more than its main street. The merchants may be trying to raise hell but get a couple of blocks off Lewis Street and it isn't that big a deal."

Glenn nodded. "That makes a lot of sense. If the businessmen want a weekly, let's give them a weekly. We'll let them have the *Pasco Herald* again. What do you think of that?"

"What will that do to the *Tri-City Herald?*"

"Nothing that I can see," Glenn replied. "People want a daily newspaper. We'll give them a good product on a daily basis. The weekly may buy us time. Those merchants who don't want to pay the daily rate can have the weekly advertising rate."

The old *Pasco Herald* masthead was dusted off and Bill Bates was named editor of the new publication. Bates, who had worked a year on the *Pasco Herald,* was on familiar ground.

But it was soon apparent there was also going to be resistance to the new paper. So Glenn hired a publisher for it. He was Arthur Hagman, a newcomer to Pasco who was in the Tri-Cities attempting to organize an Exchange Club. Hagman had a pleasant appearance, met people well and claimed to have a background in printing. Glenn had some favorable reports on him. He seemed like a person who could "front" for the new paper and create some goodwill in the business community. He had several meetings with Glenn and happily accepted the job offer.

Before long, however, some disquieting reports began to be received about how Hagman was spending his time. Finally, in March of 1949, after he had been on the payroll for about four months, it was confirmed that rather than creating goodwill for *The Herald*, Hagman was spending his time organizing a movement—with the blessing of the Pasco Chamber of Commerce—to establish another weekly in Pasco. Glenn summoned Hagman to his office and confronted him with the information. Hagman shrugged his shoulders, resigned, and returned to Pasco to do what he was doing, although now on his own time and money. Bill Bates was promoted to publisher and stayed until he left for Kelso with Hugh Scott in 1949.

There was no discounting Hagman's promotional abilities. Under the sanction of the Pasco Chamber he moved about Pasco and Kennewick attempting to win support for his new newspaper to be called the *Pasco Empire*. Those who supported him permitted their judgment to be clouded by their animosity towards Glenn and *The Herald*.

Hagman, of course, recognized the elementary fact that he couldn't print a newspaper without a plant. That led him to Kennewick Avenue, where he talked to Rolf Tuve, publisher of the weekly *Kennewick Courier-Reporter*. Tuve purchased the paper in 1945 on a conditional sales contract from Ralph E. Reed, its founder.

Tuve was unhappy with the *Tri-City Herald* for a number of reasons. He shared one thing in common with Pasco leaders, which was *The Herald's* move to Kennewick, but for a different reason. Tuve disliked having a daily newspaper within a block of his plant. He was also dismayed at the way *The Herald* had been cutting into his advertising and readership. He wished *The Herald* had stayed in Pasco so he could request loyalty from Kennewick businessmen for their hometown newspaper. Now that particular sales point had been taken from him. For this and other reasons Tuve was having a hard time meeting his bills.

He thus was ripe for Hagman's proposition that they form Mid-Columbia Publishers, Inc., with Tuve as president. Hagman got 26 percent of the stock for his idea while Tuve got the same amount for putting up his newspaper on which he still owed $15,000.

In the 1945 conditional sales contract drawn up between Reed and Tuve when the latter purchased the Kennewick weekly, was a clause reading:

"If the buyer shall fail to make any said payment or should any said goods or chattels be taken from the buyer's possession or removed from 217 Kennewick Avenue, the contract will be terminated and all payments theretofore made to the seller by the buyer shall be retained by the seller."

Tuve called the operation the Kennewick Printing Company. To improve his new newspaper he bought a large linotype at a cost of approximately $15,000 which he had installed in his Kennewick plant. He bought other equipment also not included in the Reed-Tuve contract. He was paying for them on a separate contract.

Perhaps if Tuve had printed his weekly paper alone and watched more carefully his commercial plant, which had at least one lucrative job from the Hanford plant, he would have made a comfortable living. Instead, he got involved in the new newspaper and lost it all.

What happened is a fascinating tale, although it likewise proved costly for *The Herald* too.

Mid-Columbia Publishers, Inc. announced in April, 1949 that they planned to begin printing papers in Pasco and Kennewick, and eventually in Connell, Lind and Othello.

With much fanfare, the *Pasco Empire* came to life. The new paper was an interesting operation. Its type was set in Kennewick by the *Courier-Reporter*. The forms were then locked up and hauled to the *Empire* plant in Pasco to be printed on an eight-page flatbed press. The press, it later developed, was purchased with corporation funds but owned by O. H. (Ole) Olson, leading state legislator from Pasco, and Bill Krudwig, a Pasco tavern operator. Through an unusual arrangement, they put $4,500 in the Mid-Columbia Publishers bank account. Then a Mid-Columbia check, supposedly using these same dollars, paid for the press. Title to the press was issued to Olson and Krudwig, who then mortgaged it at the Seattle-First National Bank in Pasco.

Tuve had thought the press belonged to the corporation but learned differently when the corporation went into bankruptcy. Olson and Krudwig got preference on the list of creditors and eventually got their money back.

Mid-Columbia's use of Tuve's facilities proved a heavy drain on his limited resources. All of Tuve's holdings were thrown into "the pot" with Mid-Columbia Publishers, Inc., including Tuve's interest in the Reed-Tuve contract which was now also the property of the corporation. That was the situation as the critical days of June 11 and 12, 1949 arrived.

On Saturday, June 11, the Kennewick Printing Company could not meet its payroll and stockholders and officers of Mid-Columbia Publishers had a day-long meeting in Pasco. Among those invited was Ralph Reed.

Many things bothered Reed that day. As a long-time resident of Kennewick and founder of the newspaper, he didn't hold much affection for Pasco and was perturbed his newspaper somehow was tied into a Pasco-dominated corporation. He also was surprised to discover that Tuve no longer was president of the corporation. Tuve had been removed but apparently had not been notified. Tuve later was to testify he couldn't remember when it had occurred or whether he had resigned or had been removed.

Then, too, there was the matter of not meeting the payroll, something that during all his years of operation,

Reed had never failed to do. Tuve's past week's checks had "bounced" because of insufficient funds and the current checks were overdue. The printers were in the plant but refused to work until they got paid. Now Reed heard at the meeting talk of putting Mid-Columbia Publishers into bankruptcy.

Reed angrily demanded that the payroll be met.

In his opinion, as he later expressed in court, the meeting was "a mess."

"Everybody was talking," he said. "People were entering and leaving the meeting. But at no time did I make any agreement on the contract I held on the *Courier-Reporter.*"

The payroll checks were finally personally underwritten by E. S. (Somme) Johnston, Pasco grain dealer and officer of the Mid-Columbia Publishers. Johnston claimed he had an understanding that if he met the payroll the operation would continue, but Reed denied any such agreement.

"I made up my mind to sell the business on the way home from the meeting," Reed was later to testify. "I saw no possibility of the group getting together."

According to Reed, he drove directly to the *Courier-Reporter* office to tell the workers their checks were coming. Next, he told Mrs. Tuve, who was in the front office, that he would have to take the business back.

In the lawsuit which was to grow out of the evening's activities, Reed testified that Tuve arrived while he was talking to Mrs. Tuve, who told her husband what Reed had said. Tuve put his head down on his arms on the desk and started to cry, Reed recalled. This happened at about 7 p.m.

On the other hand, the Tuves denied any meeting with Reed in the *Courier-Reporter* office and Tuve testified further that he hadn't returned to Kennewick until 10 p.m.

Reed next recalled he telephoned his attorney at 8:30 p.m. and asked whether there was anything to prevent his selling the shop. He was advised there was not. He then called Glenn and said:

117

"Do you want to buy the *Courier-Reporter?*"

"Is it yours to sell?" Glenn asked.

"Hell, yes," said Reed.

"Well, come on down. Let's talk about it," Glenn said. "I'm interested in buying it."

This was not the first time Glenn had been approached about buying the *Courier-Reporter*. A few days before, Reed's son, Jim, had asked Glenn if he would be interested in such a purchase, which would indicate that Reed had been uneasy over the prospects for his property for some time. In addition, Glenn had also been approached by Tuve, three days before, to see if he would buy the paper. But after hearing Tuve's story, Glenn told him, "Rolf, I don't know that you've got anything to sell."

Jim Reed accompanied his father to Glenn's office on June 11. Glenn had his mechanical superintendent, B. T. Russell, sit in with him.

Reed outlined his reasons for the sale.

"I'm insecure with Tuve's proposition," he said. "He has violated the terms of our agreement so I have taken the paper back. If you want it, you can have it."

"What kind of a price are you placing on it?" Glenn asked.

"I want $15,000. There's a balance due on the contract of $12,000."

"I'll tell you what I'll do," Glenn said. "Let's draw up a sales agreement and I'll write you a check for $500 earnest money to make it binding. How does that sound to you?"

Reed didn't blink an eye. "Draw it up," he said.

And so the *Courier-Reporter* was sold to the *Tri-City Herald* for $15,000 with a balance due Reed on his contract with Tuve of $12,000.

What Glenn did not know, however, was that a Linotype, which had very little paid on it, and some other equipment, did not actually belong to Reed. Perhaps Reed, himself, was unaware of the status of the equipment purchased after he sold the shop. At any rate, it was not mentioned the night of the newspaper purchase by the Scott Publishing Company.

In court, Reed testified he went directly home and stayed there. Other witnesses said Reed went to the *Courier-Reporter* office and told the group, which included Tuve, that he had sold to the *Tri-City Herald.*

Glenn, Bernie Russell, Verne Husk and Dick Galbraith, business manager of *The Herald*, went to the *Courier-Reporter* plant on Sunday to take inventory and Monday, *The Herald* took possession of the plant. It continued to print the *Courier-Reporter* and the Hanford Project News — which the Kennewick weekly had been printing on contract.

The Herald continued to pay Reed on the contract. It also kept up the payments on the Linotype and other equipment Tuve had bought.

Purchase of the *Courier-Reporter* brought a heap of trouble to *The Herald*, most important of which was a costly lawsuit. It also brought into *The Herald's* ranks some mechanical employes who became among the most vocal supporters of a strike against the newspaper a few months later. This was certainly ironic, for when they were absorbed into *The Herald* they gained an immediate 20-cent-an-hour increase. Tuve had run an open shop. *The Herald's* was a union shop. Furthermore, whereas they had been faced either with pay checks for which there were insufficient funds or a lack of pay checks, now they were paid in full and on time. Despite their economic tribulations, Glenn and Bob were proud of their record of never missing a payroll or of never delaying one.

The *Courier-Reporter* purchase also gave *The Herald* some printing equipment for which it had to pay twice because of a subsequent lawsuit. Finally, it caused Glenn and *The Herald* to be blamed for the ensuing bankruptcy of Mid-Columbia Publishers, although they were, in effect, bankrupt before he purchased the contract from Reed.

"We were really buying time," Glenn says of the purchase. "My reasoning at that time was to purchase the

Courier-Reporter, take control of it, and then *The Herald* would be in charge of the composing room facilities of the *Pasco Empire*.

"We knew the squeeze play against us was on. I figured that the purchase of the Kennewick paper would throw a curve at them, stop them in their tracks, and we would gain some time. We were fighting and bargaining for time."

The *Courier-Reporter* lost money rapidly when it became tied to the twice-weekly *Pasco Empire*. It really didn't need any help. Its records showed it was skating on financial thin ice before Hagman put up his idea and Tuve put up his newspaper.

Whether Glenn could have revived the financially weakened publication will never be known because he never received the opportunity to try. Obviously, Glenn and Bob weren't in a position to spend a lot of money operating another newspaper. However, if the paper could be made to pay its way they might have salvaged it.

The *Courier-Reporter* continued to be published but it was only a shadow of its former self, chiefly because Kennewick Postmaster Walter Woehler refused to deliver its mail. Woehler's decision was puzzling. On the witness stand he adamantly denied he was "coached" in making up his mind to withhold the mail. He had decided, he said, that the *Courier-Reporter's* mail was "in dispute" and thus refused to let anyone have it. As a result, the mail piled up and up and despite frantic efforts, pleas and threats, Woehler would not let loose of it until September, 1949, almost three months after he had made his decision.

The backlog of accumulated mail was a sight. Especially disheartening were the packets of insertion orders from national advertisers, correspondence from advertising agencies, and correspondence from subscribers.

"You can't operate a weekly newspaper without access to the mail," Glenn testified in the lawsuit that followed. A thick exhibit of complaints from advertising agencies was entered in evidence.

"National advertising all comes through the mails as either mats or insertion orders," Glenn testified. "National advertisers want tear sheets to show that the advertisement has run."

Woehler insisted he made up his own mind concerning the mail. Asked if anyone but Glenn or his employes had sought the mail, Woehler said they were the only ones. But, he insisted, the paper "did not meet the requirements" which would cause the postmaster to give it the mail.

Loss of its mail was the body blow from which the *Courier-Reporter* never recovered. It was suspended some weeks later.

Mid-Columbia Publishers, Inc. could hardly be cited as an example of a model corporation. In the court suit there was ample testimony that nobody even knew who its officers were. Johnston, who wrote the $1,000 payroll check, testified that he was not one of the officers, yet later evidence showed that he indeed was one.

The June 11 meeting which Reed described as a "mess" assuredly was that. For instance, no one could even say who presided. One stockholder testified that he thought Johnston had presided. Johnston, however, testified that Cliff Churchman had presided, which Churchman later denied on the stand. Pasco lawyer, James Leavy, said he couldn't remember who presided and added it was a "highly informal" session, a masterpiece of understatement!

Pasco businessman and former Mayor John Beck testified, "I said that under the present organization there was no direction, no centralized authority or responsibility and I couldn't see how it could be a successful operating business. I said that as far as I was concerned, I'd recommend we go into friendly bankruptcy."

Mid-Columbia filed for bankruptcy shortly after the June 11 meeting. The referee had appointed Spokane attorney Tom Malott as receiver for the defunct organization. Malott candidly stated that he considered *The Herald* the corporation's chief asset. As it worked out, he was correct.

Malott sued *The Herald* for $85,000 on grounds Mid-Columbia Publishers was bankrupted when the Scott Publishing Company took over the *Courier-Reporter* plant. This skirted the fact *The Herald* had offered to print the *Pasco Empire.*

The lawsuit officially went into Franklin County court records as "Crutcher as trustee vs. Scott Publishing Company." Ernest Crutcher, a Kennewick accountant, was acting as trustee for the defunct corporation through appointment by the referee in bankruptcy.

The case was not tried until March 1952. Superior Judge Richard Ott of Ritzville, who had heard the Columbia Construction Company libel suit, presided. Part of the delay in trying the suit was caused by Malott. He had first filed the suit in Federal court and, when it came to trial in 1951, discovered he was in the wrong court. So he had to refile it in state court.

The trial lasted nine days and was tried in a charged atmosphere, for *The Herald* had been on strike since March 3, 1950. The striking printers filled the front row—"ITU Row," Glenn and Don labelled it—and some of them testified for Mid-Columbia. The financial manipulations of Mid-Columbia Publishers and the deficit financing of the *Courier-Reporter* got a thorough airing. But, in essence, it boiled down to whether Reed had made a valid foreclosure on Tuve before he sold his company to *The Herald.*

The jury decided Reed had not and rendered a verdict against *The Herald* of $22,033. Their verdict stipulated the following:

1. That aggregate value of all tangible personal property and equipment taken over by the defendant was determined at $27,974.

2. The total value of property and equipment claimed to have been converted that was in the Reed-Tuve conditional sales contract was listed as $13,000.

3. The amount of property claimed to have been converted that was acquired after the date of the contract was listed as $14,974.

4. The award for damage or destruction of the business of the *Courier-Reporter* was set at $17,000. Against this a jury deducted $12,150 as the amount owed on the Reed-Tuve contract; $8,550 owed on a Model 34 Mergenthaler Linotype and $2,241 owed on a loan to Tuve by Kennewick wheat rancher Henry Smith.

But the jury, in turn, gave no award to *The Herald* for damage sustained through wrongful actions of Mid-Columbia Publishers. Chief among this was the tieup of the *Courier-Reporter* mail which had caused the death of the newspaper.

The jury held there was a valid contract between Tuve and Reed and that Reed did not effect a valid repossession of the property. Thus the jury gave credence to the testimony of Mr. and Mrs. Tuve that Reed did not tell them the night of June 11 that he was repossessing the newspaper.

It wasn't over yet. There were more problems in store for *The Herald*. It appealed the verdict to the State Supreme Court which, in April, 1953, upheld the verdict and added on another $8,550, boosting the total verdict to $30,533.

The additional sum involved the Linotype that Tuve had been buying on a separate contract. The supreme court held that this was property that belonged to Mid-Columbia Publishers. Thus *The Herald*, which had assumed and was making the payments on the machine, was ordered to pay the full amount to the bankruptcy, but it also still had to pay off the contract to the Mergenthaler Company or have the Linotype repossessed.

So the crowning blow was that *The Herald* had to pay for the Linotype *twice*.

Upper photo is first office of *The Herald* in Richland. This unheated shack belonged to the Richland Jaycees who used it for evening meetings. Lower photo shows *Herald* office built when GE-AEC finally gave permission to purchase land.

9   *Richland*

"I'VE COME to love this town so much I wouldn't live anywhere else," Mildred Lindgren, a friend of mine in Richland, told me one day while we were having coffee in her home.

Her view was typical of those expressed by so many of the "transplants" from around the nation who came to Richland with tens of thousands of people during World War II to work with a project so secret that no more than a handful knew what it was.

At Richland, those "20th Century pioneers" braved most of the elements that made them vow that once their job was done, they would be among the first to leave. There was the intense heat of summer without shade trees or air conditioners when they literally baked inside or outside of their homes. And the subzero temperatures of winter when they huddled inside their hastily constructed houses. There were the dust storms—"termination winds" some realist on the Atomic Energy Commission staff called them—and such things as the torn-up, dusty streets without a sidewalk as far as the eye could see.

Most of the newcomers were from the Eastern Seaboard or the South, and they had been transplanted into the middle of a desert. Hanford was a mammoth project, the success of which is a testament to American ingenuity, technical know-how and inventiveness.

They were to learn in August, 1945, that they had built and staffed the facilities that produced plutonium, the vital ingredient in atomic bombs. They were part and parcel of the Manhattan Project, as it was labelled, and they were an army unto themselves, ranging in skills from nuclear scientists to janitors.

They either worked for the duPont Company, which at that time had the construction and operation contract, or they were employed by what later became the Atomic Energy Commission. Or, they worked for one of the subcontractors, building either the reactors and supporting facilities on the Hanford project or the homes and commerical buildings in the new town.

They didn't know why what they were doing was so vital to the war effort, and some wild stories circulated. Yet, surprisingly, the secret was well kept and speculation about the project was limited because of national security. Ironically, after the atomic bomb was dropped and the secret was revealed, it was still difficult for them to talk about it.

A favorite story that is still told, involved the youngster who announced in school, "I know what they are making at Hanford because my daddy brings some home every day in his lunch pail."

"What is it?" the teacher asked.

"Toilet paper and light bulbs," the student replied.

There is a familiar ring to the story that Mildred Lindgren tells of her early experiences in Richland. Familiar, that is, because other than changing the names of the persons and the circumstances that brought them to Richland, the stories are very much alike, when told by Richlanders who were there during World War II.

T. L. (Sandy) Lindgren, her husband, was employed by duPont in Wabash, Indiana. He received his Richland assignment in February, 1944. It would be three months at least before a home would be available for his family, so Mildred and their 5-year-old son, Billy, went to California to visit her mother. Sandy moved into the men's barracks.

Sure enough, three months later a house was available.

Probably to accommodate government bookkeepers and in the style of government efficiency for that time, each home bore an alphabetical designation. The Lindgren's home was an "A" house, a three-bedroom, two-story duplex. Another common home was the "B" house, a one-story, two-bedroom duplex.

Hundreds of these homes were built. As contractors received orders for blocks of new homes of a different design, they assigned another letter to them. Twenty-five to 50 homes were built at one time and the bleak rows of houses extended farther out into the desert.

Mildred Lindgren's first view of the Tri-Cities was one that most of the newcomers experienced. First, there was the crowded Pasco depot, with people bunched together, some sleeping on the floor. Train stations in World War II were the busiest places in town, but the Pasco station couldn't contain everyone.

The trip to Richland was by car. Only a work train operated near Richland.

While waiting for their furniture, the Lindgrens moved into the Transient Quarters, later remodelled and renamed the Desert Inn after the war. The Desert Inn was Richland's hotel for about 20 years. Then it was torn down and the Hanford House was constructed on its site.

Looking out the window from the Transient Quarters one could see dust in all directions from the construction activity. Heavy equipment hurried up and down George Washington Way, the main street in Richland. By 1944, the street was blacktopped but there were no curbs or sidewalks.

The Lindgrens lived in their "A" house for several months and then moved to an "F" house in the same neighborhood on the 1500 block of Johnston Street. It was just north and up the hill from what is now the Uptown Business District, but which at that time was arid flatland. By this time Sacajawea school was built and Billy started kindergarten there. He would catch one of the inter-city buses in his neighborhood to school.

Mildred's shopping days were Monday, Wednesday and Friday. She and her neighbor, who also shopped on those days, traded off driving to conserve rationed gas. When they reached the Downtown Business District containing the only commercial buildings, and these were few, they stood in line for everything. Lines formed in front of the post office, the laundry and the grocery store checkout counter. Groceries were sold so quickly the store didn't bother to put canned goods on the shelves. The Richland shoppers just took what they wanted out of cardboard boxes on the floor. But they didn't really mind for shopping was a sociable time. It was here they visited together.

Of course there were no lawns, trees or shrubs, except what the new arrivals managed to plant themselves. The residents had trouble finding their own homes, since they all looked alike. Sandy Lindgren planted a tree beside his home and when it died, Mildred would not let him remove it. She used it to find their home.

Mildred's introduction to the speed of a dust storm came on a day she was entertaining dinner guests. The day started out warm and sunny. Unsuspecting, Mildred left her windows open and walked to the store. When she got there she noticed a dark cloud forming. By the time she reached home the storm was blowing a full gale. Her floor and furniture were covered with sand almost two inches thick. In only a few hours her guests would arrive. She was frantic. One of her guests, however, had lived in Richland long enough to know the frustrations of dust storms. She anticipated Mildred's situation and called to reassure her.

"Whatever you do, don't go out of your mind trying to clean your home," she said. "We've lived around here long enough to take dusty homes for granted. No one's going to be shocked."

The early experiences of Frank and Dottie Gabel, who came to Richland in July, 1943, from Childersburg, Alabama, were also typical. Frank was with Construction Cost Accounting and Dottie was a secretary. Having heard that Washington was the "Evergreen State," she expected to see trees and grass. She also expected a cooler climate and in her heavy garments she wilted under a July sun.

The Gabels were lucky; they were among those who were able to secure one of the 200 trailers in the government trailer camp in Pasco, near the railroad bridge. Had they not obtained the trailer they would have had to live in barracks at Hanford—Frank in the men's barracks, Dottie in the women's, which was the lot of many husband and wife teams. Rent for the trailer was a dollar a day. Linens were furnished and the trailers were heated with gas or coal oil heaters. This arrangement lasted until November when they were able to move into an "A" house. Only top employes in management and construction were housed in Richland. Construction workers were either put up in a large trailer camp or in one of the many barracks at Hanford. Both were inside the reservation some miles north of Richland.

Unlike the Lindgrens, the Gabels did not ship furniture. Their house was furnished with only bare essentials. As the supply of furniture increased they received more. It was not unusual for them to come home from work and find a lamp, a chest of drawers or a dining room table that had been placed in their absence. Their neighbors called it "G.I. furniture" but it was Eastern rock maple. For their homes, the Gabels and Lindgrens, like the other residents, paid only token rent, $43 a month if furnished and $30 a month unfurnished. This included all utilities.

People arriving about the time the Gabels did were discouraged from bringing their cars. If they did bring them, they had to make their own arrangements for enough gas to cross the United States. Consequently many sold their cars before coming to Richland, only to find when they arrived that cars were desperately needed. There was no other means of transportation except for buses.

Then there were the people who arrived in Richland to

take up residence after The Bomb had been dropped on Japan and everybody was aware what had been going on at Hanford. Security, however, was still rigid. The reaction of these newcomers to Richland was much the same as earlier arrivals.

The barrenness of the country may have repelled the newcomers but they were warmed by the cordiality of the people, and like the Gabels and Lindgrens came to love Richland so much, they stayed on.

Uncle Sam had collected a unique assortment of people and talents and transplanted them to the desert. There, once they had adjusted to the move, they spent their spare moments busily engaged creating organizations that would both entertain them and make a demand on their talents. Among the first of these were the Richland Players, a dramatic group, still abundantly successful and owners of their own theater; the Richland Light Opera Company, the Community Concert, and along with the other two cities, the Mid-Columbia Symphony. The cultural climate did indeed thrive, even in the desert.

The Federal Government was selective in its recruiting. It also exercised care in the numbers and types of businesses that could operate within the "Atomic City." Controls were strict. Those merchants allowed to do business had an exclusive franchise. Not only did they have a captive market, they also flourished by being able to obtain the war-shortage items that were absent from store shelves in other cities. It was a can't-miss situation. There was one jewelry store, one department store, one shoe store—in fact, one of everything—with each having to pay AEC-General Electric a percentage of the gross for its franchise.

The only newspaper was the *Richland Villager.*

Until the Scott Publishing Company purchased the *Pasco Herald, The Villager* was printed on *The Herald* press. It had no composition or printing facilities of its own. When *The Villager* had to discontinue being printed in the Pasco

130

plant it aroused bitter animosity from the Atomic Energy Commission and General Electric Company officials. Against such opposition *The Herald* faced almost insurmountable odds in Richland. The new daily was accepted by residents but not by management.

Another bone of contention was the fact that while *The Herald* was desperately hunting for sources of newsprint, and being forced to go on the black market for high-priced, inferior products, AEC and GE used their influence to obtain paper for *The Villager* through the International Paper Company of New York.

Glenn verified what AEC-GE were doing in June, 1948 when he visited the Green Hughes Company in Spokane. In the plant ready for use by *The Villager*, Glenn discovered newsprint rolls with shipping instructions stenciled on the side stating: "U.S. Atomic Energy Commission, care of Green Hughes, Spokane." This shipment amounted to 50 precious tons of newsprint.

Glenn argued that if AEC and GE could assist *The Villager* in obtaining newsprint, they should also rightfully assist *The Herald*. *The Herald* represented free enterprise and *The Villager* was a non-profit, non-tax paying publication that competed with *The Herald* for the advertising dollar, not only in Richland but in Pasco and Kennewick, too.

Another aspect that grated on *The Herald* was management of the news by AEC and GE to accommodate *The Villager*. Howard Sanstadt, the first *Herald* reporter assigned to Richland, had difficulty getting news released. Instead, the news was tightly held and given out just in time for the *Villager's* weekly deadline. All official releases came through Milt Cydel, the AEC information officer, or from George Brown, his General Electric counterpart.

As Women's Page editor, I found it difficult to gather Richland's social news. Richland women were reluctant to give their news to any paper other than *The Villager*, such was the sinister effect of the subsidized newspaper.

One example was the meeting report of an early-day organization, the Dr. Samuel Taylor Orthopedic Guild. The Guild was named for a Richland doctor who lost his life while attempting to rescue a swimmer on one of Washington's ocean beaches. Most women who would be eligible for any Richland "social register" belonged to the Guild.

The Guild president and charter member, Mrs. Ralph Sachs, was most cooperative in giving me the story, but emphasized it had to be held until the same day *The Villager* would print it. *The Villager* published every Thursday and the meeting took place on Monday.

My Richland cousin, Virginia Gast, saved the day. She belonged to the Guild and would be at the meeting. I asked her if she would invite two guests, myself and Barbara Smith, who would soon replace me as Women's Page editor.

Virginia was delighted to take us, so the story with a picture appeared in *The Herald* the next day.

It soon became apparent that a person with more leverage should be assigned to Richland, such as the editor himself. Hugh Scott took on the job in early 1948. He sold circulation, advertising, wrote news stories and most important, helped build the image of *The Herald* in the Atomic City.

It was Hugh who wrote a series, the first on the Atomic Energy Commission and Hanford Works, which had never really been covered locally, because security had been extremely tight and because *The Villager* didn't care, or didn't dare, to get into it.

One experience *The Herald* had concerned the meeting of the Community Council which Hugh attended. Like everything else in Richland, the Community Council was also controlled by the AEC and GE. Its purpose was to bring a measure of democracy to the administration of Richland. But it had no authority. Anything the council did could be over-ruled by General Electric which administered Richland, or by AEC which was over GE.

The question came up of when and where news of the Community Council meetings should be printed.

The chairman asked, "When does something become news?

Ted Best, who had replaced Paul Nissen as editor of *The Villager*, said, "It becomes news when we print it," meaning on Thursday when *The Villager* came out.

George Brown, the public relations representative for General Electric, responded, "No. It becomes news when we release it."

Hugh got up and said, "It becomes news when it happens. We intend to print the story of this meeting in tomorrow's *Herald*." Everybody looked around in amazement. No one challenged Hugh. That ended the discussion.

Other organizations began giving *The Herald* stories of meetings when they happened and didn't wait until Thursday.

Another incident which helped *The Herald* gain a foothold was the arrival of the American Federation of Labor in Richland. Its organizer, Kenneth Scott of the AFL's United Trades Council, received a cool reception and encountered difficulty getting his story across until he met Hugh. *The Herald* carried several hundred stories about Scott and his efforts, which culminated in a mass rally at the high school with approximately 1,000 people attending. Scott lauded *The Herald* and the newspaper received some rounds of applause. More important, it received a rash of subscriptions too. It was the beginning of a friendship and working understanding with organized labor that would continue until March 3, 1950.

From the beginning, the office arrangement in Richland had to be improved. Yet, whenever a request was made to Richland management, which Glenn did repeatedly, he was put off with the excuse that a "master plan" for Richland was being drawn up and it had not been decided where *The Herald* office could locate.

Weary of getting the run-around, Glenn decided to see how such things were handled in other AEC controlled communities. He flew to New Mexico, and visited the newspaper operating in Los Alamos. There, dressed in a pair of old slacks and a sweater, he got into a truck with the circulation manager from Santa Fe and went onto the government atomic reservation, where strict travel and visitor restrictions were in force.

Glenn delivered newspapers around Los Alamos with the circulation manager, eventually getting to the weekly newspaper office. He discovered that the weekly had a beautiful plant layout and was renting its building from the AEC for only $1 a month.

From New Mexico, Glenn flew to Oak Ridge, Tennessee. He could enter the government town only if he knew someone he could telephone from the gate. He called the publisher of *The Oak Ridger* and got in. He enviously looked over the paper's operation. When that project was booming the government had installed a laundry. Now the laundry was shut down and half of the building had been given to *The Oak Ridger* for a very nominal rent. Oak Ridge was delighted to have the new daily.

His eyes opened by this information, Glenn flew to Washington, D. C. and through Washington's junior senator, Harry Cain, obtained an appointment with Commissioner Sumner Pike of the AEC. Glenn explained the problem he was having gaining an office for *The Herald* in Richland or even a piece of land on which he could build an office.

Pike told Glenn that the problem couldn't exist because of AEC. It had to be the fault of General Electric, he said sympathetically.

Glenn hustled back to National Airport, boarded a plane and flew to the GE head office in New York for a meeting with Lemuel Boulware, vice president in charge of corporate relations. Boulware assured Glenn that the reason *The Herald* couldn't get an office wasn't because of GE. GE was for free enterprise, Boulware declared. Glenn's problems had to be caused by the AEC.

Back in Washington, D. C., Glenn went to see Commissioner Pike. He again assured Glenn that AEC wasn't to blame. The AEC official insisted it had to be GE. This time Glenn sent Boulware a telegram informing him of what Pike had said, then he boarded a plane and made another trip to New York to see Boulware. He got the same answer.

Tired of being batted back and forth like a ping pong ball, he stopped off at the national convention of the American Newspaper Publisher's Association in New York. There he made two requests. One was whether he could join. The other was whether he could have a few minutes to tell his story. ANPA Board of Directors explained they had a full agenda but spared him 10 minutes. The Board listened attentively to Glenn's story. They couldn't believe such a thing could happen. Glenn assured them it could, and that it had.

ANPA got in touch with the Small Business Committee in Congress led by Rep. Clarence Brown, who owned newspapers in Ohio. Brown's committee took up the cause. At last, *The Herald* was getting some muscle and identification.

Glenn then returned to Washington, D. C., this time to try and get newsprint. He discovered the national convention of the United States Chamber of Commerce was going on and decided to attend.

By chance, the convention had a panel discussion of government intereference in free enterprise. After the speeches were over and comments were invited from the floor, Glenn moved to a nearby microphone. In the presence of about 1,000 people, he recited the story of his problems in Richland. He was bombarded with questions, and when the discussion was completed he was interviewed by reporters from newspapers across the country and by *Time* magazine.

When Glenn got home, the story had been printed in newspapers from coast to coast. This really caused an explosive reaction in Richland. Ted Best, of *The Villager*, threatened to sue the Scott Publishing Company for libel because Glenn had labelled *The Villager* a "house organ." The end result, however, was that *The Herald* got its office in Richland. The Scott Publishing Company built a building in downtown Richland, north of the former C. C. Anderson store.

AEC and GE had good reason for opposing *The Herald* for it would upset the status quo. They had a mouthpiece in *The Villager*. That little weekly published the news releases issued through Cydell's and Brown's offices. They could *manage* the news. But *The Herald* was a different matter. It printed the news when and where the reporters found it and made its own decision on what was to be printed or what was not to be printed, and how prominently the stories were to be displayed.

The "atomic curtain" atmosphere which existed during the war, when it was vital to the security of the country, continued and the men in charge of Richland held tightly to their authority. It was the cold winter of 1949-50 and a chain reaction to their publicized inefficiency which opened the eyes of the nation.

In 1949, thousands of Hanford workers were losing their jobs and more thousands had a feeling of insecurity.

After repeatedly denying mass layoffs, AEC and GE were finally forced to admit the facts. They cited "technological improvements" as the reason for wholesale dismissals. But the workers, the people who were feeling the axe, had a totally different explanation. They told of wastefulness in time, material and taxpayer's money.

The Herald listened to the stories and began to check on them.

Bill Bequette was assigned to investigate and with his usual competence, wrote a series of shocking articles. One covered the construction of a wooden bridge over the

Yakima River south of Richland. Those in charge refused
to heed the advice of the old-time residents who warned
that a wooden structure would be threatened with the
winter ice buildup.

It required only one winter, that of 1949. Ice built up
and extended upriver more than half-a-mile from the
bridge. In no time at all, the ice crunched through two of
the bridge's center pilings. Afraid the ice would wipe out
the whole structure, workmen tore down a 165-foot section
of the new bridge, to save the remainder of the span.

The second story was about an AEC-GE error that cost
a half-million dollars.

The headline which introduced this particular situation
said: "Filtration Plant Was Started, Then Halted Reporter
Discovers."

The story explained that Richland almost had a water
intake and filtration plant the year before. A contract for
$2,509,450 had been awarded. The project was started and
then was abandoned. *The Herald* estimated that work and
materials on the abandoned job cost between $500,000 to
$550,000.

The Herald published a survey of what had been done
and then contacted GE officials. A GE spokesman said the
project was abandoned because test borings and exploration originally indicated a satisfactory foundation did not
hold up. So GE sought expert advice from Alcord, Burdeck
and Howsan, Chicago consulting engineers. They recommended the existing well system be expanded to fit the
present need. Since Richland had grown considerably in a
year it became certain more water would have to be
found.

Another *Herald* headline read, "Acute Water Situation
Faces Richland As 'Experts' Ponder Pump That Won't
Pump."

The story said:

"A pump that won't pump—a water system
that top brass insisted over numerous protests to

be the 'stuff' is gradually losing its efficiency and now Richland faces a critical water shortage that even gigantic expenditures may fail to remedy.

"The impending shortage is a simple problem in arithmetic. Richland's water system capacity is gradually failing to meet the increasing demands of population and season. GE-AEC experts, however, have little respect for elementary arithmetic . . . Top level disagreement between AEC-GE experts, huge expenditures in trial and error methods as well as loss of time involved have combined to bring about what could be a disastrous condition . . . A number of . . . persons are said to have resigned . . . because a contract was awarded for a system that would have done the job and work was begun. But top brass interpreted the problem differently—so they tore it down and started all over again on a project—like the bridge—that wouldn't work.

"The pump described by confidential sources as a 'Rube Goldberg contraption' only cost about $20,000 but it is a good example of how the entire problem of Richland's water supply had been mishandled.

"The water system—wells, which are recharged with water pumped from the Columbia River and ditched from the Yakima—cost about $500,000, several sources estimated. It may have to be abandoned and a river pumping plant and filtration plant built. The wells are fast filling with sand—volcanic ash. Many of them are producing less than 50 percent of their originally intended capacity."

On April 6, a headline story announced that Senator Cain asked the Congressional Joint Committee on Atomic Energy to investigate the Richland water system.

"If some of the methods now being used at Richland and

Hanford to supply water are a sample of the trial and error methods of making atomic bombs it is a wonder the country has any at all," Senator Cain said.

The Seattle *Times* commended *The Herald* for exposing the waste. In an editorial, *The Times* said:

"Things have been going on behind the atomic curtain at the Hanford project that one neighboring newspaper doesn't like. *The Tri-City Herald* has been exposing what it calls 'startling examples of waste' at the nearby atomic energy plant.

"Necessarily there has been much secrecy in connection with Hanford operations. That should not be permitted to cloak needless extravagance with public funds.

"In such circumstances a vigilant newspaper, alerted to ferret out instances of waste that otherwise would never come to light, wields a salutary influence and performs a valuable public service for American taxpayers."

Bill Bequette's article on April 10 concerned another blunder. It warned: "Unfinished $75,000 Cafeteria is Mute Testimony of Waste."

High points of the article read: "North Richland's Cafeteria No. 3, uncompleted and useless, gives mute testimony to the waste found in many places on the Hanford project.

"How much taxpayer's money was 'sunk' in this monument to GE-AEC planning? A GE spokesman says $75,000. Others who cannot be quoted range from $110,000 down to $55,000. Most common unofficial estimate was $90,000. However, one informant said this figure included the cost of some of the barracks which were never used."

This latest disclosure "hit the fan" in Washington D. C. Senator Cain had been asking for an investigation. Now Senator Arthur Vandenburg, the Republican Senate Leader from Michigan, called for a complete inquiry of the Atomic Energy Commission, and its chairman, David E. Lilienthal, on all security problems. A congressional committee proceeded to look into the commission's operations and one investigator, Senator Bourke Hickenlooper of Iowa, called for Lilienthal's resignation.

Some of the headlines which appeared in this regard included "Hickenlooper Asks To Prove AEC Charge. Says He'll Back Up Mismanagement Tag," "Lilienthal To Face Congressional Group On Incredible Mismanagement Charge," and then in June the headline: "Iowa Senator Ready To Wind Up Case Against AEC."

This was the first time that *The Herald*, considered small by most daily newspaper standards, caused enough of a splash to attract the attention of powerful federal officials in Washington D. C.

The next chapter in the Richland Bridge story developed that winter. As ice piled up behind the bridge, GE figured that if dynamite were used to break up the ice west of the bridge, the smaller chunks could easily pass downstream. The dynamite was timed to go off and the fuse lighted. Unfortunately, they had neglected to consider the river's current. It carried the dynamite downstream and directly under the bridge, where the dynamite exploded, blowing up the bridge!

Hugh Scott was successful in creating good will in Richland, although it was an uphill monumental task, particularly when his newspaper would blow the whistle on AEC and GE. When Hugh resigned, Bob Philip moved to Richland from Seattle. He quickly made many friends. One of his main problems was to be friendly, yet not allow those friendships to influence news policy at *The Herald*. It took a tactician and Bob was a master.

In 1951, the pendulum began to swing the other way. This time the powerful AEC and General Electric Company turned to *The Herald* for what help it could give in solving an impossible situation. This time GE and AEC began feeding tips indirectly to *The Herald* about the slowing down of projects at Hanford and the soaring cost of overtime due to shortages of skilled workers.

Don and reporter Hill Williams met with Hanford

officials and received an outline of the problem. Then Hill was assigned to uncover the facts and to present them in a series of stories. He painstakingly began to dig into the situation and prepared a very readable group of articles that detailed what was going on and why.

His articles zeroed in on the construction of a huge chemical separation plant for the Hanford Works labelled as of top importance to the nuclear program. The plant was nearing completion but was five months past the target date and dragging. The AEC said the project represented about 20 percent of the total cost of their current expansion program. The total program was running into hundreds of millions of dollars. Authentic sources revealed that the overtime in construction and delay in finishing the facility were costing about two million dollars a month.

One cause for the delay was a shortage of skilled workers of one union, the AFL's United Association of Plumbers and Steamfitters. The shortage was apparently created while plenty of qualified workers were in the area.

Factors which made this possible included:

1. The Washington State Agreement between Master Plumbers and the AFL's U. A. of Plumbers and Steamfitters, which created a virtual monopoly in the plumbing business and practically made employer and union one and the same.

2. Traditional construction practice of hiring only through union halls which put tremendous power in the hands of the union leaders.

3. Failure of the AEC at Hanford to insist upon enforcement of the Taft-Hartley Act, designed to take this "life and death" power out of the union's hands. But in the majority of labor disputes at Hanford the unions demonstrated they had more muscle in Washington, D. C. than the AEC.

Vincent H. Larish, business agent of the United Association of Plumbers and Steamfitters Local 598, had notified two piping subcontractors of the Atkinson-Jones Construction Company of the union's desire to open their agreement for negotiation. The two subcontractors were Hanley Company, Chicago, and Urban, Smyth and Warren Company. At that time Hanley was nearing completion of its contract while Urban, Smyth and Warren USW was moving into a phase of construction which would require hundreds of plumbers, pipefitters, steamfitters and welders — all controlled by Local 598 in Pasco.

Hanley began to lay off men highly trained in these crafts. However, for some reason they were not reporting for work with USW. Normal procedure was for a man to report to the Pasco local and then be reassigned to existing jobs.

USW had submitted a requisition for 85 plumbers and steamfitters to the union in April. By the middle of July, one man had been dispatched by the union to the job. During this time Hanley had laid off 75 men who, presumably, became available for other jobs.

As early as July 15, 1951 field supervision reported that the vital job was "beginning to hurt" because of a lack of steamfitters. The company took action to obtain workers under procedures outlined in the Washington State Agreement with no result.

Early in August, after more than a month had gone by with no steamfitters being dispatched by the union, six more were sent out. Of these only two reached the job due to other circumstances. A few more men began to report for work from the union hall and by the middle of August the union had supplied 59 men but the work still lagged. By this time Hanley had reduced its force by 346. Requisitions for men still on file at the union hall totalled 137.

During these weeks, negotiations between the union and USW concerning a new contract were being dragged out, but about the middle of October agreement was reached. Shortly after that, men began to be supplied to the job and work began slowly moving ahead.

Few working men have the financial backing necessary to "hang tough" waiting for their union to send them to a job. Most of the former Hanley workers were forced to move away to seek work elsewhere.

Of the more than 600 men laid off by Hanley during these Summer and Autumn months only about 100 ever showed up at Hanford again. After they dispersed it was difficult to assemble a large group again.

The AEC said the job never had been fully staffed by the United Association of Plumbers and Steamfitters.

David F. Shaw, Hanford manager for the AEC at that time, said the shortage had definitely slowed down completion of the vital chemical plant. He said that other difficulties might have set the completion date back to around the first of the year, but the other three months of the delay could probably be wholly chalked up to the shortage of steamfitters and welders.

In explaining how the shortage of one craft could so completely throw a job off schedule, Shaw said the chemical separation plant involved a great deal of plumbing. Much of the work consisted of setting vessels in concrete with highly complicated connections of close precision. He said the shortage of steamfitters and welders came unexpectedly during June and July when practically no men were supplied by the union despite the hundreds being laid off by Hanley.

When the AEC complained to the union local or to the international, the "official" answer was that requisition from other jobs "blotted up" the surplus men available before they could be sent to work at Hanford. Shaw answered that the AEC received allegations that idle men were in the area and were unable to get a work dispatch, but no substantiation could ever be obtained.

Expensive equipment for new Hanford plants—secured on a rush basis at premium prices—arrived only to sit and gather rust because of the slow-down.

Three former top supervisors for Atkinson-Jones Company, contractor on the chemical separations plant, told Williams they felt they were removed from A-J's payroll because of pressure applied by the union. They had opposed certain tactics of the union which slowed down the construction work. The trio signed a notarized statement that outlined:

1. How they were suspended by the A-J Construction Company.

2. How the shortage of plumbers and steamfitters on the USW project had slowed the job.

3. How men on the job had participated in a "definite slowdown" after a change in supervision.

4. How equipment had been procured under emergency conditions only to have its installation delayed for long periods by this slowdown.

Two key employees of USW who were opposed strongly to Larish's methods in operating his union, claimed Larish had "absolute control" of their company at Hanford. One said that when Larish wanted a man removed from USW rolls he merely telephoned and said, "Get rid of . . . . . ." The man would be discharged.

One man, who would send requisitions to the union for workers, said Larish dispatched no more than three steamfitters to USW while during the same period Hanley was terminating approximately 400. This man and his supervisor had refused to take orders from Larish so Larish had gotten them fired.

More and more information came out that provided insight into Larish's methods and tactics in handling contractors and in ruling his workers. He would levy a fine on members if they didn't go to work where he told them, usually to jobs in other parts of the region or state. He also had a procedure for getting rid of men he didn't want in his local for any number of reasons. His method was to send such workers to the state unemployment office in Pasco to apply for unemployment compensation. There was a one-week waiting period. At the end of the week, the office would give the worker a card for his business

agent to sign certifying there was no work for him. When
the man appeared with his card, Larish would tell him a
job had just turned up and send the man to one of his
favorite plumbing contractors. The contractor would pay
the man "show-up time" set at four hours pay by union
law, and then tell him he had no work for him.

Very few men had the financial assets to stand this
treatment long and were forced to leave town to seek other
work.

A favorite contractor could pick his own men for any
job. This gave him a big advantage over contractors who
had to take workers Larish would send to them.

Hill Williams also learned from a key Hanford official
that Larish had the AEC "backed up against the wall." His
weapon in keeping the AEC in line was the threat of
pulling out his men. Most of the construction then in
progress hinged on work by steamfitters, so a walkout by
steamfitters would have been disastrous. Asked why AEC
didn't do something about it, Williams was told there was
"a lot of politics mixed up in it." No one wanted to get in
bad with labor. Also, AEC wanted to get this particular
project done as quickly as possible and therefore would
knuckle under to almost any Larish demand.

The Federal Bureau of Investigation was called to investigate Larish after the steamfitters had caused so much
trouble and so many slowdowns that subversive elements
were suspected. The FBI reported that although Larish
was troublesome he had not violated federal law. However, they continued to keep a close watch on him.

Meanwhile, Larish curtailed operations by carefully
screening all men who applied for work. Those he knew
were against him, he'd send to jobs out of the area. Those
who favored him he sent to Hanford. The object of this
was to perpetuate his own regime and to build a strong
local. One steamfitter at Hanford circulated a petition
condemning Larish and his practices. When this was
uncovered, the man was blackballed and lost his union

card. He was unable to get another plumbing job. Those who signed the petition did not lose their cards but were sent out of the area. The incident served to illustrate the tremendous power of the union official as well as the strong feeling of the workers who objected to his tactics but who were unable to change them.

Hill Williams' articles exposing Larish and his maneuvers with the vital construction at Hanford never appeared in *The Herald*. While Hill had been doing his investigative work, Don and Glenn had been investigating the Kennewick School District. Don's articles had set off an explosion that was reverberating across the state. Lawsuits had been filed and the investigation was continuing. *The Herald* had one wild tiger by the tail. Could it handle two at the same time?

The decision was to hold up the Larish-Hanford series not because of their controversial nature but because two major investigations running at the same time might be too much to shove at the reader. In other words, one might detract from the other to the extent that both would lose.

The Herald would learn there would be many other labor situations at Hanford that would develop and be covered but none quite so unique as that of Vincent Larish and Local 598 of the United Association of Plumbers and Steamfitters. The articles on his methods would have served to hold up to public view the dangers inherent at that time in Big Government and Big Labor. The public was the loser because the series was not carried.

On the other hand, it became known shortly thereafter that Larish had a brain tumor and had only a short time to live. Whether the tumor accounted for his erratic behavior no one would know. Regardless, Larish's practices soon came to an end.

10 *Five Cents On The Dollar*

"REGARDING the Pasco situation, we have concluded we should take no more action at this time in buying the *Tri-City Herald*. Some day that will probably be an excellent one-paper market. Based on the information we have been able to obtain, it is my opinion the three cities involved in the immediate vicinity, will go through a long period of 'battling' with several newspapers of different types before the area settles down and really supports one good one."

In othed words, Harry Green, chief executive officer of the John Scripps Newspapers, was saying, "Don't call us, we'll call you."

Others in the newspaper business were saying that also when the broker authorized by Glenn and Bob contacted them to see if they were interested in purchasing *The Herald*. It is ironical, because within four or five years there was to be a continual patter of feet to *The Herald* doorstep to see if the paper would consider selling. That request is being currently asked with great frequency.

Glenn and Bob definitely had themselves a "tiger by the tail" as the year 1948 wheeled to a close. They didn't know if they could hold on and yet they didn't dare let go.

From the standpoint of public acceptance, things couldn't have been better. This despite the hostility of the various local power groups who didn't trust anything they couldn't control or that wasn't completely aligned to their interests.

From the standpoint of finances, things couldn't have

been worse. Following the economic impact of the flood, there seemed nowhere to go but up. But that didn't happen. Instead, there was a severe loss in total advertising volume in September, 1949. This resulted from periodic layoffs at Hanford. By the fall of 1949, instead of having a substantial gain in advertising, *The Herald* actually suffered a decline.

The problems confronting the newspaper were many. Every effort was made to borrow additional working capital, sell capital stock and to continue making payments on debts for machinery and equipment. To make matters grimmer, the Tri-City economy worsened during the last quarter of 1949.

In December, 1948, Glenn had become acquainted with Arthur W. Stypes, a newspaper broker from San Francisco. In an exchange of letters between them in late 1948 and early 1949, Glenn had emphasized his search for more investment capital for his newspaper. Stypes said it probably would be impossible for a new newspaper to obtain investment capital, but he wanted to know if Glenn and Bob might be interested in selling all or at least the controlling interest in *The Herald*.

It was a big decision although a necessary one. Glenn wrote that the partners were in accord. They would sell.

The first prospective purchaser was Lincoln O'Brien from New England who had money and a newspaper and business background. O'Brien had decided to seek his further fortunes in the West. He appeared in the Tri-Cities in 1949 to survey *The Herald* and its circulation area. He spent two days in the Tri-Cities—probably because he couldn't get away any sooner—and stopped by the office long enough on his way out to tell Glenn he was not interested in the proposition.

O'Brien had written a three page analysis of the situation for Stypes which he supplied to Glenn at the latter's request. It was hardly a "selling tool" for *The Herald* or the Tri-Cities, O'Brien was disenchanted with both. First

148

of all, he wrote, he wouldn't want to bring his family to live there. The appearance of Pasco was somewhat like a tough part of Lynn, Mass., to him.

As for the newspaper itself, the plant and equipment were in terrible condition and entirely inadequate. The paper had a poor office in Richland and was unable to get government permission for better quarters. It had no newsprint contract and was buying newsprint on the black market for as high as $140 a ton whereas the price through regular channels was $45.

O'Brien's report noted that the company's books were not very well kept and its operating statements were confusing. He correctly noted that the newspaper was getting desperate because, although its monthly losses were small, it had no resources to take care of such losses.

O'Brien was favorably impressed with Glenn, however. He considered Glenn an enthusiastic, hard-working young man who had done amazingly well with the newspaper against tremendous obstacles.

Ever the optimist, Glenn wrote to O'Brien to thank him for his analysis and see if he would be interested in buying $10,000 worth of common stock or investing $20,000 in six percent preferred stock! Glenn never received an answer.

Now Glenn wrote to Stypes and authorized him to sell *The Herald* for $400,000. Stypes then was able to interest Harry Green in a deal. Green sent Julius Gius, editor, and Alex Ottevare, business manager, of Scripps' *Bremerton Sun* to look over *The Herald.* After they reported back to him, Green wrote his polite, but firm, reply in the negative. Glenn and Bob could only tighten their grip on the tiger's tail and continue their quest for a buyer or for some means of financing their newspaper.

One of the real ironies is that had Glenn and Bob lost their newspaper at this juncture, they would have shown how the Tri-Cities was the right spot for a daily newspaper. Having demonstrated this, they would have had to step aside and watch somebody else reap the benefits.

On the other hand, the emerging Tri-Cities presented as much of a financial threat as it did an opportunity to the investor. Which city would be the dominant one and which newspaper would dominate? There was no good answer to this equation in 1948 and 1949. Nor would there be for some time. This is why Scripps backed away. There was an underlying community of interest between the cities but it didn't manifest itself clearly to the outsider, or, for that matter, to many of its citizens. Subtle changes were taking place and though they would prove decisive, they would not be dramatic.

The financial troubles of *The Herald's* owners and the woes they were experiencing in their struggles with General Electric, the Atomic Energy Commission and now Pasco, didn't go unnoticed elsewhere. It only served to heighten interest in the Tri-Cities as a newspaper prospect. Like the dying man in the desert, *The Herald* also could hear wings overhead. Thus, while Glenn and Bob were busy making contacts and trying to find additional working capital or prospective buyers, unknown to them a survey of the Tri-Cities newspaper potential was being made by Earl McCallum for a small group of Seattle speculators.

McCallum was an experienced newspaperman in management and advertising. He had had experience in making studies in various parts of the Western United States to determine whether a given area could support a daily newspaper. McCallum was asked to make the survey by Howard McGowan, a Seattle businessman, and was paid $1,250 for his work.

The Tri-Cities newspaper situation was "complicated," McCallum conceded in his report, and then set out to try and explain what made it complicated. The crazy patchwork quilt-type newspaper situation made interesting reading but it likewise served to complicate the report. Of course, the situation was not an easy one to explain. Here was a weekly Pasco paper converted to daily that moved to

Kennewick. Then it restarted the weekly Pasco paper. Meanwhile, another Pasco weekly was started unsuccessfully. Thus the daily was circluating its weekly and daily in Pasco and Franklin County and for a time its daily and a weekly — *Courier-Reporter* — in Kennewick. Both weeklies were in financial trouble and so, as a matter of fact, was the daily. Meanwhile, in Richland, eleventh largest city in the state, another weekly was circulated by a civic organization. This weekly was printed in Spokane and it also was in financial trouble.

The area was difficult to present optimistically to outside newspaper investors. McCallum tried gamely to do so. He noted the primary source of employment in Pasco was the Northern Pacific Railway, but it always had been. Agriculture would do much for Pasco, particularly when the Columbia Basin was developed, but that was years away.

Kennewick was the bedroom community for Hanford with no major employment source of its own. And Richland was supported by Hanford, which was supported by government spending.

It was a "boom" area and, although McCallum didn't say so, the question hung there for the investor — could it also turn into a "bust" area?

McCallum wrote: "*The Tri-City Herald* is very aggressive and it has created, by its contentiousness, almost what might in some quarters be called, hatred, or, at least, a great dislike among some citizens of Pasco because their daily has moved to Kennewick."

McCallum recommended that a weekly newspaper be established in Pasco at a minimum cost and developed to stand on its own feet. He did not propose that McGowan's group come into the area and compete with *The Herald* as a daily, but that they put out a weekly and probably graduate into a semi-weekly doing a localized job primarily in Pasco and Franklin County.

It was his thought that such a move would develop earnings and prove economically feasible. He guessed the *Tri-City Herald's* worth, because of its rapid growth and

151

expansion, to be close to $300,000. If the new weekly or semi-weekly became strong enough it might eventually enter the daily field, and either force consolidation with *The Herald* or take over the field, McCallum explained.

It was a long way around to get to the obvious conclusion of either running *The Herald* out of business or getting strong enough to force a consolidation with it. Strangely, he didn't list purchase of *The Herald* as a possibility.

McCallum gave his summation to McGowan, who later took him and his report to realtor Henry Broderick, one of the key men in Seattle's power structure and a person of tremendous wealth and influence. Broderick suggested they take the report to Howard Parish, former publisher of the suspended *Seattle Star* and owner of the Craftsman Press, a large commercial printing plant in Seattle. They did, and Parish read the report with intense interest. A peculiar set of circumstances seemed to provide Parish with information on the Tri-City market, a market on which he was not uninformed. Right now things seemed to be playing into his hands. Coming his way, among other things, were Bob and Glenn.

Bob and Glenn were unaware of McCallum's report in the Spring of 1949. Their quest for financing had led them to California, where they met with vacationing S. A. (Sam) Perkins, publisher of the *Bellingham Herald* and the *Daily Olympian*. They contacted millionaire Perkins regarding possible additional financing for *The Herald*. They got no money from Perkins but they did get some advice and part of it was the suggestion that they go to see Parish, whom Perkins recommended as an experienced newspaperman who might be able to give them some ideas.

So on a Spring day in 1949, Bob and Glenn had lunch in Seattle with Howard Parish in the coffee shop of the Benjamin Franklin Hotel. After listening to his visitors spell out their problem, Parish said:

"I might be interested in buying your newspaper. What do you think it's worth?"

"A fair price would be about $400,000," Bob answered.

"Impossible," Parish snorted. "That's an absurd figure."

"What do you think it is worth?" Bob asked, of course not realizing McCallum had estimated its worth at about $300,000.

"Maybe I'd give you $250,000 for it. Maybe," Parish replied.

"That wouldn't cover our investment," Bob said. "It won't bail out the stockholders and their investment."

"Your property isn't worth any more than that," Parish retorted. "That's all I'm prepared to pay and I recommend you consider the offer."

"Hell, $250,000 would be a steal," Glenn said. "Here, look at this," and Glenn took the paper placemat and quickly made a rundown of the assets of *The Herald*.

Parish shrugged his shoulders and waved off the figures.

"I would never give you more than $250,000 for your paper," he said. "And you'd better give it some serious thought. Otherwise I will come over there and start a newspaper and run you to the wall. When I do, I'll buy you for five cents on the dollar."

Perhaps it was a bluff, a maneuver to try and drive down the price. Or, perhaps, Parish was prompted to act as he did because he fancied himself as quite a newspaper expert while, in his opinion, Bob and Glenn were a couple of novices who could be handled easily in newspaper competition.

Whatever it was, Parish had sadly misjudged the two men with whom he was meeting. By the time this was resolved they would all be wiser but, for Parish, he would be both sadder and wiser.

Bob and Glenn looked at each other in amazement and anger. They stood up, signifying they were through talking.

"You come on over, Parish," Glenn said tightly. "You come over. We'll see who gets run out of there."

Parish had succeeded in doing one thing. He had filled

Bob and Glenn with a resolve not to sell to him at any price.

Back in the Tri-City area in the first half of 1949, *The Herald* made its final attempt to gain an office in Richland. It had been rebuffed at every turn by AEC and GE and tempers had flashed repeatedly as *The Herald* jabbed aggressively at the Hanford establishment.

"We just don't think you people would make good neighbors," Milt Cydell, the AEC's information officer, told Don once during one of their discussions.

"Why don't you fellows just concentrate in Kennewick and Pasco?" Cydell and his assistant, Lloyd Wier, asked during another discussion with Don.

Whether the AEC wanted any daily newspaper in Richland that they could not control is questionable. But even if they did want a free enterprise newspaper in Richland, obviously the free wheeling, hard-hitting *Tri-City Herald* didn't begin to approach what they had in mind. Yet they were faced with the embarassing knowledge that the *Richland Villager* was getting to the point where it was losing money despite all the protection they were able to give it. So the Hanford AEC made its move.

Cydell approached the Allied Daily Newspapers of Washington, and asked them to assist AEC in drawing up specifications so various newspaper publishers could bid on an exclusive franchise for a daily newspaper and printing plant in Richland. The newspaper association through Lew Selvidge, its secretary manager, quickly refused and followed its refusal with a strongly worded resolution, adopted May 13, 1949, condemning the move as violating our First Amendment guarantee of a free press. Furthermore, said the Allied Dailies, an attempt to limit newspapers was a "transgression on the American concept of freedom." Richland should be open to any loyal American to establish a newspaper, whether daily, weekly or semiweekly, or, for that matter, for an individual to establish any type of legitimate business institution, the newspaper organization told AEC.

But these were times when the Atomic Energy Commission considered itself all-powerful and Richland was its dominion. It went ahead anyway and advertised for bids.

There was only one bidder for the exclusive franchise, Mort Frayne, a Seattle printing shop owner. Frayne also was, of all things, a State Republican Party leader who was an outspoken proponent of the free enterprise system. Frayne's bid specified several exceptions to the terms set forth by GE and AEC. One exception would require that any other newspaper having its principal distribution in Richland must "edit, publish and print" the paper in that community.

Frayne explained that this exception was not intended to exclude newspapers like the *Portland Oregonian* or the *Seattle Post-Intelligencer* from circulating in Richland because, obviously, this was but a small part of their total circulation. His move apparently was aimed at the *Richland Villager*, which was published in Spokane, and *The Herald*, which was published in Kennewick.

Frayne's paper would be called the *"Richland Record"* and would be published by the Record Publishing Co. It was proposed as a weekly with the privilege of expanding to a bi-weekly and a daily when desired.

AEC and GE officials sat tight with Frayne's bid for 10 days. It was as if they had a slow-ticking time bomb in their hands. Meanwhile, *The Herald* kept up the pressure with a series of Page One editorials regarding the "unusual newspaper bid," as the newspaper labeled it. One editorial on Tuesday, July 19, 1949, read:

"Many people are asking a lot of questions since the unusual newspaper bid was opened by General Electric Co. in Richland, July 12.

"Literally, the unusual bid was a request for a 'monopoly in reverse.' It asked that AEC-GE ask other newspapers if they wanted to 'edit, print, publish' a newspaper of principle circulation in Richland, to duplicate the 'unusual bidder' investment in plant and equipment in Richland.

155

"The questions asked us most frequently and our replies are:

"1. Are AEC-GE, who claim they will establish a Free Press in Richland, actually considering the bid?

"Answer: Yes, they must be or an announcement would be made promptly tossing out the bid.

"2. Is the bid designed to put the community paper, the *Villager*, out of business?

"Answer: AEC-GE may want to 'eliminate' the *Villager*, but the people of Richland and the people who make-up the *Villager* board, want to keep the *Villager* in publication. They should have the right to do so. But economically if the unusual bid is accepted it signs the death warrant of the *Villager*.

"3. What action will the Scott Publishing Co., Inc., take if the unusual bid is accepted?

"Answer: If the unusual bid is accepted and the death knell of the *Villager* is sounded, the Scott Publishing Co., Inc., will commence weekly newspaper coverage and service for the community of Richland to supplement its existing daily newspaper coverage.

"4. Is AEC-GE sincere about carrying out the promise to give the *Tri-City Herald* a plot of land in Richland for the construction of appropriate offices?

"Answer: Yes, we think so. Negotiations in this respect started at once after the unusual bid was opened. GE officials in charge of the negotiations have given every indication of being helpful and cooperative and it is hoped early results may be obtained. If the selection of *The Herald*— and GE is approved by AEC, the 'wooden shack' days of *The Herald's* operation in Richland will soon be over.

"We submit that AEC-GE have many large and pressing problems. We choose to believe, however, that the newspaper situation in Richland will soon be cleared up so a free press, in every sense of the word, will function in Richland."

A few days later AEC-GE officials rejected Frayne's bid and on July 27 *The Herald* announced that it had been awarded a ground lease in Richland for construction of an office building. A milestone had been reached. At that time, the development seemed almost unbelieveable, although it also presented the problem of having to locate the financing to construct the building. That, however, was the type of problem *The Herald* always had.

From time to time, *The Herald* had made efforts to obtain the printing contract for *The Villager*, but always without success. Angry words had been printed and spoken in months of heated atmosphere and *The Villager* board never forgave *The Herald* for terminating its contract to print *The Villager* at the time it went to daily publication. However, having *The Villager* printed in Spokane meant the staff was compelled to travel to Spokane constantly. The early deadlines for both advertising and editorial copy severely limited the paper. The whole process was inconvenient, and expensive.

The Summer of 1949 saw a momentary thawing in relations, however. When *The Herald* approached Ted Best, then publisher of *The Villager* and later to be a Seattle City Councilman, and some of *The Villager's* Directors, they agreed to talk. The talks were fruitful and the two sides decided to "bury the hatchet." It was decided to work out an agreement between the two newspapers so *The Villager* could be printed at home. The matter was settled in a verbal understanding. *The Herald* was to print the first issue of *The Villager* in *The Herald* plant, Wednesday night, August 31, for delivery September 1, 1949. A contract was then signed by officers of *The Herald* and turned over to *The Villager* group. Peace seemed truly to be at hand, but *The Herald* hadn't figured on Howard Parish. He had been busy with plans of his own.

The web of newspaper intrigue which Parish wove in the Tri-Cities was started early. Later, as it was gradually unravelled, the discovery was made that Parish had been on the scene, at work, long before Bob and Glenn met with him at the suggestion of Sam Perkins. Eventually, a federal court suit would trace Parish's early efforts and show that when Exchange Club promoter Hagman was hired as publisher of the *Pasco Herald*, Parish already was making trips to the Tri-Cities and the two were secretly working together.

It was Parish, court testimony would show, who sold Rolf Tuve on the idea of combining his newspaper with the *Pasco Empire.* When this arrangement eventually lost Tuve control of the *Courier-Reporter* and bankruptcy ensued, Parish purchased for $2,500 the press Mid-Columbia Publishers had installed in Pasco at a cost of about $10,000.

In Seattle, Parish told McCallum he was interested in getting into the Tri-City newspaper field in a big way. He revealed that he had just completed the purchase of the Green-Hughes Printing plant in Spokane, which printed *The Villager.* He planned to move the Spokane plant to Pasco and print a weekly much like the one McCallum had proposed. He would call this paper the *Pasco News*—later to be renamed the *Columbia Basin News. The News* also would have *The Villager* printing contract. Parish emphasized that he planned to get the *Pasco News* into the area in "a big way." He also confided to McCallum that in a year or two he would be in position to give the *Tri-City Herald* competition "right across the board." He expected to create a situation that would either cause a consolidation or a possible purchase of the control of *The Herald,* just as McCallum had spelled out in his report.

"I've also received information from a trustworthy source

that *The Herald* is trying to get financing," Parish said with a wink to McCallum. "It's badly over-extended."

At Parish's direction, McCallum went to Spokane to look over the newly purchased printing plant and then to Pasco where he met with Hagman. Hagman was offered the position of business manager of the new operation but he turned it down. He agreed, instead, to install the new plant for Parish.

Parish titled his new company Columbia Basin Publishers. He was right on target and everything seemed to be going his way. The contract which *The Herald* turned over to the *Villager* board to confirm the printing of *The Villager* was never signed. Instead, *The Villager* board made a deal with Parish. They bluntly stated they did not wish to enter into a contract with *The Herald* if any other way could be found to have *The Villager* printed.

Parish had now fully surfaced. He was observed in the Tri-City area frequently during the Summer and Fall of 1949. At the same time a source *The Herald* had in Richland reported *The Villager's* financial troubles were mounting. Rumors persisted that the paper was up for sale and *The Herald* soon had information that Walt Smyth of *The Villager* board and Parish were talking about the ultimate disposal of *The Villager*. This was just prior to Christmas of 1949. So that Christmas season, like the one that preceded it and some that would follow, contained an ominous chill that had nothing to do with the weather. It meant long, long hours without seeing Don. It also meant that during the time he was home he always seemed glued to the telephone.

11   *The Strike*

"And coming events cast their shadows before."
                    Lochiel's Warning (1802)

There is little likelihood Glenn and Bob were thinking of
old Scottish poems, despite any application they might
have had in 1949 and 1950. Undoubtedly, though,
Lochiel's warning should have been recalled by Glenn that
December day in 1949 when Harold Whittemore, one of
The Herald's linotype operators, approached him.

"Mr. Lee," said Whittemore, "I represent the boys in the
backshop and we'd like to talk to you about more money
in the paycheck."

"I'd be glad to meet with them, and talk about anything they wish," Glenn replied. "But it's going to be
difficult for us to pay more money at this time, Harold.
You know what business conditions are, and I'm sure you
see the paper's hurting."

"Well, the boys wanted me to get the message to you
that they want to talk," Whittemore said.

"Okay, but just give me some time. I've got some real
problems right now. I'll get with you just as soon as I can,"
Glenn said.

Perhaps Glenn's radar didn't activate itself because his
mind was preoccupied with all the other things that had
been happening in such a rapid-fire sequence. For instance, there were the rumors of an impending sale of *The
Villager* and that Howard Parish would convert his weekly
Pasco News to daily publication at almost any time.

160

Ted Best had suddenly resigned as editor of *The Villager* and was going back to Seattle. The *Pasco Herald* and the *Kennewick Courier-Reporter* had been merged to cut costs, but they were still losing money even though they were being printed on *The Herald's* press. The area's economy was shuddering under the continuing layoff of thousands of construction workers. Some 5,000 persons were on relief and men were hunting jack rabbits and winter-fishing the rivers for food.

A few days after his talk with Whittemore, Glenn received a letter from Local 831 of the International Typographical Union giving a 60-day notice that they desired to negotiate a written contract. At this time *The Herald* employed 10 journeymen printers and five apprentices in the composing room. The press and stereotype department had one journeyman and four apprentices.

There was still the problem of finding qualified printers, a problem that had nagged *The Herald* from the day it began. Now, the newspaper had boosted its apprenticeship program to train its own printers.

Parish had only four men employed in his Pasco backshop. The fact that most of the union men were in *The Herald* plant plus the fact that he had never negotiated with a union before, also contributed to Glenn's seeming lack of priority to the union request. He had gone to extreme lengths to recruit a composing and press room force and *The Herald* was paying in excess of the Walla Walla scale in an effort to keep printers. The Tri-City printers had been under the Walla Walla local. Near the end of 1949 it was announced they had formed their own local. So Glenn kept busy financing *The Herald* and trying to keep track of what Parish was doing with the Richland Board of Villagers, Inc. and their newspaper. He was soon to learn that the menacing union situation was just another in Parish's bag of tricks.

In January, 1950, C. L. Bushell, general manager of the Printing Industry of Seattle, Inc., wrote to Glenn stating that Parish had asked him to review the typographical union's proposal. Among other things, Bushell said he hoped Parish and the Scott Publishing Co. could get together on negotiations. The letter gave Glenn a jolt. Negotiate in concert with Parish! Glenn would rather swim in a river of crocodiles and he expressed himself very bluntly on this matter in the plant. He rebuffed any suggestion that he and Parish negotiate together.

"Parish is out to steal our newspaper," he said. "I'll talk to the union but I want nothing to do with Parish. I don't like him. I don't trust him. He's using the union as a tool."

In a conversation with Lew Selvidge, manager of the Allied Daily Newspapers of Washington, Glenn spelled out his plans.

"Who have you got to handle your negotiations?" Selvidge asked.

"I plan on doing it myself with Bernie Russell," Glenn said. Russell was *The Herald's* production manager. "Do you have any suggestions?"

"Glenn," said Selvidge, "you'll be making a mistake not to go in with an experienced negotiator."

"I know these printers pretty well. Some of them have been with us since we started the paper," Glenn said.

"You may not know them as well as you think you do," Selvidge replied.

Selvidge recommended D. S. (Scotty) Haines, an attorney who specialized in labor relations for the Pacific Northwest Newspaper Association which was headquartered in Portland, Oregon. Glenn telephoned Haines and sent him a copy of the ITU letter of 60-day notice.

Later, after Glenn's five-year pursuit of the union, first in Superior Court and then in Federal Court, testimony would verify the suspicions held during those early months of 1950. Parish and the union were to deny vehemently that they had conspired in 1950, but documentation would show something else. For instance, in 1957, in Chicago, a deposition turned up a letter from Parish to Hagman about Bushell's January, 1950 letter to Glenn.

"Dear Art," Parish wrote. "The attached letter will be of

interest to you, I am sure. Bud Bushell is the manager of our local printing industry set-up working with the print shop owners . . . Howard."

In 1956, Glenn talked to Bushell in Seattle concerning Parish. Bushell recalled that Parish had talked to him about the negotiations and Parish had asked Bushell to get certain information for him. Bushell made phone calls to daily newspapers in Aberdeen and Vancouver, about wage scales and he also contacted Clarence Lafromboise in the weekly newspaper field in regards to the same matter. Because Parish operated the Crafstman Press and had been publisher of defunct *Seattle Star* he was familiar with wage scales and hourly arrangements for printers both in the metropolitan and non-metropolitan fields.

In those early months, the advantage belonged to Parish. His experience in newspapers and in business showed through. He was on the offensive and he moved speedily and adroitly. With great flourish, he signed his contract with the union in February. He was very generous and gave the union just about everything it asked for: a scale of $90 per week with two-weeks vacation, six-paid holidays, and a work week of 38 and 3/4 hours. A quick calculation showed this would cost *The Herald* from $18,000 to $20,000 annually. For Parish, with four people, the increase was nominal.

The union and *The Herald* were to commence their negotiations on February 22. The ITU let it be known they wanted from *The Herald* the identical contract that Parish had signed. *Herald* management was notified that otherwise there would be a strike.

Glenn had placed a hurried call to Haines and on the morning of February 23, Haines flew to Yakima where Glenn met him. They drove to Kennewick together. Sure enough, it was not just the "boys from the backshop" who were negotiating. Present was Walter Marvick, a skilled union negotiator. Marvick was surprised to see Haines. But there really wasn't anything to negotiate. Instead, the union repeatedly stressed that the contract already had been established. *The Herald* was told to sign for what the others had signed.

Glenn and Bob protested that they were the major employer and had the most at stake. Other than Parish, there were only a couple of commercial plants, one with only an owner and he was in the union. So he had merely signed to give himself a raise. That could hardly be used to bind *The Herald*.

Glenn and Bob's arguments got them nowhere with Marvick, who insisted the competing newspaper had met the demands, now it was mandatory *The Herald* do likewise.

"It is simply the fact that we can't pay that new contract," Glenn said. "We have been fair in the past but this is the Seattle scale. The contract is not fair and we can't afford to pay it."

Marvick looked at him coldly. "Then why don't you sell to somebody who can?"

Glenn's eyes shot fire. For a moment it looked like he was going to jump over the table.

Haines told Marvick, "I'm sorry you said that. I'm sorry that reflects your attitude. But am I to understand that we shall be deprived of the chance to even submit a counter offer?"

There was a discussion among the union delegates. They finally announced they would agree to hear a counter offer. They also made it clear it was little more than a courtesy. Their position was that a contract had been established for the Tri-Cities and they couldn't "favor" one employer over another. *The Herald* must meet the contract signed by the *Pasco News*.

It was clear the union wasn't bluffing. In his talks Marvick emphasized that the ITU's position was practical and had to be devoid of sympathy. The union wanted the best contract it could get. It was not interested in who might win out in a newspaper fight. There was no room for sentiment.

On the other hand, *The Herald* wasn't bluffing, either. Its financial position as of January, 1950 was an over-drawn bank account of $2,200. For the month of January, the operating loss was $3,182.26. Contracts payable were $69,262 with monthly payment of $2,500 and notes pay-able of $30,539. Because of economic conditions, two printers had to be laid off. They were Frank Cummings, a holdover from the *Courier-Reporter* plant, and Linn Hebron, in *The Herald's* composing room.

During the negotiations both Glenn and Bob had several opportunities to impress upon Marvick and the ITU scale committee the difficult economic situation in the Tri-Cities and the fact *The Herald* was not making money. Marvick merely shrugged this off. Unless the contract was signed, he told them, he and the ITU members were "going outside and start throwing rocks."

Marvick had good reason to be unbending with *The Herald*. What the newspaper's management didn't know was that on February 12, he had met Parish in Seattle and had discussed in some detail what would be done if *The Herald* had a strike. The strike would be Parish's "signal" to go daily, Marvick dutifully wrote in a letter to the headquarters of the typographical union in Indianapolis. So Marvick wasn't worried. Strike or no strike, there would be a daily newspaper published in the Tri-Cities.

Marvick next went before the Tri-City membership of ITU prior to a strike vote and told them the *Pasco News* would help them out in case of a strike. He explained that the printers would get their strike benefits from the ITU strike fund plus one day's work each week with the *Pasco News*. This figured out to be approximately what they were making at *The Herald*. Some of the printers candidly explained to Don how it would work and they could show that they would be making more money on strike than when they were working.

Everything seemed to be going Parish's way. One of his windfalls would be a ready-recruited composing room staff that had taken *The Herald* two years to recruit and many headaches to assemble. Undoubtedly this figured in his reasoning not to attempt to purchase *The Herald*. From all appearances, he could take over the field without the expense of buying the existing newspaper. Certainly Parish had the financial backing to have purchased *The Herald*. *The Seattle Star*, which he organized in the 1930's and then sold to the *Seattle Times* in the 1940's, had made money for his Seattle backers. Parish moved in the better circles of Seattle society. He lived near William Boeing in the exclusive Seattle Highlands and he was active in affairs of the Seattle Rainier Club.

Among his financial backers in the Tri-City venture were realtor Henry Broderick; Rainier Brewery owner Emil Sick; John X. Johnson, owner of a fish-packing plant; Wilbur Scruby, officer of Seattle-First National Bank; attorney and civic leader Ernie Skeel; bottler Paul Glaser; insurancemen Charles Parker and Van McKenny, and E. B. McGovern, G. P. McNamara and T. V. Dempsey. Most of them originally bought stock and others were later tapped for loans by Parish when money ran short. Dempsey, for one, became disturbed about his investment early in the game. The one man who contributed the largest amount over the first year was Johnson. These men were merely investors in Parish's proposition. They were not involved in its operation.

The time was now ticking away for the "showdown" date with the ITU of March 3. Unless there was to be a break in the stance of either side, a strike seemed inevitable. Parish had maneuvered *The Herald* where it had two options, both dire. The easy one was to sign the contract and then economically bleed to death from the increased costs of higher wages and feather-bedding clauses in the contract. The other was to take a strike and fight it out, hoping that *The Herald* could continue to publish and that the advertising and circulation losses wouldn't bankrupt the paper.

The difference, as Don often described it when questions arose as to why *The Herald* had taken a strike, was:

"We could either play Russian roulette or become afflicted with economic leukemia. Neither choice was desirable but Russian roulette seemed more sporting."

The atmosphere in the plant was charged. Work slowdowns became frequent and it was necessary to continually remind non-ITU employees not to get into arguments with those who belonged to the union. Among the editorial workers especially, there was a fierce loyalty to the newspaper. They were keenly aware of the various moves by Parish. Advertising department salesmen and news reporters were the eyes and ears of *The Herald* during these days and they were constantly relaying important morsels of information to Bob and Glenn.

This loyalty was important because after the strike began Parish made overtures to hire salesmen and reporters, a procedure he followed during the life of the *Columbia Basin News*. He was rarely successful, although his staff at times contained several ex-*Herald* employees. For the most part, these were employees who had left voluntarily, by request, or had returned to the area after being away. Don lost only one man to the *Columbia Basin News* during all the years that newspaper operated and the man proved as unsatisfactory there as he had at *The Herald*.

Meanwhile, on the economic front there were still answers to be sought, for unless local business picked up, the matter of what was in a union contract was going to be moot anyway. This problem, of course, didn't belong just to *The Herald*. The Central Labor Council, headquarters for Tri-City unions, also was making inquiries through senators and congressmen trying to learn the reason for the Hanford layoffs and when hiring would start.

The situation was best spelled out in a front page editorial of February 28, titled, "No Answers Yet." The editorial pointed out that many small businessmen in the Tri-Cities, without the necessary reserves, were being forced to the wall and had taken bankruptcy in record numbers during the preceding 60 days. The Hanford layoffs had been so heavy there were almost 5,000 persons on relief. By April 1, it was expected that 4,000 would be cut from relief lists because of insufficient funds.

The editorial asked the question that was a household topic at that time, "When will hiring start again and how many will be hired?"

But from AEC and GE no answer was forthcoming, which wasn't unexpected in view of the fact they had repeatedly denied that the layoffs were taking place. However, it was entirely possible that the reason they had nothing to say at this time was that they didn't know, either.

As the "countdown" to March 3 approached a scramble started to answer the question: "How do we get out a newspaper if we have a strike?"

One unknown was whether any of the backshop would remain. There were some question marks but the decision was made to go on the basis that no union employee would stay with the newspaper. There would be plenty of help from the editorial and advertising departments but these were also unskilled.

One thing worked in *The Herald's* favor on the matter of personnel. The ITU had caused a series of strikes across the nation and in Canada. Some strikebound newspapers published despite their strike and the ITU responded by financing a strike organization which it named "Unitypo." This arm of the ITU established and operated its own newspapers in those cities on strike. The result, however, was that eventually a non-union pool of printers was established that could help striking newspapers. The

The Strike

American Newspaper Publishers Association (ANPA) called them "floating printers." The ITU called them "scabs."

These non-union printers did, however, float about the country taking advantage of the strikes which grew out of the rising militancy of the ITU and the resistance of many newspapers to the contract the union demanded. Strikes were a bonanza to them for they got plenty of overtime work. Then, when the strike was settled, they would move on.

Several printers were obtained a few days before the strike and housed in the Desert Inn. They proved competent enough to do a variety of jobs and thus, with assistance from the staff, they were able to keep the paper publishing. However, it became apparent that they were a temporary, though necessary, device. Permanent people were recruited from the Tri-Cities and trained in the plant. These trainees became so capable that Parish attempted to hire some of *The Herald's* "scabs" for his own plant.

The period of negotiations—if it can be called that—lasted from February 23 to March 3. The union had been receiving $80 a week for 40 hours with one-week vacation and four paid holidays. The ITU wanted $90 for 38¾ hours, with six paid holidays and two weeks of vacation. *The Herald's* counter offer was $85 for 40 hours with two weeks of vacation and six paid holidays. There was contract language to which *The Herald* objected and for the most part, this was the subject of most of the deliberations in the 10-day period of negotiations. Whether this contract language could have been mitigated, no one can say. The burning issue was that $5.00 a week difference and the one-and-one-fourth hours less work per week. Looking at it from today's viewpoint, it seems like a trifling difference. For that matter, the next day, Saturday, March 4, Marvick and Jack Whiting, another international representative at the final meeting, went to Yakima, only 85 miles away, and settled with the *Yakima Morning Herald* and *Yakima Evening Republic,* both published by the same family, for $85.00 a week the *Tri-City Herald* had offered!

The March 3 meeting began at 4:35 p.m. in the conference room of the Kennewick Chamber of Commerce, then located on Auburn Street just north of Kennewick Avenue. This marked the first appearance of Whiting. He and Marvick were accompanied by the union scale committee. *The Herald* representatives were Glenn, Bob, Don, Scotty Haines and Bernie Russell. Also present was P. A. Lind, a state mediator, who presided.

Was there a chance *The Herald* would increase its offer, Lind wanted to know? Haines told him *The Herald* was unable to go any higher; in fact, had difficulty in going as high as it had and would have difficulty sustaining that scale. Whiting restated the union's position that a contract already had been established for the area and they would not give favored treatment to one employer over another.

There were long exchanges but the union held firmly to its position and refused to discuss the counter proposal made earlier by *The Herald*. Lind pursued concessions from *The Herald* during a recess, although he conceded he would have a hard time selling the ITU on any changes or concessions.

Haines pointed out the scale committee was under fixed instructions to get what they had originally asked for and nothing could be changed in this respect.

The recess ended at 7 p.m., but there was little to talk about afterwards and finally the union delegation stood up.

Haines asked:

"Will the union agree to submit this matter to arbitration?"

"What do you say to that?" Lind asked Whiting.

"Our response is no," Whiting answered. "We have never fared well in any arbitration. We are not interested in it."

"If you leave the room will it mean a strike will exist?" Lind said.

"Yes, that is correct," Whiting said. And then he said, "Well, let's go. Let's get out of here."

The union delegation moved to the door. It was 7:20 p.m.

"Well, gentlemen," said Lind, "you've done nothing else but negotiate yourselves a strike. Everybody's bluff is called. No one is holding back anything. I'm sorry."

The Herald delegation remained seated as the union filed out.

The newspaper plant was only two blocks from the Chamber office but it was a long walk back. The night crew was on its regular shift, but within 30 minutes the plant was empty except for two persons, production manager Russell, and O. J. McCloud, composing room foreman. The union put a lot of pressure on McCloud but they were unsuccessful in getting him to leave.

The strike had begun and now Parish had his "signal" to go daily. He lost no time. Parish had carefully mapped his moves and they seemed to be going like clockwork.

On Tuesday, March 7, the *Pasco News* announced in a front page editorial that it would change its name to the *Columbia Basin News* and commence daily publication the next Tuesday. Two days later, March 9, the newspaper announced it had purchased the *Richland Villager* for $2,000 and was merging the Richland paper with the new daily so Richland would have its own newspaper.

Meanwhile, pickets from Local 831 were on the job bright and early Monday morning, March 6. They picketed the Kennewick and Richland offices. The Pasco office was omitted because it was in Verne Husk's commercial printing plant. Those first days the picketing was a novelty, both for the pickets and for *The Herald* employes. There was some good-natured banter, sheepish looks and even some friendly conversation. It would be a mistake to think all employes wanted the strike because they didn't. Most stayed to work for Parish. Some, however, left the area and obtained printing work elsewhere. As a matter of principle they would support their union in its strike and not cross the picket line. But also as a matter of principle, they would not work for the *Columbia Basin News*.

On some occasions there would be as many as six pickets. Other times there were four. For the first few months of the strike there were always at least two. As the summer wore on it was reduced to one picket at the Kennewick plant.

One of the pickets, Paul Hathaway, a member of the *Courier-Reporter* staff who had stayed when *The Herald* took over that operation, became a constant picket, sometimes sleeping in his car in front of the Kennewick plant.

A lighter side of the strike came one hot summer day when *The Herald* moved onto the sidewalk in front of the plant a circular metal table with a beach umbrella, a Coke machine, and a couple of metal outdoor chairs. The table had a radio and some cigars. During hot days the pickets took advantage of this and would sit, and have a Coke and a smoke. Before long, high school students were leaning out of cars and jeering at them. Then some students found it more entertaining to wheel quickly around the corner and throw peanuts at the pickets. So some of *The Herald* employes placed a sign on the sidewalk facing the street which read: "Please don't feed the pickets."

For the pickets, that was the last straw. They boycotted the sidewalk facilities, which were then withdrawn.

As the years went by, the picketing became more infrequent. It finally stopped altogether except for one "die hard" who stayed on the picket line long after the others had left. He was Frank Cummings, an officer of the union. He read books as he slowly paced in front of the Richland office, so slowly that it appeared he wasn't moving. Undoubtedly he came out of the strike as the best read person in town, judging from the amount of material he went through. The picketing was friendly. When his family wished to get in touch with him, they would call the Richland office and ask that the message be relayed, which it was. Cummings wouldn't return the call from *The Herald* office even though the offer was often extended.

When the strike started the union went to work on *The*

First days of strike, 1950, ITU pickets march at entrance to Kennewick plant.

Concessions supplied for ITU pickets by *The Herald* on the sidewalk in front of the plant, 1950.

A broken window by Don's desk made by a rock thrown during the strike.

Glenn picketing the pickets. Former Northern Pacific Railroad Depot is in the background.

Howard Parish, founder of the *Columbia Basin News*, who schemed to drive *The Herald* to the wall, talks to Frank Cummings, ITU picket, in front of *The Herald*.

Herald with a vengeance. *The Herald* hadn't missed an issue and as the paper continued to publish the friendly greetings between pickets and staff members began to dissipate. Each side began to recognize that it would be a long uphill struggle. For the pickets there was the frustration of seeing the paper come out without them. For the staff members, there was the continual harrassment they faced in the community. They were constantly being called upon to defend the newspaper and there was mounting tension on both sides.

Within a matter of weeks, efforts by the ITU to embarrass and harm *Herald* employes became chronic. Automobiles parked adjacent to the building began experiencing flat tires. Tacks and nails were strewn about the parking lot and additional flat tires were experienced.

On another occasion a homemade bomb was thrown through a window of the pressroom. Fortunately, it failed to go off and immediately heavy boards were nailed across the windows both in the press room and around a portion of the warehouse in which several carloads of newsprint were stored. Soon, the remaining warehouse windows were smashed, so all lower windows were boarded up. Extra lights were placed around the building as the damage continued.

Then another fortuitous thing happened. One of the great fears was fire because the warehouse was merely a big wooden barn that had contained the machinery for the old cannery. It now housed the newspaper's mechanical department. By a stroke of luck, Glenn made a swing around the outside of the building before going home one night and discovered rags, soaked in oil, had been stuffed under the wooden siding of the building. They apparently had been set on fire, but for some reason the flames had gone out. There was some speculation that the arsonists had been startled—maybe by Glenn, although if so, he wasn't aware of them—and hadn't been able to finish their job. Whatever the case, a night watchman was hired. Immediate steps were taken to cover this portion of the warehouse from the ground to about a four foot level with aluminum sheeting.

Later the glass in the front door and a window beside Don's desk were smashed by rocks. Someone also climbed up the building and cut all telephone wires. So little by little, *The Herald* building began to take on the appearance of a besieged fortress.

Personal harassment to our family included telephone calls late at night. The callers would immediately hang up as soon as someone answered. Don was working long hours and late into the night. The calls were timed to interrupt his sleep. But the phone had to be answered for it might have meant an emergency at the plant.

Eventually, this led to a hot exchange of words one night between Don and a couple of pickets. When Don got home for dinner, he noticed a picket's car driving slowly through our alley with about five men in it. The car circled the block and then came back through the alley. The only gun in our home happened to be a broken shotgun that my father had left for repair. Don grabbed it and sprinted towards the car. Tires screeched and gravel flew as the driver accelerated wildly.

The telephone calls stopped after that!

The union went on radio to stress that *The Herald* was on strike and to request Tri-City residents not to purchase it, advertise in it or to support anyone who advertised in it. Local 831 also sent letters throughout the Tri-Cities telling people *The Herald* was "produced by scabs behind the picket line," and urging them not to read it.

The Herald had campaigned hard for professional baseball. April, 1950, marked the start of the area's first team in the new baseball park, Sander's Field, located in the Kennewick Highlands. There was a touch of irony in the fact that many of the thousands who saw that first game also received cards, passed out at the entrances, containing a schedule of the baseball games on one side and Jack London's definition of a "scab" on the other.

The union also decorated a car with large posters

blazoning that *The Herald* was "Unfair to Organized Labor" and entered the car in Tri-City parades. The union also fashioned a floating sign proclaiming *The Herald* as "unfair" which they anchored in the river by Highway 410.

In addition, the union circulated, both personally and by mail, a list of merchants who had placed advertisements in *The Herald*. At first, the list was printed weekly. Later it came out semi-weekly. The list was about eight inches wide and 15 inches long and was often printed in different attractive colors. A typical paragraph read:

"Are Your Dollars Supporting A Scab? If you are patronizing the advertisers of the *Tri-City Herald* you are helping to support a scab. Do not patronize these firms!"

This was followed by the list of firms that had advertised in *The Herald* that preceding week. On the bottom of the leaflet was the usual reminder:

"Remember, every nickel spent for the *Tri-City Herald* helps support a scab."

Members of Local 831 also distributed the leaflets to various merchants and business houses and placed them in automobiles and under windshield wipers. It was a mammoth undertaking and the enthusiasm for this type of program waned quickly.

At other times, the union would wage a telephone campaign in which they would call all persons having classified advertisements in *The Herald* and advise them to cancel such advertising because the newspaper was unfair. Large-sized advertisements were placed in the *Columbia Basin News* and published over a period of many weeks, conveying messages against *The Herald*.

Later, in 1951, a regular publication was printed and sent through the mail entitled "The Picket Line." This was a small, magazine-size newspaper consisting of from four to six pages with various messages, articles and editorials about *The Herald*, Glenn, and the strike.

Glenn was the union's favorite whipping boy. He was a constant subject of ridicule. Over the years he was labeled "Old Ironhead;" as "cut-throat;" one given to "childish prattle;" "malicious;" one who "undermines public confidence;" one who "gnaws at the foundations of institutions;" one who "distorts the truth;" one who "wrecks people and communities just for nickels;" one who is a "loose spark in a powder keg;" a "licensed mud-slinger;" and one "operating a vehicle of lies, distortions and unfair innuendos worthy of the attention of a Russian Commissar."

One attack labeled his actions "old as the slanderers of Socrates, and as modern as Malik." Malik was a much despised Russian diplomat at that time.

On other occasions he was accused of "luring suckers;" of being a "carnival barker;" of "creating malicious hoaxes to viciously dupe the voters;" and as "Little Cedric of Cascade Street." This latter usually was accompanied by a caricature of a frenzied man looking like he was about to pounce on someone.

The Herald was described as a newspaper which was "unfair and destructive;" a paper "striving to dominate through fear, plumbing the depths of infamy to attain its questionable ends;" "wielding its power to force individuals and communities to bow to its will;" it was called a "fountainhead of scandal;" a "spawning ground for scurrilous rumors;" a "cesspool of untruths, half-truths and innuendo;" and a "disgrace to the great Fourth Estate;" a "blot on the name of a community that allows it to exist."

Parish's newspaper blared: "That paper has bravado and braggadocio but not courage. Words of the editor hold the people in thralldom. Unfair and filthy and destructive methods of competition are carried on."

The venomous attacks continued for years, as bitter as any of the insults in the storied newspaper wars of earlier American history. There is a limit, however, to how much the human mind can absorb—or will absorb. In time, these verbal assaults had an opposite effect and only too late did the *Columbia Basin News*— CBN it called itself— begin to realize this. But it proved to be a habit so ingrained, it couldn't be changed.

The union activities were not without their effect, particularly in the early months of the strike. The overwhelming percentage of Tri-City residents were members of some craft and they faced fines or other penalties if they subscribed to *The Herald.*

There were those staunch union people who would have nothing to do with an "unfair" newspaper. They made themselves known at once. The whole basis of *The Herald's* strategy was to keep publishing. The longer it could publish in the face of a strike the stronger it would become. When it became strong enough—and if it became strong enough—it could publish with or without a union. The test would come on whether a non-union newspaper could operate in a highly unionized area. It is not an experiment to be recommended. But if you have no choice, surely it is worth the gamble; at least Glenn and Bob thought so.

There were ways to measure the effectiveness of the union's sanctions. One was in circulation. It was climbing in 1949 and the first two months of 1950, despite economic conditions. In the nine-month period from June 30, 1949 to March 31, 1950, it climbed from 10,214 to 11,218. The Sunday paper was even more outstanding, and it must be remembered that the Sunday edition was started only in February, 1949. Sunday went from 9,374 to 10,882.

The circulation started to dip from the day of the strike and by the end of September it had fallen on a daily basis to 9,550, a loss of 1,668, and to 9,679 on Sunday, a loss of 1,203. These were severe dips but hardly dramatic in view of what was happening, or what should have been happening. Furthermore, by the end of September, Parish was in financial trouble himself. He had run through most of the $150,000 his backers had put up and he had been back for more money with little success.

But circulation wasn't the only thing that bit into *The Herald.* The union had undertaken a campaign of writing letters to national advertisers and national advertising agencies with some degree of effect, although not large. It had merit, however, as a harassment tactic, for it kept

Glenn and his national advertising representatives busy putting out the brush fires that this campaign caused.

In addition, members of the union made personal calls on merchants to get them to stop advertising, or, to split their advertising between *The Herald* and CBN. Some merchants dropped from *The Herald's* pages. Those who stopped advertising included all other unions or organizations connected with labor unions; for instance, firms in such fields as painting and electrical contracting, most of the restaurants, and musical organizations.

One grocery market quit advertising for several months. The proprietor told Bob the union had promised him that if he did so, he would get all of the union grocery trade. Needless to say, he didn't.

So advertising and circulation were down and costs were up.

The Herald was always a busy place. The strike made it even busier while radically changing the duties of most people. No one was immune. Glenn worked long hours in the composing and press rooms. Bob sold advertising, delivered advertising proofs, worked in the circulation department and delivered bundles to the carriers. Don handled the news staff, got the news content of the paper out and then went to work in the backshop. Business manager Dick Galbraith helped in the press room and the circulation department. Glenn's sister, Myrtle, went to work as a perforator operator and I went to work in the women's department.

Perforating machines and Teletypesetters had only recently been introduced to composing rooms and the ITU had fought them. The machines cut a tape that operated a Linotype keyboard. Anyone who was a good typist could run a perforating machine with little training. Perforating machines made a big difference in *The Herald's* successful fight for existence.

But in essence, it was people who won out. It required a tremendous effort over a long period of years. Everybody had a part in making the operation work. Department heads took a voluntary 10 percent salary cut. The staff in some departments was reduced. This meant fewer people to handle the work load. Reporter Jim Grant was transferred to the advertising department. Glenn made arrangements with the Linotype company and the Ludlow Company, which produced a headline type casting machine, to reduce payments on machinery so the drain of cash could be curtailed.

On the other hand, a perforator operator was forced to leave *The Herald* when she was told that unless she quit, her husband, who was a carpenter on McNary Dam, would lose his job. A proofreader, an editorial man, and later a man in the stereotype department quit and went to work for the *Basin News*. Allen Cooke, an advertising salesman, left because CBN offered him more money as advertising manager.

One move that failed early involved the American Newspaper Guild, a union for non-mechanical department employes. The strike wasn't very old when Don received a telephone call from a Guild organizer in Seattle. They met the next morning in a Kennewick coffee shop and reviewed the strike in detail. The ITU, he said, had suggested the Guild look into organizing *The Herald*. But before he left Seattle, one of the officers of the Guild on the *Seattle Times* suggested he talk to Don.

"I don't want any part of this and I'm going to tell the ITU as much," the Guild organizer told Don. He disclosed that he had talked to Paul Busselle, former editor of the defunct *Tacoma Times*. Busselle, who had been one of the charter members of the Guild in Tacoma, was news editor of *The Herald*. Busselle had told him much the same story that Don had.

As he left, he said, "Don, settle with those guys. They'll break you. You can't beat them. I admire your fight, but it isn't going to work."

One factor that hampered the CBN and continued to help *The Herald* was credibility. The *Columbia Basin*

News simply wasn't fully trusted or believed. Furthermore, it unwittingly aided this through its attacks on *The Herald*.

The Herald had been a controversial newspaper and continued to be one. But it suited the mood of the Tri-Cities to a large degree. With such wide bureaucratic control over the major economy of the region, citizens didn't mind having a feisty newspaper that would battle AEC and GE, blow the whistle on shoddy construction practices, and lash out at county and city officials. *The Herald* had also enjoyed good relations with labor unions. Now all of a sudden it was being blacklisted and there were conflicting responses from the unions. Some were reluctant to issue sanctions against the newspaper. All went along with the strike but many only gave it lip service and had to be constantly prodded to keep disciplining their members.

In many cases this reluctance came about because the members were suspicious of the strike and of the new paper. This carried over to many Richland residents who, although they subscribed to *The Villager*, nevertheless considered it a company newspaper. Some felt obligated to take it. All the bickering between *The Herald* and *The Villager* hadn't gone unnoticed. They had some questions. Thus when Parish purchased *The Villager* and the sale was announced in the method it had been, it greatly strengthened *The Herald's* position.

And indeed *The Herald* was sounding off, loud and clear. It started very politely on March 5 with a front page statement signed by Bob and Glenn. This explained that *The Herald* could not meet the terms demanded by the union. Advertising and circulation rates had been raised several times and the newspaper was only 28 months old. It expressed the hope that the employes would soon be back at work.

In addition, the front page also carried a news story announcing the strike and explaining what the issues had been. Don telephoned Local 831 and offered to publish any statement they wished, but they declined.

A few days later, when the sale of *The Villager* was announced, an editorial titled "No Wonder The Sale Was Silent" blasted the transaction as a give-away. The $2,000 price "wouldn't buy hamburgers in the newspaper game," the editorial said, adding, "There would be no limit to the number of takers at twice, three times or four times that sum. By the way, keep your eye on the investigation of the sale. A good old-fashioned whitewash job is already under way . . . and it won't be slopped on. It will be applied with the noble touch of a Hanford 'Rembrandt'."

From then on *The Herald* was quick to challenge actions of the union and the *CBN* or their contemplated moves and to set forth *The Herald's* position.

At the same time, in his column, Glenn had a busy time telling readers about the moves by "Parish and his Seattle millionaires" to take over the Tri-City newspaper field. In Glenn's parlance, they were the "Seattle Rainier Club's silk-stocking set" and the term got across well. In a way, it had to, there was seldom a week when Glenn didn't use it.

The News expected to fall heir to *The Villager* circulation but discovered instead the ill feeling over the way *The Villager* had been purchased. Richland residents felt they had subscriptions paid for a year to their local weekly newspaper. Then, overnight, they discovered their subscription was paid only for one month to a new daily newspaper which had absorbed the weekly. *The News* had automatically taken over *The Villager* circulation list and distributed its newspaper to all on the list whether they wanted it or not. Their expectation was to get readers to take the paper and pay for it eventually.

To satisfy its main advertiser, the C. C. Anderson department store, *The News* blanketed Richland once or twice a week. Its circulation staff then followed up and tried to sell subscriptions. Their success was spotty.

Finally, in August, 1951, a campaign was started in which members of Local 831 and other union volunteers began a systematic practice of following *Herald* carrier boys and motor route drivers to learn where *The Herald*

185

was being delivered. The union would then contact these families in an effort to have them stop the paper. If they were union people they would be threatened with union retaliation. Many were fined by their respective unions.

The practice of following carriers had some initial results because of the concern by parents. Thus, quite a few boys quit their routes. This angered some parents and they commenced following the union cars. They wrote down license numbers and reported them to police.

The most popular time for carrier surveillance was Sunday morning, and some of the carriers showed lots of enterprise. They gave no indication that they were being watched and would carefully place the paper on the porches of non-subscribers. After the cars had moved on, they would then retrace their steps, pick up the newspapers and distribute them to their regular customers.

Public reaction to this surveillance forced the ITU to make a series of radio announcements. Typical of these was one given by Jim Reed on February 13, 1952. He said, in part:

"The advertising rates of a newspaper are based on circulation. Circulations of newspapers are audited in March and September. Both newspapers have their circulation audited. The audit is done by the Audit Bureau of Circulation. Since we of the ITU had been locked out since March 3, 1950, the unfair *Tri-City Herald* has been using false circulation figures, constantly claiming to have more circulation than we know it has.

"When the audit came out in September, the ITU boldly went out and we proved the circulation was less than *The Herald* claimed. Because of the new audit coming out in March we will again have our survey cars out, properly marked. We are not out to harm children and so forth. If the *Tri-City Herald* would give the ITU the names and addresses of the subscribers it gives to Audit Bureau of Circulation, it would not be necessary for us to make this survey."

The broadcast only served to point up the union's and

Parish's frustration. For Parish, it was an especially galling experience. Just about everything he tried had worked, yet *The Herald* continued to publish and grow. Parish was winning the battles but *The Herald* was winning the war.

12   *Showdown At Kennewick*

I N THE FALL of 1951, with the strike at its height, quite by accident *The Herald* walked into an explosive situation. In running down the facts the newspaper became involved in one of its largest and most costly campaigns, resulting in six libel suits. The campaign sapped the paper's meager financial resources and drained its limited manpower reserve. Despite this, *The Herald* emerged bloodied but still breathing. There were those who questioned its judgment, but its credibility was strengthened.

William Allen White, the weekly Midwest publisher who was such a critic of President Franklin D. Roosevelt, wrote upon Roosevelt's death, "We, who hated your gaudy guts, salute you."

The Herald's successful campaign to change the Kennewick school administration, in effect, brought the same salutation from citizens in all walks of life. Except, of course, the paper was very much alive and growing.

Of the libel suits, four were brought by one person and were eventually joined into one suit with four causes of action. A total of $400,000 damages was sought.

Overall, depending upon how the legal situation is viewed, *The Herald* fared well, at least in the four causes of action. It won three and lost $5,000 on the fourth. But two other lawsuits emerging from the campaign were decided for the plaintiffs.

Even more important than the judgments, was the tremendous financial outlay required to finance the suits and the appeals. It couldn't have come at a worse time for the newspaper. The unions were working to organize boycotts against *The Herald,* both with readers and with advertisers; in secret, at this time, union money was financing the competing *Columbia Basin News* and enabling it to operate at a loss. It was a desperate time, but as Glenn has often remarked, "There is an advantage in being too dumb to know you can lose."

The chain of events was triggered by a column, "The Way I See It," that Glenn had written in November, 1951, during National Education Week. It was well into 1955 before all the legal cases were settled. The whole complexion of the campaign and its resulting suits would have been changed had the present U.S. Supreme Court decisions on libel stemming from the Sullivan vs. *New York Times* judgment been in effect. But in the 1950s the interpretation was vastly different and the odds were not with the publisher.

Glenn heard a speech by Seattle Attorney Frank Holman, who was then president of the American Bar Association. He was disturbed by a reference to some school textbooks. So Glenn contacted his friend Lowell Poore, a Richland school official and an officer of the Washington Education Association, and obtained a copy of "American Government, 1950," by Magruder. He found some passages that disturbed him and, as usual, his comments were blunt and direct.

"There is a textbook being used in local schools that I think ought to be examined by school authorities and parents and maybe tossed into the ash can," he wrote.

"The title of the book is 'American Government, 1950,' by Magruder. I understand that the author is dead and that some portions of the book have been revised. I would like to know who revised it. Perhaps he is the person who put some of the 'socialistic ideas' into the book.

"This is American Education Week and it would be a good starting point for a committee of businessmen, teachers, school authorities, and parents to get together and

189

study this book. I am sure of surprise and amazement on the part of anyone who will read the book . . .

"I think the text is dangerous. I think it ought to be examined."

It was written in Glenn's typical slam-bang style and drew its usual number of cheers and catcalls. But it also drew two interesting reactions.

The first was from the Richland and Pasco school districts. They appointed committees to study the book and this resulted in its eventual removal from the two high schools. The second was in Kennewick where, one by one, school authorities cancelled their subscriptions to *The Herald.*

First to cancel were Superintendent E. S. Black; business manager Samuel Lamanna, and T. L. Bennett, principal of Kennewick High School. They encouraged school district employes to follow suit and as more and more employes of the school district cancelled their subscriptions, *The Herald* began printing a daily "Box Score" on Page 1. Glenn wrote a second column. The school district printed a mimeographed message saying *The Herald* was "attacking" the district, and the intra-school campaign to have teachers, administrators and general employes to cancel their subscriptions was accelerated.

Surprisingly enough, after Glenn's second column, there was a procession of people into *The Herald* office, each with a complaint about the Kennewick school system, some dating back a few years, but all within the time frame of Black's superintendency.

Until then, *The Herald* and Kennewick school authorities had enjoyed a somewhat normal and pleasant relationship. Not long before the subject of Magruder's book came up, Black had praised the newspaper at a Chamber of Commerce meeting for the services it had rendered in a successful building bond campaign.

In view of all the unexpected public discontent that was surfacing and the number of stories that were being related, it was decided Don should take a look at the minutes of the Kennewick School Board Meetings to attempt to verify some of the tales coming to the newspaper's attention.

In those days, *The Herald* editorial staff was too thin to cover all school board meetings. However, it turned out that even if the paper had the reporters available, they would have had a hard time determining when and where the board met.

It was December 20, 1951, when Don first went to the superintendent's office. He was told he couldn't see the minutes because school was dismissed for Christmas vacation, although the business office remained open. The second time, he contacted business manager Lamanna and was told he must first get permission from Phil Heffelfinger, school board chairman and one of the owners of the Richmond Farm Implement Company. Don contacted Heffelfinger for permission. He returned to the school the following day.

He went again to Black's office and the superintendent produced the minute book but would not let Don read it. Black had changed from the smiling, affable man of Chamber of Commerce meetings into a seething person who stalked about the office in a rage. Alone in a charged atomsphere and apprehensive as to what a continued confrontation might cause, Don decided to leave without looking at the minutes.

He was puzzled why the Magruder affair would bring about such a change in Black's attitude. Then he and Glenn remembered another incident in which *The Herald's* investigative reporting and editorial comment had thwarted Black in one of his schemes.

The departure of Jerry Ballaine, Don and I for Seattle during the 1948 flood was from the Twin City Airport, owned by Herb Henne. The airport was located in southeast Kennewick just north of the Fairgrounds.

Black had decided he wanted the airport location for the site of an elementary school. Henne refused to sell but Black, who was accustomed to having his way, insisted on

191

the site. In an attempt to break the deadlock, Black was able to have the school district buy a piece of land just west of Gum Street, downhill from the airport and below its runway. He then went to the Federal Aviation Administration and insisted the airport be closed because a new school would be in the flight pattern.

The Herald discovered what he was trying to do, exposed it and blocked the school district's chances for acquiring the airport site. Although the Eastgate School now occupies the location that was once the airport, it was not until Henne decided to sell out and leave the area that the district was able to purchase the land.

This temporary setback, current at the time of the minute-book hassle, had to be a key factor in Black's wrath which had been smoldering just below the surface of his forced friendly behavior. It took the Magruder textbook controversy and then the newspaper's request to see the mintues to bring it out.

The Herald's next move was to seek an attorney and obtain a court order for permission to read the minutes. Attorney Powell represented the school district as well as *The Herald*. Because of the conflict, he asked to be excused. He told Don about a new attorney in town, Edward Critchlow. Don went to Critchlow's office but he was out, so Don went down the street and retained Charles Morbeck.

Black also went to Powell and from there also went to see Critchllow. This time Critchlow was in. We have often wondered if Critchlow would have become so personally involved in the fight if he had represented *The Herald* instead of the school district in this initial legal action.

About three years ago, in a chance meeting with Critchlow, Don remarked about this. Critchlow said he hadn't known about Don's visit to his office. He was amused by the information but was unable to say what might have been the trend of events had he started out by representing *The Herald* and not the school district.

The hearing on a court order to produce the minute-book was held in Benton County Superior Court in Prosser before Judge Orris Hamilton. Judge Hamilton ordered the minutes opened, but first he heard testimony as to why the records had not been made available. Don listened in amazement as Black described Don's demeanor in the superintendent's office. Everything was in reverse regarding the conduct of the two.

Until the court hearing, Don's involvement with the school district was that of a newspaperman doing his job. But in that courtroom when he heard Black's version of what went on in the superintendent's office, the conflict between them intensified.

Even though the school district minutes were sketchy, they nevertheless provided clues and tips. Don went over them repeatedly, but now whenever he went to review them he was accompanied by Bill Bequette. Each time Don and Bill were seated at a table with the minute book, three or four school employes sat around and closely watched them.

Black later said it was the first time in his 19 years in Kennewick that anyone had wanted to see the minute book. Don went over a total of 57 minutes. Among the things he uncovered and which he wrote into one of his investigative articles were:

1. Black and Business Manager Lamanna both made motions and voted by proxy when some members of the school board were absent.

2. Only once in 57 meetings did the board fail to vote unanimously. The charge that Black had a "rubber stamp school board" was one that Black and some of his directors hotly protested. But the minutes gave the charge credence.

3. Attempting to keep track of meetings of the board would have been nearly impossible. Much of the business was taken care of in special meetings, held at various places: the cafeteria, the gym, the library, and even in the Arrow Grill, a combination cafe and cocktail parlor. Sometimes the board meetings were held in different places on the same day.

4. The district did business with only one architect. Don recounted the case of another architect who had canvassed members of the school board in an effort to gain an audience with the board and to show his work. The architect finally blurted his complaint at a general meeting of the Kennewick Chamber of Commerce and so embarrassed the district that it agreed to listen to him.

However, the minutes showed that the school board had already hired the architect for the project three weeks earlier. It seemed unnecessarily cruel to have the young architect stay in hot pursuit of a job that didn't exist. It also led to the natural question of why the board wouldn't merely state it had hired an architect?

There was also the discovery that a page had been taken from the minute book; from all appearances it had been sliced with a razor. No one realized it had happened, but during a State Auditor's hearing into the conduct of school district affairs it became evident whatever was on the missing page was written during the period when the School Board had been negotiating a contract with its architect.

The architect admitted a building contract for the district was altered without knowledge or consent of the School Board. The three members of the board who appeared could not recall any authorization by the board for changes in the contract.

The minutes also tersely recounted that the School Board had voted to sell a surplus truck for four band uniforms. At the time of that transaction, trucks were hard to come by and surplus trucks were a prized item. Something about the wording of the minutes excited Don's curiosity. The transaction was handled in two somewhat vague sentences which read in their entirety:

"A resolution was made by Harvey Owens that the 1943 Ford surplus truck be traded for four band uniforms. Seconded by Vina Hudson and passed unanimously."

Don went back and forth through the minutes, but that

was the only reference to the truck. What truck? Everyone was vague on the matter.

Eventually, the story behind that brief item was unraveled. The truck had been sold to Black and was on the superintendent's 120-acre farm near Mt. Vernon, Washington. When examiners for the State Auditor's Office challenged the purchase, Black returned the truck to the school district stating, "It was too light for farm work" anyway.

So although terse, vague and, at times, skeletonized, the minutes had value. So did the information that was pouring into *The Herald's* offices.

Don spent two weeks travelling about the state creating a file of information on past activities of Black. He visited three other communities where Black had been connected with their school districts—Stanwood, Bothell and Mukilteo. He talked to former school board members in those communities. He visited the Black dairy ranch in the rich farming country at the little town of Bow. He went to Olympia and interviewed the State Auditor. He obtained copies of Kennewick School District audits and interviewed some of the men who had conducted those audits. He went to Spokane and called on a former High School Principal under Black and received more information and more leads.

Meanwhile, in Kennewick, Glenn was carefully listening to all the stories being volunteered and making detailed memorandums. Glenn also was anxious to undertake a detailed examination of the school district's vouchers which were filed in the Benton County Courthouse with County Auditor Ralph Wise.

Glenn was in close contact with candidates in the upcoming school board election. Two longtime members of the board, Harvey (Pat) Owens and Ben Blair had filed for re-election. Owens, a cattle and wheat rancher, had been on the board for 12 years. Blair had been a member for five years.

Three men filed against them but one, Clement Cejka, sales head for a trucking firm, decided to withdraw lest he pull votes away from the other two, Dr. Jack Freund, physician, and Ezra Hollister, a Hanford engineer.

Cejka had been contemplating filing and on January 28, 1952, Black contacted him and warned he had better not file.

"I warn you that I am going to show partiality to keep the two boys up for re-election on the board," Black said. "I will do everything in my power to keep you off the school board."

The situation of campaigning for his own selected school board had been going on for the 19 years Black had been in Kennewick. This is how *The Herald* discovered Black's school machine worked: Teachers and other school employes were each given a list of 10 names and told by Black to get the voters out. Against such odds the independent candidate had little chance.

A teacher who had recently left the district wrote: "I refused to canvass the neighborhood and tell the taxpayers how to vote in a school board election. I considered this above and beyond the call of duty of a teacher who valued professional ethics above such iron curtain tactics. I had to find another job."

Black also contacted Dr. Freund and hinted that his medical practice would be hurt if he ran for the board.

"I didn't file for the school board because I was against anybody," Dr. Freund said at the time. "I felt I could be of service to the school district. I filed in good faith, but trying to scare me out by hinting my practice would be damaged if I ran is shocking to me."

By this time, with all the material he had compiled and carefully documented, Don prepared a series of four articles on the Kennewick school district. The first article, under a headline of "How Good Is Kennewick's School System?" appeared February 24, 1952. The other three articles followed on successive days.

They completely unmasked the school district and its operation. The way it handled its employes, its records, its money, its building programs and its election. It was a stunning exposure that burst like a bombshell on school district patrons. Some of the things had been known and forgotten. Some had been suspicioned or hinted but this was the first time it had been all put together. Mostly, however, the information was all new.

The articles were written in low key for their substance contained the dynamite. They were the result of dogged leg work. Only a portion of all the information uncovered could be used, but the tremendous investigative effort involved was obvious.

Furthermore, they covered a wide range of activities and actions over a period of years. Most Kennewick residents, for example, learned for the first time that every audit conducted by the State Auditor's Office over a period of 10 years was adverse and that one had actually been suppressed. They learned that Kennewick had gone about to smaller school districts and recruited outstanding athletes by promising jobs to them and their parents. The articles outlined how the school machinery hand-picked its school board and perpetuated board members in office. How school board members did business with the school district and/or had spouses or relatives on the payroll was explained.

The articles stunned the community and caused the largest voter turnout in its history for the March, 1952, elections. The two incumbents, Owens and Blair, were voted out of office by a lop-sided majority and Dr. Freund and Hollister replaced them on a tidal wave of votes.

Interestingly enough, although Black and others threatened to sue for libel, the articles were never challenged in court. They were factual, direct and on target. They presented no opening for a lawsuit. As so often happens, when the libel suits came they involved articles and editorials written during the heat of the continuing campaign that developed to remove the school administration.

Then too, with the benefit of hindsight, what wasn't so apparent at the time, the articles spelled doom for Black and his administration. Everybody was reading and listening. The evidence was too overpowering. It couldn't be explained away. A lesser man than Superintendent Black would have faded away and licked his wounds while he made a stake elsewhere. But Black showed he would not cave in to anything, not even the power of the printed word. He didn't budge an inch and he had around him fierce, diehard supporters who stood by him. The battle was truly joined at this point and for Kennewick it was like civil war with families, friends, business associates and relatives bitterly divided.

Glenn and Don had never anticipated the emotion that would be generated. But they could have done nothing differently and now they were past the point of no return. They put their heads down and kept boring away.

There was one unfortunate incident. Back in November, during National Education Week, Glenn had written a column critical of a textbook. Black's reaction to the column is still puzzling but nevertheless it triggered the school investigation and eventual overturn of his administration.

Textbooks, of course, played no role in the controversy. But somehow word circulated throughout the state that the battle was over textbooks. *The Herald* and Glenn and Don were labelled as "textbook burners." They were painted as "Hitlers" and "storm troopers" out to censor and to dispose of textbooks. They were called "enemies of education." Explanations became useless because they only seemed to fan the flames and the rumors.

An old lawyer once said that when the evidence is on your side, emphasize the evidence. When the evidence is against you, argue the law. When both are against you, pound the table. Millions of dollars worth of World War II surplus had been distributed to school districts and other municipalities. Those old enough to remember, will recall that in the years immediately following the war there were many scarcities in building materials, electrical supplies and in all phases of the automotive field. It was to be expected that an investigation of the disposal of surplus materials once it left the Federal Government's hands would touch off nervous reactions all over the state.

Thousands of cars, trucks, and appliances—everything that would equip a farm, an office, a household or a factory—were up for grabs and agencies such as school districts had high priorities which gave them first call. Some districts kept detailed records. Others didn't. So there was much statewide "table pounding" defense and it undoubtedly proved convenient and effective to dismiss the Kennewick controversy as a fight over textbooks.

At home, however, a "Kennewick Citizens Committee" had been organized and it was energetically engaged in rooting out Black, his administration and his school board. They had supported the election of Dr. Freund and Hollister. Next, following the public hearing in April conducted by the State Auditor, they began recall proceedings against the remaining school directors.

Board Chairman Heffelfinger, a quiet, sensitive man, had resigned, leaving a two-to-two split on the board. The four board members could not agree on his replacement. In June, 1952, charges against Mrs. Jennie McHenry and Mrs. Vina Hudson were filed in Superior Court to get the recall rolling.

Leading the citizens group were insurance man Harold Riggins, and two wheat farmers, Ted Reese and William Blair. Blair was the brother of Ben Blair, who had just been defeated for his position on the board. A measure of the depth of feelings is the fact Bill had opposed his brother's re-election on the basis that he was too friendly to Black.

The recall petition required 1,056 names, or 35 percent of the voters in the last school district election. The petition charged "malfeasance" and "misfeasance" in office. The charges against the women were:

1. In permitting Black to expend school funds without supporting vouchers.

2. Permitting expenditure of school funds upon the construction of school properties without a written contract.

3. Permitting use of school property by private interests.

4. Failing to procure or cause the discharge of Black for improper conduct in office.

5. Failing to correct improper accounting practices of the school district after being so requested by the state auditor.

Mrs. Hudson's petition contained the additional charge that she permitted the employment of her husband by the school district.

Untoward incidents took place during circulation of the petitions. Harold Riggins was threatened with bodily harm by a man whose wife was employed by the school district and Glenn wound up in jail.

He was arrested and temporarily lodged in the Kennewick City Jail on July 13. He was released on $250 bail. The complaint was signed by Don C. Isham, Kennewick accountant who charged Glenn had violated the law by advertising in *The Herald* that signatures would be solicited for the recall of the two directors. The complaint was based on a column Glenn had written on July 9 and a news story on July 6, both of which concerned circulation of the petitions.

The matter was heard in Benton City before Justice of the Peace John Delere, and he dismissed the suit.

But if that seemed bizarre, there was more to come. Lamanna, business manager of the district and also clerk of the school board, set the whole thing off when he announced the recall election had failed because of insufficient signatures. However, the furor was raised because there were petitions that had not been canvassed by Lamanna. Furthermore, the canvassing delay was caused by Lamanna who had questioned the manner in which the city clerk had certified the petitions.

Don fired off a hot front-page editorial titled "Boot Them Out" which eventually resulted in a libel suit. The irony of the situation was that Mrs. Hudson and Mrs. McHenry also obtained a restraining order in Superior Court charging the petitions were legally insufficient to support a recall vote because they were not sufficiently particular or definite in alleging misfeasance or malfeasance. The court upheld them.

Meanwhile, in response to requests from the Citizens Committee for investigation of the surplus situation, Herbert Haseltine of San Francisco, assistant surplus property officer for the Federal Security Agency, was assigned to ascertain the whereabouts of the surplus materials. He spent two weeks investigating and among highlights of his report were the discovery of insulation from the Farragut Navy Base in Idaho in Mrs. McHenry's home and a "swap" —in which no records were made—of surplus lumber to a construction company for a lot, the value of which increased each time Haseltine spoke to the parties involved. The contractor placed the value of the lot at $350. His bookkeeper estimated the value at $500 and Black told Haseltine the value was at least $2,250.

Haseltine said he crawled under some of the homes to confirm surplus materials had been used. He also was asked to reinspect Mrs. McHenry's home about a week later and discovered the insulation had been removed and returned to the school district.

Haseltine's report stressed his investigation should be treated as preliminary because he felt the irregularities warranted a full scale probe into surplus use and disposal by the school district. This never came about. But now the months were running along and the school election of March, 1953, loomed large ahead.

Two positions were open. Mrs. Hudson's term had expired and she did not seek re-election. The other position was the one vacated by Heffelfinger. Mrs. McHenry was the lone holdover of Black's regime.

The two candidates chosen by the Kennewick Citizen's Committee were Dr. Paul O. Stone, a retired Kennewick dentist, and Glenn. Glenn was not anxious to run but with *The Herald* so directly involved he felt an obligation to the community and the Citizen's Committee.

The candidates favored by Black and his supporters were contractor Frank Dunham and Marvin E. Johnson. H. Ed Clary, business agent for the Painters' Union, also filed but withdrew a week before the election.

Pre-election activities were vigorous although somewhat subdued compared to the 1952 election. But feelings were intense, interest was high—in fact, even the interest of voters in Richland and Pasco focused on Kennewick, not on their own school campaigns.

Another landslide vote took place and Dr. Stone and Glenn won an overwhelming victory. Dr. Stone, a resident of Kennewick for more than 20 years, piled up 2,207 votes. Glenn was right behind with 2,062. Johnson had 1,590 and Dunham 1,467. Dr. Stone and Glenn carried 15 of the 19 precincts. It was in the large rural areas that they gained their greatest victory, carrying them better than 2 to 1.

In three of the precincts captured by Dunham and Johnson the voting was close. Stone trailed in one by a lone vote and Glenn by three.

That set the stage for March 30, 1953, the night the new school board was to be seated. The meeting was held in a multiple-purpose room in the school and it was a standing-room only crowd. Outside, police and deputies were on patrol and inside the tension was keen. Yet the crowd of about 200 was attentive, orderly and, for the most part, well mannered.

I sat in the meeting with two friends. Our neighbor, Leonard Stampe, a brawny Alaska gold miner, wanted to attend so he went with us. We couldn't find seats together, particularly down in front where Don wanted to sit. Leonard got a seat behind Don.

A friend asked me, "Aren't you afraid for your husband?"

I nodded towards Don and said, "No. Do you see that big fellow sitting behind him? That's his bodyguard."

Stampe always loved that story. And, although it was hardly the reason he was present, nevertheless he was big enough and strong enough to have been quite formidable.

Dr. Stone and Glenn were confirmed and for the first time Black had a school board he could not control. The crowd sat tensely as Board Member Hollister said to Dr. Stone, who had just been named chairman:

"Mr. Chairman, I hereby move:

"That the employee of this board, Erwin S. Black, be immediately suspended from all of the rights, privileges and powers of any nature whatsoever, which he may now have by reason of his employment as Superintendent of Schools of this district, with the express and only exception that his right to compensation under the contract entered into by the previous board of directors of the Kennewick School District, shall continue until further action thereon be taken by this board."

Hollister continued in a clear, even voice that gave no indication of his feeling from being in such a strange and strained setting. Black was restrained from exercising any authority whatsoever; removing or exercising any control over property; disbursing moneys. The list of particulars contained in a three-page resolution continued on and on. Then Hollister said:

"The causes for this suspension are that it is my opinion, and the opinion of those voting with me for the passage of this motion, that no official occupying the high position of public trust of Superintendent of Schools, should be allowed to continue in office while being sued by the State of Washington for a return of funds owing to this school district after investigation and report by the Auditor of the State, and while a recent report of surplus materials given to this school district, made by an official of the office of the Federal Security Administrator, recommends that further investigation be undertaken by the U.S. Department of Justice . . ."

Black, Hollister continued, was placed in a fiduciary capacity and there was now a question as to whether he had lived up to its standards.

Hollister also moved that Assistant Superintendent Lamanna be suspended, because he was an "inseparable part of the actions (of Black) acting under his directions . . ."

There wasn't a stir in the room when Hollister finished his resolution. Dr. Freund seconded the motion. It passed 4 to 1, with Mrs. McHenry dissenting.

"Inasmuch as this board has not invested me with Mr. Lee's rubber stamp, I vote no," she declared. She was striking back, as best she could, at the oft-repeated claim that Black had a "rubber-stamp" school board.

The second bombshell was unloaded when Dr. Stone moved "that the present name of this building be changed from Erwin S. Black to Kennewick Senior High School." This also carried by 4 to 1.

Dr. Stone continued: "And I further move all locks on the school business office and the superintendent's office be changed tonight." Four "yes" votes carried the motion. This time, Mrs. McHenry declined to vote.

Black left the meeting when the first vote was taken and when the board finally adjourned they found him in his office busily stuffing papers into cardboard boxes. Altogether there were five boxes he was trying to take, but the board stopped him. He was hotly defended by Donald Coates, the junior high school principal, who was watching.

At its next meeting, the board also suspended Coates. Eventually all were removed from the district's payroll.

Black, Lamanna and Coates fought in the courts to gain the pay still due on their contracts. This went on over a long period of time.

Mrs. Pearl Wanamaker, State Superintendent of Public Instruction, who sided with Black throughout the school controversy, held that the three were entitled to all their pay.

However, in 1954, Superior Court Judge Charles T. Wright of Thurston County ruled that the evidence showed the board had adequate reason for the firings and it was justified in its action.

The libel trials were something else. Financially, they were a tremendous drain on *The Herald*. The amount of time required was enormous. Glenn has always said, "Time is money." That is correct, but he wasn't overlooking that the libel suits required both time and money. In addition, they exacted a terrible price in draining emotions, too.

It was an exhausting but necessary experience.

"We can probably afford the verdicts if the lawsuit expenses don't kill us," Glenn said.

It wasn't just the expense in trying the cases. First, there was the seemingly endless time and costly ordeal of nailing down every shred of information included in the offending stories on which the libel cases were based.

It is quite a different thing from being sure of your facts for a news story or editorial and supporting these facts in court. It required a mass of evidence, and it also required bringing together a wide array of witnesses from all parts of the state.

In addition, it meant having to deal with some reluctant witnesses, for many people become surprisingly elusive when it appears that they will have to tell their story to a judge and jury. So frustrations over the reluctance of witnesses also took their toll.

Then there was the libel law, itself. Today, a newspaper has a fair chance. That wasn't true then.

In going back 20 years and being able to review matters in a more objective manner, it appears that Superintendent Black got the worst of it. He sued on four different items; three columns by Glenn and an editorial by Don. He sought $50,000 for each cause of action. For trial purposes they were lumped together. In addition, he asked $200,000 for damages to his professional reputation based on the premise that the articles had caused him to lose his job and prevented him from getting another one. The total judgment sought was $400,000.

The trial was held in Spokane in January, 1954, before a jury of seven women and five men. Superior Judge Raymond Kelly of Spokane heard the case. The trial lasted three weeks. In addition to full coverage in *The Herald* by reporter James Grant, it was also staffed by the two Spokane newspapers, *United Press International* and *Associated Press*.

Don's editorial, titled "No Answers Yet" had appeared on the front page of the March 10, 1952, *Herald* and summarized the many facts uncovered in the School District that the newspaper felt should be answered.

Glenn's columns concerned the disposal of surplus materials by the school district which was printed April 6, 1952; a column concerning the district's management and the visit to Kennewick of Dr. Robert Skaife of the National Education Association, published on June 6, 1952; and a column on May 19, 1952, regarding an alleged altercation between Black and a Kennewick resident at a school board meeting. This column pertained to Black's physical prowess in meeting opposition.

This last column was the one that almost resulted in a hung jury. After deliberating for more than 24 hours the jury sent a note to Judge Kelly stating: "We have reached a verdict on three complaints and are deadlocked on one since early afternoon. What do we do now?"

Judge Kelly had the jury returned to the courtroom, where he told them they should go back and deliberate some more. He pointed out that the parties had gone to considerable expense in presenting the case and if the jury was not able to reach an agreement it might necessitate another trial going over the same ground.

The jury returned to its deliberation. The next morning

at 10:30 it was ready with a verdict. Black was not in the courtroom when the jury returned. One of his attorneys, Critchlow, was. Glenn and Don were present.

Black was awarded a judgment of $5,000 on the column pertaining to his physical prowess. But the jury ruled *The Herald* had proved the substantial proof of the charges in its editorial and in Glenn's other two columns. It also rejected Black's claim for $200,000 damages to his professional reputation.

It was a tremendous shot in the arm for the struggling newspaper. It was not yet out of the woods, but this was the suit that the paper feared, not only because of the amount involved but also because it followed a setback *The Herald* had taken in Franklin County in May, 1953.

For Black, it was a stunning defeat. He had retired earlier to his Mount Vernon farm after suffering a heart attack. He did not appear well during the trial and occasionally suffered what appeared to be heart seizures during the trial. He died in Mount Vernon in October, 1954.

Undoubtedly there will always be some question over the wisdom of having tried the first libel case, a $100,000 suit by ex-School Director Pat Owens, in Franklin County. But at the same time Glenn's decision, made when it was and based on the reasons then apparent, still seems logical.

The Herald attorneys were John Gavin and Hal Halverson of Yakima, two lawyers from different firms, and a young Pasco attorney, George Fulk.

Gavin and Halverson recommended a change of venue to some other area, citing the difficulty of obtaining a jury in Pasco because of the wide publicity given the school controversy. They also pointed out that Pasco was the bastion of the unions and *The Herald* was in the throes of a labor dispute. They cited the articles and editorials blasting *The Herald* and Glenn almost daily in the *Columbia Basin News*. They were worried that a residue of bitterness still remained because *The Herald* had moved its publishing plant from Pasco to Kennewick.

The Herald was a "Kennewick" newspaper to Pasco, which now had a "Pasco" newspaper in the *Columbia Basin News,* they argued.

These were all very genuine concerns and Glenn had weighed them often. But he felt *The Herald* should not seek a change of venue in order to save face and to show faith. It would appear, he said, that we were afraid of our own people if we moved the suit. We would, in effect, be announcing that we could not obtain a fair trial in the Tri-Cities.

Owens' suit was based on a front-page column by Glenn. The column ran across the top of Page One. It was titled "Was The School District A Clearing House For Surplus?"

Glenn and Don went into that first libel suit fearful yet confident they could win. They knew they were in trouble when it became obvious they were going to have serious difficulties in selecting a jury. Prospect after prospect disqualified himself or was excused because he admitted to having formed an opinion of the case.

When the regular jury list was exhausted, deputies scurried around to locate new prospects. They even brought in farmers right off their tractors. There was a parade of citizens through the Franklin County courtroom until 12 were finally picked.

Judge Ralph Edgerton of Spokane replaced Judge Horrigan, who had removed himself from the case.

Owens' chief attorney was Peter Tonkoff of Yakima, assisted by Critchlow, a combination that continued throughout the lawsuits.

The $100,000 total was arrived at, Tonkoff told the jury, by multiplying the number of *Tri-City Herald* readers by $2.50. The newspaper had about 12,000 subscribers. The U.S. Post Office estimated there were about 3.5 persons per family, so Tonkoff figured we had 40,000 readers.

Both *The Herald* and the *Columbia Basin News* carried reports on the trial and it was the main topic of conversation all over the Tri-Cities. Everyone eagerly followed the case.

The trial lasted two weeks and went to the jury on Thursday, May 14, 1952.

Where there had been a parade of prospective jurors through the courtroom, now it was a parade of witnesses. Virtually everyone who had played a prominent role in the Kennewick school controversy got a chance on the witness chair.

Owens presented himself as a broken and shunned man who could no longer even be elected to offices in organizations in which he was a longtime member. He was followed by witnesses who testified that although their feelings towards him were unchanged, they had heard him discussed in unfavorable terms by others.

Black was not a part of this case. The former school superintendent made no appearance, although in the other libel cases Owens, or members of his family, presented testimony.

But this time it was Owens' lawsuit and perhaps not surprisingly the first witness called was Glenn. The strategy was obvious—Glenn was the publisher of *The Herald* and was a controversial figure. Had a different man been at the helm it would have been a far different newspaper. Perhaps there would have been no newspaper at all. So if there was ill will towards Glenn, attorney Tonkoff intended to exploit it.

Tonkoff and Gavin, the major spearheads in the lawsuits, were vastly different in their courtroom styles. Tonkoff made his mark as a plaintiff's attorney. He was flamboyant, crafty, a showman. Gavin, a big-boned man, had a wry sense of humor and a penetrating mind. He could relentlessly pursue a witness, although he had a deft style which made him appear deceptively gentle.

There was nothing to be held back now and the loose practices of the school district got a thorough airing. It is difficult to recreate the atmosphere of that courtroom.

Judge Edgerton was hearing the facts for the first time and was not informed on the local situation. When Tonkoff rested his case, Gavin immediately moved for a dismissal on grounds that a substantial case had not been made and that the defendants had already proved the substantial truth of their articles.

Judge Edgerton wavered for a moment. He appeared on the verge of dismissing the case right then and there. Later, in an informal conversation with *The Herald's* attorneys at which Don was present, Judge Edgerton revealed he had indeed almost ended the case at that point. He didn't, and it continued for more than a week before it got to the jury.

The jury deliberated for 24 hours and returned a verdict of $40,000 for Owens. This figure was arrived at by giving a dollar for each reader of the newspaper. Gavin requested a poll of the jury. Each juror was asked, "Is this your verdict?" Two of them, former city councilman, Ted Overlie, and Mrs. Ada Savage, stated it was not their verdict. Mrs. Savage broke down and cried as she gave her answer.

I was sitting in the courtroom with Catherine Riggins, wife of the leader of the Kennewick Citizens' Committee, and Opal Graber, one of the persons who had circulated the recall petitions. The three of us witnessed a scene that was used as evidence to prove *The Herald* could not be tried before a fair and impartial jury in Franklin County.

As the jurors passed the lawyers' table, Pete Tonkoff embraced one of the male jurors and said excitedly, "We knew you'd do it for us." They marched happily out of the courtroom with their arms around each other.

It was because of this shocking performance, plus other factors, that *The Herald* was able to receive a change of venue to Spokane for the other libel trials.

The Owens lawsuit was far from over. It carried on for three more years and eventually provided an even more costly judgment.

Judge Edgerton threw out the verdict on grounds it was not justified by the evidence. He also ruled that it was too excessive and had been reached "by passion and prejudice." Within months, a Spokane jury ruled in Black's libel case that *The Herald* proved the truth of the charges contained in this printed material.

Owens appealed Judge Edgerton's ruling and the State Supreme Court overruled Judge Edgerton. However, it ordered a new trial to determine if Owens had sustained any damage. It was a fantastic ruling because it stripped *The Herald* of any real defense. The newspaper was limited to trying to prove Owens wasn't damaged. The only way was through cross-examination of those called to testify · that he was injured. Always in the foreground loomed the awesome fact that the State Supreme Court had ruled the article was libelous.

The trial for damages was held in Walla Walla in the summer of 1956 before Judge Albert N. Bradford. At the pre-trial hearing, Judge Bradford told the attorneys that he had read the testimony of the Pasco trial and that he didn't think the evidence would bring much of a verdict. As a matter of fact, he continued, if the jury brought a substantial verdict he would probably throw it out.

Unlike the Franklin County jury, the Walla Walla jury didn't need 24 hours to reach a decision. It went into the jury room and right out again. It gave Owens the full $100,000.

Judge Bradford said he could see no passion or prejudice in the jury. It was, he said, a "blue ribbon" jury. He admitted he was shocked at the verdict. "All I could see was zeroes," he said. One of his aides had told him, "Don't look so sick."

Judge Bradford said he thought he would reduce the size of the judgment but on further consideration felt he had no right to invade the privacy of the jury. He thought the jury was attentive during the trial, and even though they had deliberated only a little over an hour after electing a foreman and reading the instructions twice, he ruled the verdict should stand.

The verdict did stand. After going back to the State Supreme Court and attempting to gain a hearing before the United States Supreme Court, *The Herald* had nowhere else to go.

The libel suit of Lamanna also posed its special problems. Spokane was his home town. He had starred in football at Gonzaga University. The courtroom behind the plaintiff's table was packed with his relatives and friends. Their partisanship was apparent.

The wily Tonkoff seldom missed any bets. Lamanna was business manager of the school district and as such was also clerk of the school board. That was all Tonkoff needed. Lamanna became merely a school "clerk" hounded by a newspaper "corporation."

During one recess Don got a jolt when he noticed one of the jurors walk over to an elderly man with the Lamanna group, greet and talk to him.

I attended the trial and being usually the only person in the spectators section behind the defendant's table I felt rather lonely.

During the recesses, when the women on the jury visited the ladies' room, Lamanna's female supporters filed in behind them. It was suggested by John Gavin that I also go to the ladies' room to make sure that information of a prejudiced nature did not pass between the jury ladies and the relatives of Sam Lamanna.

There was no room for me at the basins or in front of the mirror and the looks I received were not friendly. I retired to one of the stalls where I stood unnoticed, listening.

Lamanna asked $50,000 for a September 25th editorial on the front page, written by Don. The trial, two years later to the day, lasted six days. The jury, by a 10-2 vote, awarded him $29,600. This was divided as $15,600 general damages and $14,000 special damages. However, later

Superior Judge Carl C. Quackenbush set aside the $14,000 judgment on grounds it could not be held that Lamanna's discharge from his school position was attributable to the editorial. He allowed the verdict of $15,600 to stand.

The foreman of the jury was the juror who Don had seen shake hands and talk to one of the Lamanna group. What was the connection and who was the man to whom he had spoken?

When everyone went home, Don stayed in Spokane and began an investigation to find the answers. He registered as "Don Taylor"—my family name—because there had been considerable mention of the lawsuit in the Spokane newspapers.

Gradually, Don pieced the puzzle together. He drove to Priest River, Idaho, where he went through old volumes of the weekly paper, and then to Potlach, Idaho, where he called on the juror's father-in-law.

He also poured through newspapers in the Spokane library. He spent so much time in the Gonzaga library and asked for so many records that the University finally refused to give him any more. By this time, he had enough information to know he was on to something big. He obtained a court order demanding that the college reveal the student transcripts of Lamanna and the juror. This was done and it was disclosed the juror and Lamanna had not only attended Gonzaga at the same time but had been classmates.

Determining the man the jury foreman had greeted in the courtroom proved a real chore. Eventually, though, Don boiled it down to a choice of two of Lamanna's uncles. But it was a guess. He couldn't be sure. Don spent much time near the homes of the two men hoping to see them, but that didn't work. Time was running out. Don decided on a more direct course. He purchased four different magazines from a nearby market, walked up to a home he knew was occupied by a relative of Lamanna's, and rang the doorbell.

"Good evening," he said pleasantly to the lady who answered the doorbell. "Would you be interested in any of these magazines?"

He recognized the lady, but the man seated in the living room had his back turned. Don was nervous, and this increased for the woman seemed to be studying his face.

"We don't want any magazines," she said.

"But you might ask your husband about this one," Don said, holding up a copy of Argosy. "They claim this is a wonderful man's magazine."

The man turned and Don's heart jumped. His ploy had worked. He had found his man—Lamanna's uncle.

It was to be his only satisfaction.

When Judge Quackenbush summoned the juror during the October 22 arguments for a new trial, the man testified he had no knowledge who Lamanna was or that they were in college together. He said he had no recollection of having ever seen him at Gonzaga. In fact, he didn't even know the man he greeted was Lamanna's uncle or that he had been seated with the Lamanna family and friends.

"I didn't look at the people in the audience," he testified.

The conversation, he admitted, was over some lots Lamanna's uncle wanted the juror to purchase for him so he could build homes which the realtor was to list.

In the end, Judge Quackenbush decided there wasn't enough reason to doubt the juror and the verdict stood.

And thus ended the libel trials and the Kennewick School controversy. It made an indelible impression on the *Tri-City Herald* and on the community. On the "plus" side, new administrators took charge of the district, new policies were instituted and a progressive, well-managed school system resulted.

When the question is asked, "Who won the Kennewick School fight?" the answer Glenn and Don give is, "The Kennewick School District."

However, like most conflicts, it exacted a tremendous price. Undoubtedly, some collision between *The Herald* and the school administration would have taken place, at least so long as Black was superintendent.

Yet one cannot help but wonder, what would have happened had not Glenn read and commented on "American Government, 1950," by Magruder?

13   *A Momentous Disclosure*

GLENN has frequently said that when he grows old he intends to entertain himself by reading Howard Parish's correspondence with the International Typographical Union.

He won't run out of material, only time enough to read it. He has a file drawer full of Parish's letters. If he should read his way through the letters, he also has files filled with 157 depositions, numbering 8,230 pages, and 3,688 exhibits, totalling 160,865 pages, regarding the ITU and the *Columbia Basin News*. Plus two months of transcripts of a Federal Court trial in Seattle.

But the letters are something else. They bring Glenn's most repeated accolade to his former competitor:

"That Parish was one helluva letter writer."

You'd better believe it! In a period of about nine years, Parish was successful in having the ITU give him some $1,178,000 with which to operate the *Columbia Basin News*. The union paid Parish's salary and expenses; paid all the salaries at the newspaper; purchased the plant and equipment; paid the taxes, and financed all other expenses.

Howard Parish was indeed "one helluva letter writer."

His letters usually ended with the request: "Send me another $20,000." Or, "Send me another $30,000." Or, "I haven't seen your check yet but I know it's coming. I could use another $25,000."

Without fail, the union mailed the money to Parish at his Seattle address for his Seattle account of "Howard

216

Parish and Associates." Then he would write personal checks to finance his Tri-City newspaper.

"Lee and his partner are 'cracking up' from all reports I can gather," he wrote on October 26, 1953. "The pressure we keep on him is wearing him down pretty fast. We can begin to expect most anything to happen at any time now.

"I hope I am not wearing you out with all the letters I have been writing your office recently, but damn it, Larry, we are winning this battle and things are happening so fast I just feel you should be fully informed all the time."

"Larry" was Larry Taylor, who was at ITU headquarters in Indianapolis and was in charge of the ITU-sponsored newspapers. The union had a $12,000,000 war chest to establish, finance or assist newspapers operating in communities with ITU-struck papers. Parish had had financial "angels" before, but this time he struck a gold mine.

Parish was nobody's fool. He was crafty, skillful, a good promoter and salesman, and every inch an opportunist. In the Tri-Cities, he seemed to have it all—backing, money, connections. He could almost taste victory, but it kept eluding him.

"I've got Lee on the ropes," he wrote exuberantly to the ITU, "we'll turn the corner any minute now."

Parish and the ITU never turned that corner. He was an utterly frustrated man. Time and again he must have rued the day he turned down that $400,000 price tag for the *Tri-City Herald*. That would have been the cheapest money he would ever have spent and the wisest too. Now he used every device, every trick, every scheme he knew or that was presented to him and none of them worked. Sometimes he would gain a degree of success but only momentarily at best.

As so often happens, after the first blush had died away, Parish discovered he, as well as *The Herald*, was in a fight for survival. Both sides knew that the area could support only one newspaper. Parish's announcement of a daily newspaper had been greeted by cheers among Pasco leaders. He learned, just as *The Herald* had learned earlier, that this enthusiasm did not necessarily extend to their pocketbooks. Thus his costs mounted but his income didn't.

Some of the advantage he had gained by absorbing *The Herald's* printers was diminished by the fact he had to go through the throes of giving birth to a new paper and start from scratch on building circulation, editorial coverage and promoting advertising. There is a period of trial and error that even the best planned organizational chart can't avert.

The News quickly ran through a succession of employes, and a few months after it began it had hired W. E. Scheyer, a circulation promoter, who was named general manager about 30 days later. For advertising manager, Scheyer had Francis Hilton, who had held a similar position for *The Herald* before being dismissed.

They soon launched a new advertising program called the "New Deal." The scheme was designed to slice into the advantage *The Herald* held by virtue of the fact it was a member of the Audit Bureau of Circulation. The ABC is a national organization which audits the circulation records of newspapers and thus attests to the accuracy of their paid circulation figures. This, in turn, enables national advertisers to have confidence they are not being sold on bogus circulation claims. In order to obtain much national advertising, therefore, a newspaper has to belong to the ABC. This is no immediate process. It takes time, so *The News* devised a shortcut. Here is how it worked:

In order for *The News* to get certain major advertising accounts, Hilton and Scheyer would approach a local merchant in each field with a special offer to become a "bell cow" or leader, for *The News* in that field. They figured that if they could obtain the major portion of the advertising from these firms, their competitors would then be forced to advertise in *The News* too.

The advertisers were to get a special reduced rate and

the arrangement was to be kept confidential. As Scheyer explained later in a court deposition, "We were scratching for every bit of advertising we could get."

The News' national advertising was handled through the firm of Gilman, Nicoll and Ruthman. Through this firm the paper would tell its national advertisers that *The Herald's* circulation figures were inflated, and that its editorial policy had created considerable ill will.

Another advertising practice *The News* started in 1950, stepped up a year later, and really got into full gear in 1952, was its treatment of cooperative advertising with local merchants. It was seen in the drug, clothing, heavy appliance and the furniture fields. In these areas, *The News* sometimes was receiving more display cooperative advertising than *The Herald*. It hurt and it was puzzling.

Cooperative advertising involves the splitting of the advertising bill between the local merchants and the manufacturer or distributor of the product advertised. For instance, if the local merchant features a name brand in his ad, the manufacturer will pay half the price of the local bill.

The News began a system of a "double billing" arrangement. Double billing isn't complicated. It also isn't ethical. *The News* would issue two bills, both of which were stamped "paid." These were given to the advertiser with copies of the advertisement as proof that it ran. The merchant would mail one bill to the manufacturer with the copy of the ad, and he would be reimbursed for 50 percent of the price of the ad.

One of the bills marked "paid," however, would be at a special low rate that had been worked out with the local advertiser. The other bill—the one he mailed to the manufacturer—would be at the much higher national rate, enough so the local man would get his advertising for little or nothing and sometimes he would even make a profit on the ad.

The advertisers who were selected to get special rates did

not know that other advertisers were also getting special consideration. Newspapers, like any other business, can't afford to sell their goods and services below cost. Double billing may enable a merchant to get his advertising message in the paper without having to pay for it, but the scheme isn't good business practice for the newspaper. In the case of *The News*, however, the practice did two things. First, it gave *The News* advertising it would not otherwise have had. Second, it deprived *The Herald* of the advertising.

The Herald suspected the double billing arrangement. What *The Herald* didn't know, was that *The News'* losses were being subsidized by the ITU. *The News* could afford to sell advertising below cost, especially if the practice harmed *The Herald* which didn't have a financial angel.

Circulation was Parish's long suit. He had learned his lessons well over the years, particularly with the Hearst newspapers. He recognized the value of circulation and he had a lot of tricks he wished to dust off. This he promptly did. One of the strengths of *The News* was its circulation department. Parish began an aggressive move for circulation right from the start, and as *The News* gained in circulation it promptly applied for membership with the Audit Bureau of Circulation. *The News* advertising staff scurried about telling advertisers *The News* was practically a member of ABC, and that its net paid circulation was 8,200, but, in reality, they whispered, they had 10,000 subscribers. Parish even threw a party for his staff, and cut a 10,000-subscriber cake, a picture of which he featured in *The News*. He missed no bets.

Glenn wasn't napping either. When he heard of the ABC move by *The News*, he telephoned and began corresponding with A. R. Petterson at the Audit Bureau of Circulation headquarters in Chicago.

"We have every reason to believe that ITU financial assistance is being given to the *Columbia Basin News*," Glenn wrote. "Union men have told us the State American

Federation of Labor has given large checks amounting to several thousand dollars from time to time to purchase circulation for members of the Hanford Atomic Trades Council.

"Some people in the Tri-City area are receiving *The News* and not paying for it."

These were all matters which should be brought to the attention of the auditor who would inspect *The News*, Glenn told Petterson. In his next letter he asked for an outside audit, which in ABC parlance is a second audit of circulation, separate from the first, and very thorough. If unions really were purchasing bulk circulation for *The News*, and Glenn was certain they were, then he wanted this established. It would possibly bar *The News* from ABC membership.

The Audit Bureau of Circulation agreed to an outside audit and requested *The Herald* to put up a $1,000 deposit as evidence of good faith and to guarantee the cost of the investigation in the event Glenn's charges were not supported. *The Herald* complied and the special audit substantiated Glenn's charges. ABC membership was denied *The News*. Glenn's $1,000 was returned.

Within a year, however, Parish was back again and this time he was not to be denied. Now circulation really became the name of the game. With ABC membership, Parish started cutting into *The Herald's* accounts and began either dividing the national advertising or taking it away entirely. This was true with such food accounts as Pillsbury, Brownie Cookies, Star-Kist Tuna and others. Its impact was also felt in the finance accounts, oil companies, beers, paints, Institute of Life Insurance and others.

The Herald also had a new look in circulation in Eldon R. Smith, who Glenn and Bob managed to get from the Alameda (Calif.) *Times Star* which had just been sold. Eldon had begun circulation work on the Cincinnatti *Post*. He had taken a circulation job with the Miami *Daily News* and moved to California in 1946, where he joined the San

Gabriel *Press*. Eldon had been active in the Circulation Manager's Association, where Glenn had heard of him.

On his way into the Tri-Cities, Eldon drove his wife, Maxine, and their three children by way of East Pasco, where he intentionally pulled up by an old shack on a side street with no grass surrounding it and chickens running around in the yard. He told his family they had arrived. This was the place. The children were stunned and Maxine admits even now that had she possessed a weaker character she would have cried.

Eldon soon discovered he would need his sense of humor if he intended to retain any balance in his new position. When Eldon got together with Glenn and learned all the problems facing *The Herald*, he thought Glenn was only testing him. He didn't believe things could possibly be that bad. He soon learned otherwise.

Eldon received heavy exposure to this lesson when he looked up Wendell Brown, Pasco realtor and insurance man, at the suggestion of a friend in Alameda. In fact, Brown found a home Eldon could buy in Pasco, which was a relief after motel living.

"Who are you going to work for, GE?" Brown asked. They were seated in Brown's office and Brown was relaxing, his feet up on his desk.

Eldon answered, "No, I'm going to work for the *Tri-City Herald.*"

Brown's feet flew off the desk. He rose from his chair and stated sympathetically, "If you haven't unpacked your furniture I would turn around and head back to California if I were you. You can never possibly work for that newspaper!"

Both papers were scrambling for circulation now like they had never done before. *The Herald* management was greatly concerned with Parish's growing ABC circulation. Additionally, rumors were spreading among businessmen that *The News* circulation would surpass *The Herald's* by the first of 1954.

Parish prepared a campaign he felt certain would give *The News* the leadership. As he prepared to launch it, *The Herald* uncorked one campaign of its own that proved to be the most successful circulation drive in its history. Parish tried frantically to blunt *The Herald's* attack, not only spurring the ITU to greater action, but also trying to get the other unions involved in stopping it.

However, this one proved a runaway. The other unions washed their hands of it, for it concerned baby pictures, and they had a host of angry mothers and fathers on their hands.

The promotion was the brainchild of Gordon Bentrod. He had it copyrighted and then went about the nation staging it. The contest entailed commercial printing for tickets and placards. There were 250 prizes and trophies. Extra office help was needed; extra newsprint was consumed publishing announcement, promotion and pictures. Hundreds of engravings were made as each baby entrant got his picture in *The Herald*. Mothers had a list of local photographers where they could have their baby's picture taken free, with one print for them and one for the newspaper. Merchants participated, too. It was a grandiose promotion with prizes galore.

The ITU began a telephone campaign to counter it. They contacted mothers and urged them not to participate. They wrote letters, made radio appeals and distributed placards telling mothers that *The Herald* was using their tots "to take bread out of the mouths of the babies of ITU printers."

Meanwhile, Parish launched his drive but it was no match. It centered chiefly on reduced rates, a Parish standard. Parish did, however, also inaugurate his policy for rural circulation, which was one of allowing the carrier to keep everything he could collect on his route without turning in any part of the money. Parish would even pay all car expense. As a result, *The News* reached far, far out, well beyond the normal limits of the Tri-Cities trading area.

The News ended 1953 with a circulation of 11,193. *The Herald's* was 13,743, still well in front. Parish had been foiled again.

The Tri-City economy looked healthy in 1954. The additional circulation put on by the baby contest and the participation by so many merchants in the contest continued to help the sale of advertising.

Population and business growth looked encouraging. Construction of McNary Dam, located 25 miles from the Tri-Cities, was in full swing, while at home, construction of the levees and dikes along the Columbia River, changing of the railroad and raising of the bridges because of the dam's backwater, was also under way. In addition, there was peak construction at Hanford, new farm land was being developed under irrigation, and other normal growth raised the volume of business in the area. It looked like a good year.

The acceptance of *The Herald* continued, so well in fact, that the newspaper had been averaging a larger press every two years. It started with the eight-page Goss press of the *Pasco Herald*, then moved to the 24-page Scott rotary press in Kennewick, in 1948. It rapidly outgrew the 24-page press and had purchased a second-hand, 48-page Goss press from Victoria, Canada.

Now the 48-page Goss was proving too limited, particularly with the increasing use of color in advertisements. Color was something Advertising Director Jack Gillis was pushing successfully.

Little did anyone suspect the canning plant facility which appeared so vast when *The Herald* moved into it in 1948, would start cramping up in 1954. That was the encouraging side. Because of the glowing over-all picture, it was decided to finance a larger structure to be built on the south side of the existing building. At the time, it was

truth
honesty
accuracy
fair play

Columbia Basin News

307 W. COLUMBIA ST.   PHONE 7576   BOX 528   PASCO, WASHINGTON

HOWARD W. PARISH,
PRESIDENT

Pasco, Wash., Nov. 18th, 1954.

Mr. Larry Taylor
Post Office Box 728
Indianapolis 6, Ind.

Dear Larry:-

The ABC Auditor's reports are in for the two Tri-City papers and they are very
interesting reading.   This is the way they show:-

AVERAGES BY QUARTERS	The News	The Herald
Oct 1 to Dec 31,1953	11,193	13,743
Jan 1 to Mar. 31,1954	11,634	13,917
Apr 1 to June 30th,1954	12,360	13,928
July 1st to Sept 30th,1954	12,479	13,788
TO-DAY	13,117	

Slowly but surely we are wearing him down.

Last year at this time he put on a Baby contest in which he gave away 250 prizes
to babies for votes given to subscribers for renewal and new orders.   The votes
ran into the many millions.   A lot of people paid a year in advance--some of
them ordering as many as five papers delivered to them so as to get the votes.
A lot of these orders are expiring between now and the end of the year.

Just yesterday we found Herald solicitors offering preminums to new subscribers
so we have them worried--and working.

Enclosed find adv. we ran in this morning's paper.

Sincerely yours,

Howard Parish

P.S. I don't want to bother you with a lot letters but some of the things that
are happening here a mighty important.

Ex. No. 1637 is Dep. of
Date 5-3-55
W. J. LAUCKHART
Notary Public in and for the State of
Washington, residing at Seattle. Wn

I - 8

Howard Parish was a prolific business letter writer, and he
kept the money coming for his newspaper operation from
the International Typographical Union. A Federal Judge
later characterized Parish's letters as a "sales pitch". They
usually depicted *The Herald* as faltering and Parish's newspaper as gaining renewed strength.

The ITU poured its funds into Howard Parish's Seattle bank account and he then wrote checks to cover the operating expenses of the Pasco newspaper. These checks for one month, from July 29 to August 27, 1957 totalled $22,000.

The $1,000 check to Seattle accountant Ray C. Shepherd for worthless *Columbia Basin News* stock, a transaction that eventually forced the International Typographical Union to admit its ownership of the newspaper.

Don Pugnetti and Bob Philip at Priest Rapids damsite for
ground-breaking. April 25, 1957.

Pages ready for stereotype department; Glenn at right; Larry Benjamin, mechanical superintendent, at left. In background, pressmen John W. Kirkham, Dean Haas and George Weikum.

merely a large concrete loading dock. It was ample enough to accommodate all of the newspaper's mechanical facilities.

A five-unit Scott press was up for sale by the Minneapolis *Star Tribune* Company. The new press would cost upwards of $75,000. The fact *The Herald* was involved in a strike did not make the Scott Publishing Company a very good risk in the eyes of the *Star Tribune* Company. Details were then discussed as to the possibility of leasing the press, with *The Herald* paying for dismantling and erection of the equipment. The *Star Tribune* Company wanted $10,000 as a down payment and $15,000 on delivery. It was estimated dismantling, shipment and erection would come to an additional $25,000.

Glenn and Bob discussed the problem with the other stockholders and the proposal was made that perhaps the press could be financed privately and rented to *The Herald*, rather than from the *Star Tribune* Company. The money was raised with the help of three out-of-town stockholders, Merlin Phillips of Walla Walla, and Dr. R. C. Philbrick and Tom Harman, both of Seattle. All were very successful in their fields and all were fraternity brothers of Bob, to whom he had sold stock in the company in the early days. They added the credit weight that made the transaction possible.

Again, the concern was whether union labor would dismantle the press, transport and unload it in Kennewick. That was looking too far ahead, however, for no sooner had work on clearance of the site started than the ITU placed pickets around the job. After a short huddle, it was decided construction would go ahead on a private basis. Business manager Dick Galbraith formed the "Boondocks Construction Co." of *Herald* employes and others who wanted to work, and actually started construction activity. It was a gallant gesture but so much would be involved, there was serious question whether enough skills would be available for the project and also whether *The Herald* wanted to go it alone.

Fortunately, before such a decision was made, officers of the Building Labor Trades Council and Ree McReynolds, a union building contractor, met with Bob and Don and objected to the use of non-union people on the project.

William A. Wiseman of the Building Council said the union considered the building and the newspaper as two different things. If the building was constructed by non-union labor and later the paper signed a contract with the ITU, the printers would work in the non-union-built building.

"The concern of the Building Trades Union is to put craftsmen to work," he said. "We want all construction work to be done by union labor."

"The only difficulty I can see is that if you were constructing the same building across the street or in the Highlands, there would be no difficulty at all," said Larry Brown, business agent of the Carpenters Union. 'The same situation is true here. The building has nothing to do with the ITU. The ITU is striking the newspaper operation.

"If they were to picket the new building, that would have nothing to do with the Carpenters Union. We are a building trade and not concerned with the operation of printing machinery."

Bob pointed out the paper would need a guarantee that if a contractor undertook the work the union wouldn't do anything to halt him or hold him up.

Both Wiseman and Brown assured Bob they would supply the workers. The men would not be hired by or working for the *Tri-City Herald*, but by the contractor who received the job.

McReynolds said he had a contract with the union stating they would supply him with men for contracts he undertook, but the contract also stipulated he must not make the men cross a picket line.

McReynolds had been the prime mover of the meeting which was held in Glenn's office, March 28, 1955, a little more than five years after the strike began. McReynolds had objected to a non-union project that could just as well have a union contractor.

The ITU didn't see it that way, however, and their pickets paced in front of the construction project. On April 20, McReynolds obtained a restraining order from Judge Horrigan halting picketing on that side of *The Herald* building. On May 3, Judge Horrigan made the order permanent, holding the interests of the ITU would not be impaired by being restrained from picketing the construction site area.

The year 1955 was not as good as the previous year. Construction at McNary Dam was coming to a close; large contracts at Hanford were being completed and a sudden dip in retail business was noticed towards the end of the year. The North Richland Trailer Court, largest in the state, was scheduled to close. *The Herald* management discussed ways to replace lost advertising.

This brought the decision to start the *Tri-City Herald Advertiser*, a publication designed to go through the mail to small towns and farms outside the Tri-Cities. The publication started during the Summer of 1955, and for a while was quite successful. Eventually though, the number of merchants using it declined. This, plus the cost of newsprint and postage, spelled its doom, although *The Herald Advertiser* lasted for 15 months.

Changes were also taking place on *The News*. Scheyer was replaced as general manager by Francis Hilton. Hilton decided to call himself Editor and Publisher because "I like the sound of it better." He didn't get to hear it very long, however, for he was soon replaced. There was always a constant turnover of personnel on *The News*. Most left the area, but Scheyer remained and went into business for himself.

In June, 1955, Melvin B. Voorhees arrived as editor. Voorhees, a seasoned newspaperman, came to *The News* from *The Argus*, a weekly in Seattle where he had been editor. With the exception of 12 years in the Army, Voorhees had been in newspaper work all of his adult life. His father had been an editor of *The Tacoma Times* and Voorhees was wire editor of *The Times* when Don worked there as a cub reporter.

"Sure, I remember Don Pugnetti," Voorhees would say around town, "he used to be my office boy."

I resented it every time I heard it. Don enjoyed it.

"Of course I remember Mel Voorhees," Don would say. "He was the man with the desk by the teletype machine."

Voorhees had been a member of General MacArthur's staff and had authored a book, "Korean Tales," which the Army claimed contained confidential material. It had court martialed him, but he was successful in winning the case.

Voorhees didn't mind controversy and he was an excellent writer. He especially liked to write columns, and he immediately embarked on an editorial campaign attacking *The Herald*. Just about anything *The Herald* attempted, regardless of merit, was attacked by *The News*. To offset Glenn's front-page column, "The Way I See It," *The News* started one titled, "The Truth For A Change."

Voorhees' plan was to engage *The Herald* in a running controversy in hopes *The Herald's* readers would buy *The News* to read the other side. *The Herald* knew what he was up to and declined to accommodate him.

But then came the major breakthrough for *The Herald*.

One day, as Glenn was working in the composing room in his usual attire of an ink-smeared T shirt with No. 7 on the back, he had a visitor. It was the joke in the plant that when some dignitary would come by to see Glenn, he would be ushered into the backshop where he met Glenn in his T shirt, printer's apron and arm-pit deep in ink. Glenn always carried a metal makeup rule, a basic tool of printers, which he frequently used to scratch his close-clipped head. Glenn was one publisher people remembered and remarked about.

This time his visitor was Scheyer, who happened to be in Kennewick and was curious to see the plant now that he no longer was with *The News*. Glenn took him on a tour and then they had a cup of coffee.

As they visited, Glenn began to paint a glowing picture of how *The Herald* eventually would win out over Parish and *The News*.

Scheyer disagreed. "You can't hope to win the fight with the union and *The News*," he said.

"Why do you say that?" Glenn wanted to know.

"It isn't Parish anymore. He doesn't own the paper. The union has taken over and they've got more money than you can count to beat you. It's only a matter of time," Scheyer said.

Glenn got a jolt. Each October, Post Office regulations require publications to publish their list of owners and stockholders. Glenn went to a file and got the list published by *The News* a couple of months before. The legal announcement showed: Howard Parish, James Bryce, (Parish's son-in-law); Mrs. Katherine Jenkins, Charles Johnson, A. C. Johnson, Sanford Johnson, Bruce Johnson, Annie Magnuson (heirs of John X. Johnson), Sara H. Johnson estate, Rhodes Department Store, Paul F. Glaser, Wilbur Scruby, Gerald McNamara, and Ray Shepherd, all of Seattle.

Scheyer explained that they had sold their stock to Parish and Bryce at a very nominal sum. For example, some sold all of their stock for $1.00 so they could show the loss to the government for tax purposes.

Parish and Bryce had then turned over the stock to the ITU.

Glenn thanked Scheyer for the information, hung up his printer's apron and caught a plane for Seattle.

He proceeded to talk to every stockholder listed in the legal notice. From them he learned much the same as he had heard from Scheyer. They had not held stock in *The News* since 1951 and, in some cases, since 1950. They had sold their stock to Parish and Bryce for a nominal sum or no sum at all, and had written it off as a loss for tax purposes.

Glenn encountered one exception, R. C. Shepherd, a certified public accountant. He had purchased some *News* stock as follows: from E. B. McGovern, 35 shares of preferred and 35 shares of common; from Mrs. Gertrude Bryce, mother of James Bryce, 34 shares of common and 5 shares of preferred, and from T. V. Dempsey, 68 shares of common and 5 of preferred.

"What's the stock worth now?" Glenn asked.

Shepherd laughed. "It's worthless, of course."

Glenn took out his checkbook and opened it.

"It's worth a thousand dollars to me," he said.

So on January 6, 1965, Glenn became a stockholder of the *Columbia Basin News.* Or was he? Well, there was one sure way to find out. He telephoned Bryce and said he wanted to see him.

Undoubtedly a hundred thoughts must have raced through Bryce's mind when he agreed to meet Glenn. Did Glenn want to sell? Was there a chance for a merger? Any number of ideas about the visit except the one the smiling Glenn shoved at him.

"Jim," he heard Glenn saying, "I am now the proud holder of 171 shares of common stock and 79 shares of preferred stock in your company. I have the receipts and I would like to transfer the stock to my name."

Bryce may have been caught by surprise, but he knew what to say, and he said it emphatically.

"No."

Glenn persisted but Bryce was adamant. Glenn then asked Gerald DeGarmo, a Seattle attorney, to make a request for such a transfer in a letter dated January 14. Bryce didn't answer the letter. On January 26, another Seattle attorney, Carl Johnson, wrote to the ITU in Indianapolis advising them of the stock purchase by Glenn.

The big day, however, was February 3, when Glenn and Pasco attorney George Fulk called on Parish in his

Pasco office and asked him to make arrangements to deliver the stock to Glenn. *Columbia Basin News* employes looked up in surprise and amazement as they recognized Glenn. When he and Fulk entered Parish's office their eyes really bugged.

Parish was as adamant as his son-in-law in his refusal. It was the first time since their 1949 meeting in the Benjamin Franklin Hotel coffee shop that Glenn and Parish had talked. Glenn said:

"Howard, I am a stockholder. I hold common stock in your company. I want to see the books and records of your company. Where are they?"

Parish had been cool and firm. Now he exploded. He rose from his chair, thrust a finger at Glenn, and shouted:

"You, Lee, have no interest in the *Columbia Basin News*. That stock you have purchased is worthless and in no way will you ever be able to see the books of this company, much less get title to the stock."

"Why, Howard, why?" Glenn demanded.

"Why," Parish snapped, "happens to be none of your business. Please leave."

A short time after Glenn's visit, Parish was on a plane to Indianapolis, undoubtedly to report and to explore the problem. Glenn continued doing what he called, "Getting my thousand dollars worth."

He talked to Jim Reed, president of Local 831, about the matter of ownership of *The News* by Unitypo. Reed knew nothing about it and later told Glenn he had followed up and discussed the matter with Walter Marvick. Marvick advised him there was no truth to Glenn's allegations. Thus, for its own reasons, ITU didn't want even its own members to know the actual situation in Pasco.

Glenn asked the Post Office Department to investigate that *The News* was violating its ownership regulations by printing improper names in their notice. Glenn contacted Pasco Postmaster Lon Leeper and wondered if he was going to do anything about making a local investigation.

Leeper replied it was completely out of his hands. Under Post Office regulations he had no power to make any kind of investigation.

Meanwhile, Parish, and at times his son-in-law, Bryce, continued to send a stream of letters to Union headquarters telling how "close to the end of the line" *The Herald* was and asking for more money to make up their losses. They kept assuring ITU that *The Herald* would soon have to sell out to them on ITU terms.

Parish grabbed at anything as material for his letters. One incident he used was a little friendly banter between Glenn and Don at the Pasco-Kennewick Rotary Club. Don had arranged for Glenn to be the club's luncheon speaker to discuss economic prospects for the Tri-Cities. In introducing Glenn, Don remarked how much better it was to have him speaking at a luncheon rather than testifying in court. The comment drew a big laugh from those who were familiar with the paper's numerous court appearances. Glenn drew a bigger laugh when he replied, "If Pugnetti would stop writing those libelous editorials we might not have to be in court!"

One of Parish's aides was at the meeting and it is interesting to read Parish's report on the incident. Pressure at *The Herald* was apparently getting so tense, he wrote, that Lee and his editor got into a quarrel in front of the Rotary Club that almost turned into a fight. Fortunately, cooler heads prevailed. But it was an embarrassing and shameful exhibition and illustrated how the internal situation at the newspaper had deterioriated.

As the summer of 1955 wore on without any progress in acquiring title to his stock, Glenn decided to go into court and force the issue. Assured that the Scott Publishing Company would assume all liability, Shepherd agreed to file as co-plaintiff.

The case was heard before Judge Lloyd Shorett in King County Superior Court and he decided in favor of the Scott Publishing Company. This gave Glenn and attorney

Carl Jonson the opportunity to begin the long, tedious process of taking depositions and thus uncovering the evidence which would indicate a conspiracy on the part of Parish, the ITU and Unitypo to drive *The Herald* out of business.

The ITU, by that time, had advanced Parish almost $500,000 to cover the financial losses of *The News* and had acquired ownership of the newspaper's building and its equipment.

Unitypo Inc. had been the brainchild of Woodruff Randolph, national ITU president, as a method of fighting strikebound newspapers. Because of the enormous amount of union money being spent, Randolph was under attack by some members of his union. This accounted for the appearance of Parish and H. M. (Hank) Greenspun of the Las Vegas *Sun* at the national convention of the ITU in 1955.

They were newspaper publishers who were in debt to Unitypo and were there to discredit claims of Randolph's foes that his defense policy was pouring money down the drain. An article regarding their appearance was printed in ITU's *Typographical Journal*. A portion of the article read:

"The union's interest in the *Columbia Basin News* came out when Glenn Lee, publisher of the *Tri-City Herald* in the Pasco area, purchased some *News* stock and then went to court to obtain delivery on it.

"Mr. Lee's stock purchase was 'worthless,' Mr. Randolph told the convention as he introduced Mr. Parish. 'It was pledged as collateral to Unitypo,' he explained.

"Mr. Parish, who described his career as an associate of the late E. W. Scripps and the late John H. Perry in several newspaper ventures, reported that the *Columbia Basin News* has been built from scratch in five years, from a weekly to a daily of 12,400 circulation as against the competing daily's 14,000.

" 'We will turn the corner this fall and you will have an interest in the paper,' he stated.

"His competitor, according to Mr. Parish, gets financial help from a powerful group in the Pacific Northwest. He also told how he had hired Col. Melvin Voorhees as 'a fighting editor' after the latter won exoneration in court-martial for having published a book that was critical of army censorship."

There seemed to be no end to what Parish would do to keep the money coming from the Union. Now with the ITU records being uncovered by virtue of Judge Shorett's ruling, a few other things were being uncovered too.

Glenn told Jonson to file a law suit against them in Federal Court, which Jonson did.

A lot of information came tumbling out. Parish, for example, had built a new home in the fashionable Highlands of Seattle. To help furnish it, he got about $10,000 worth of equipment and fixtures from Fred Bunch's appliance store on Avenue C in Kennewick, and from the Seattle Lighting Company, a supplier for Bunch. In exchange for the materials, Parish gave Bunch advertising space in *The News*.

The ITU wasn't aware of that until Glenn and Carl Jonson discovered it while going through the records obtained from depositions of Parish and Bunch.

The loans by the ITU went on for several more years. The records showed a clear case of intent to monopolize the newspaper field in the Tri-Cities on the part of *The News* and its allies, the ITU and Unitypo.

With this multitude of evidence, Glenn, through his attorney Jonson, decided to sue the union. The suit was filed in the fall of 1955.

14   *The Suit Against The Union*

FEDERAL Judge John Bowen of U.S. District Court in Seattle was a no-nonsense person. Thin, slight of stature, well into his three score and ten, the big chair in which he sat and the big elevated bench that he peered over made him seem small. Until he spoke, that is. He had a razor keen mind and no reticence in expressing it. And he did not believe in wasting words.

Glenn learned this early in the game. The International Typographical Union learned it too, much to their discomfort.

Time and again when the ITU placed legal obstacles in his way, it was necessary for Carl Jonson to appear before Judge Bowen. Jonson was in court 20 times on such matters. On 19 of those appearances Judge Bowen ruled in favor of the Scott Publishing Company.

At one point, Judge Bowen ordered the ITU to truck all of its records from its main office in Indianapolis to Seattle for copying and inspection. This forced the Union to open an office in Seattle to store records covering 15 years of activity in financing strike-bound newspapers.

It is small wonder the Union should have sought a different judge.

Glenn was a "traveling man" during the years 1955 to 1959. He had temporarily turned his back on the publishing business and entered the legal world to gather the facts on what he believed to be a conspiracy to drive *The Herald* out of business.

To get his data he traveled extensively to reach any possible shred of evidence that might assist the law suit. He criss-crossed the nation, at times he practically lived in Seattle, and he was always with attorneys who took depositions in Vancouver, B.C., San Francisco, Indianapolis, Detroit, New York, Colorado Springs, Santa Barbara and Chicago. There were obstacles all along the way.

On one occasion, it was necessary to go to court in Chicago to obtain an order demanding the Audit Bureau of Circulation to let him inspect its records. This marked the first time in ABC history that such a thing had happened. The Bureau had refused Glenn and Carl Jonson access to the circulation records of the *Columbia Basin News.* After they finally pried open the records, Glenn and Jonson discovered that the Union had been buying circulation for *The News.*

The trip to Colorado Springs also had a story behind it. Glenn and Carl were in Judge Bowen's court in Seattle to force a deposition of Don Hurd, treasurer of the International Typographical Union. Hurd did not appear.

"Where is he?" Judge Bowen demanded of the ITU attorneys. They informed him Hurd was in Colorado Springs, where the ITU maintains a retirement home and hospital.

"Approach the bench," Judge Bowen said crisply. The attorneys moved forward to huddle with the judge.

"Where is your witness?" Judge Bowen asked.

"Mr. Hurd is ill, your honor," he was told. "He's in the hospital."

"What is the matter with him?"

"Sir, he has terminal cancer and has but a short time to live."

The judge paused.

"All the more reason to get his deposition," he said finally. "Go down to United Airlines, get your tickets and go right now to Colorado Springs and get that deposition."

The Herald's suit was filed specifically against Columbia

Basin Publishers Inc., Howard Parish, James M. Bryce, Kennewick-Pasco Typographical Union No. 831, Unitypo Inc., International Typographical Union and its officers, Woodruff Randolph, president; Don Hurd, Walter D. Marvick, Charles M. Lyon, Harold H. Clark, Joe Bailey, Frank R. McClothlin, A. L. Wilie, Seattle Typographical Union No. 202, and the Allied Printing Trades Council.

Advertisers in *The News* such as Allied Stores Corp. and C. C. Anderson and the manager of its local store, M. G. Swain, were at first included in the suit but later dismissed when Swain died.

The original amount asked was $1,638,000.

The Herald claimed the defendants violated the Sherman Antitrust Act, Section I: "Every contract, combination in the form of trust or otherwise, or conspiracy, in restraint of trade or commerce among the several states is declared to be illegal."

Also Section 2, which provides: "Every person who shall monopolize or attempt to monopolize or combine to conspire with any other person or persons to monopolize any part of the trade or commerce among the several states or with foreign nations shall be deemed guilty of a misdemeanor."

In regards to *The News'* advertising practices, *The Herald* alleged violations of Section 2 of the Robinson-Patman Act which forbids: "Discrimination in price between different purchasers of commodities of like grade and quality where the effect of such discrimination may be substantially to lessen competition, or tend to create a monopoly in any line of commerce, or to injure, destroy, or prevent competition with any person who either grants or knowingly receives the benefit of such discrimination or with customers of either of them."

Also, Section 3 of the Clayton Act: "Unlawful for any person engaged in commerce to lease or make a sale or contract for sale of goods, wares, merchandise, machinery, supplies or other commodities for use, consumption or resale within the United States or to fix a price charged therefore, or discount from, or rebate upon, such price on the condition, agreement or understanding that the leases or purchaser thereof shall not use or deal in the goods, wares or merchandise, machinery, supplies or other commodities of a competitor of the lesser or seller, where the effect of such lease, sale or contract for sale may be to substantially lessen competition or tend to create a monopoly."

Shortly after Jonson filed the lawsuit, Glenn learned that Randolph and other ITU officials were going to be in Seattle and would be staying at the Olympic Hotel. He quickly got a U.S. Marshall and went to the hotel. They prowled the building without success before learning Randolph was over at the *Seattle Post-Intelligencer* negotiating a contract. Glenn and the marshall hurried over, arriving at 5:15 p.m.

The lobby was empty. Glenn and the marshall went to the third floor executive suites and staked themselves out. A while later John Callahan, general manager of the P-I, came out of the meeting. Callahan walked over and shook hands with Glenn.

"What are you doing here?" he asked.

"I'm waiting for Randolph. I've got something for him."

Callahan looked past Glenn to the U.S. Marshall, noticed his badge and his eyes widened.

"What is this all about?"

Glenn said, "Well, John, I've got a little lawsuit here for Randolph. I'm tired of the Union financing that paper over at Pasco and we're going to serve this on him."

Callahan recoiled.

"Oh, my God!" he exclaimed. "Not here! Not in the P-I! Don't do it here!"

"Okay, if you feel that strongly about it. I'll go back down to the lobby and catch him there when you're through," Glenn said.

"Please do," Callahan said.

Glenn and the marshall waited in the lobby for about an hour, then the indicator on the elevator started to move. They could trace the elevator's descent. It stopped on the mezzanine, then continued on down to the lobby. The door opened. The elevator was empty. Randolph and the ITU delegation had departed by a different door on the other side of the building. Callahan had tipped them off.

Glenn and the marshall returned to the Olympic Hotel. They waited until midnight. Harvey Kelly, a Hearst company executive from New York, finally appeared in the lobby. Glenn walked over and started talking to him.

"How are things going, Harvey?"

"We're having a terrible time with negotiations," Kelly told him. "We've been at it all day and we are going to start tomorrow morning at 10 at the P-I."

The next morning, a Saturday, the P-I lobby was deserted. Glenn and the marshall stayed out of sight until the ITU delegation was waiting for the elevator. Then Glenn stepped forward.

Pointing at the group, he identified the members for the marshall.

"That's Mr. Randolph. That's Mr. Marvick. That's Mr. McGlothlin." McGlothlin represented Seattle ITU Local 202.

As Glenn called off the names the marshall stepped up and served them with a copy of the complaint.

Randolph glared at the marshall. His face was red.

"You're not very fussy with the company you keep," he growled.

"Don't worry about that," the marshall said matter-of-factly. "I'm just doing my job."

It was the first big step to the final showdown between *The Herald* and the ITU. It would be another four years (and many file cabinets of records later) before the matter would come to trial. But for openers, Glenn had the satisfaction and the advantage of having personally served the complaint on Woodruff Randolph in Seattle. The Union was legally hooked.

Filing the suit was the easy part. Now came the difficult

task of processing it. This began with depositions of executives and former executives of the *Columbia Basin News.* This then led to the Union and thus the process continued, with each deposition opening new doors for additional facts.

Slowly the puzzle began to fall into place. Suspicions or "hunches" that *The Herald* had long held regarding the strike and the tactics and operation of *The News* were verified by the testimony of the participants. The double billing of merchants proved to be more common than even *The Herald* had figured.

One piece of evidence led to another. It was a long, exhaustive task of studying, digging, reviewing and digging some more. It meant long days of being cooped up in hotel rooms jammed with attorneys taking endless depositions with court stenographers and witnesses. And the scene shifted continually, for one shred of testimony might point Glenn in a certain direction, but that direction might be to New York or California or the Middle West.

Glenn would be gone for weeks at a time. Once he was gone for almost three months. At first, he tried to continue his column but this proved impractical. The column began to appear infrequently. Sometimes Glenn would telephone Don and outline an idea he had and Don would write the column for him. Glenn's reluctance to drop his daily column was apparent to the staff and they urged him to give it up. Finally, he too, reached the conclusion that he was being unfair to himself and to the column. "The Way I See It," once a fixture on *The Herald's* front page, disappeared.

It was in the fall of 1955 that Glenn pointed out the president of the ITU for a U.S. Marshall. It was four years later, September 8, 1959, when the case actually began in United States Federal Court in Seattle. By this time *The Herald* had taken 157 depositions numbering 8,320 pages, and had entered 3,688 exhibits totaling 160,865 pages. It was an awesome compilation of evidence and all of it was cross-indexed so it could be readily referred to.

Now it came down to the lawyers and the judge. Assisting Carl Jonson were Howard M. Downs and Robert D. Raven

Documents compiled for anti-trust suit against the ITU, ready to be shipped to Seattle for start of lawsuit, September, 1959. From left; Glenn, attorney Howard Downs, San Francisco; Don.

of the San Francisco law firm of Morrison, Foerster, Holloway, Shuman and Clark. This additional firm became part of *The Herald* team because of their national reputation and prestige in the anti-trust field.

Representing the defendant Columbia Basin Publishers and Parish and Bryce, was Joseph A. Barto of Lundin, Barto and Goucher of Seattle. The other defendants were represented by Alfred J. Schweppe, Martin A. Marguis and Fredric C. Tausend of the firm of McMicken, Rupp and Schweppe of Seattle.

In addition, the ITU and Unitypo Inc. were represented by M. Sidney Dickstein, of Dickstein, Shapiro and Galligan of Washington, D.C.

This time, however, it wasn't Judge Bowen who peered down from the bench, but rather Judge William D. Murray.

Judge Bowen had originally set July 20, 1959, as the trial date, but it was postponed to September 8. Postponements are common in law suits, but in this instance the September date became Judge Bowen's reason for slipping out of the case. There was need for a continuous hearing of the law suit, Judge Bowen said, which would not be possible under the calendar of his court. He advised the parties that the suit was being assigned to Judge Murray of Montana.

This was not a happy choice for *The Herald.* Judge Murray's father was a veteran U.S. Senator from Montana, well-known for pushing through legislation favorable to the unions. Glenn also learned belatedly that Judge Murray was a close friend of ITU President Randolph.

September 8 was the Tuesday following Labor Day and Bob and Don drove over to spend the weekend with Glenn in Seattle. They worked on the upcoming trial. The weekend was a continual sequence of strategy sessions.

The switch in judges was particularly disturbing. Much consideration was given to the options that were open. Should a motion of prejudice be made against Judge Murray? Should the decision not to have a jury be changed and one requested after all? Or should the case be pushed on the basis that Judge Murray would be fair and impartial?

There were good arguments pro and con. How good, for example, would a jury be and how well would it understand the complex nature of the case? And if Judge Murray was asked to disqualify himself, would his successor be any better? In other words, if, in fact, there had been some manipulation of judge choices—and in the highly strained atmosphere proceeding a trial of this magnitude one is suspicious of everything—then why wouldn't it work against *The Herald* again?

So most of the decision making began to center on the question of whether or not there should be a jury. Finally it was decided to leave everything as it was. It would be Judge Murray and no jury.

When the case began September 8 in the hushed atmosphere of the court, Don whispered to Bob, "Do you think we've been had?"

Bob grinned. "Don, my curly headed friend," he said, "there is only one person more suspicious than you and that's my partner. Just don't worry."

Don said, "I hope you're right."

Bob stopped grinning. "So do I," he sighed.

The case lasted two months and was covered extensively by the *Seattle Times* and virtually ignored by the *Post Intelligencer*. Every aspect of Parish's operation was covered, all of it in detail. Documents piled on documents and the testimony mounted as *The Herald* sought to prove a conspiracy in restraint of trade and to monopolize the field between Columbia Basin Publishers Inc. and the ITU.

In the testimony of Allen Cooke, former advertising manager of *The News*, he related that Parish told him, "Now we have got the lineage and Lee is on the ropes. His money won't last long and you know it takes a lot of money to run a newspaper. You keep plugging, get the lineage. We have got the money and the backing and we will get Lee. There's only going to be one newspaper."

There was testimony by former general manager Bill Scheyer and others to the same line of conversation. This idea was also passed along to the advertising solicitors, the testimony showed.

Jack Anderson, news editor of *The News* from July, 1950, to March, 1951, said he had learned from Bryce that "we are going to be able to buy them out, establish a single large newspaper in the Tri-City area."

Other testimony revealed that Columbia Basin Publishers Inc. lost huge amounts of money from the very start. Parish was reduced to only one of his original financial backers, John X. Johnson, but Johnson soon became reluctant to invest more money also.

As his original investors deserted him, it appeared for a time that Parish might have to abandon his plan and sell *The News.* He ran an advertisement in Editor and Publisher magazine which was answered by a C. Brooks Peters of New York, a potential buyer. In a letter dated June 21, 1950, he wrote to Peters revealing his purpose to sell: "Our competition in the field is the *Tri-City Herald,* published by a former hotel man. At first the field was so ripe he did very well before we started our daily. They are over-expanded and I think a merger can be made at the right time."

In his decision, Judge Murray used the fact Parish tried to sell his newspaper as a reason he was not trying to establish a monopoly. "It was only the serious financial position he was in that prompted Parish to take this measure," the judge ruled.

Peters apparently saw through Parish's scheme. Without buyers, Parish had to find another way to salvage his newspaper. Even if he could have persuaded Johnson to advance him more capital it was too late. Johnson had died.

That did not stop Parish. He went to Johnson's widow for more money and, either because of Parish's salesmanship or because of sentiment, the widow financed Parish again. His next move involved the Union. He did this by reminding the ITU that they had a common enemy. The fresh money from his Union allies rescued Parish.

Clarence Martin, an attorney for the ITU at Indianapolis,

personally investigated *The News* in connection with the Union's contemplated financing. He wrote, in August, 1950: "Both papers are probably being operated at a loss. Parish does not believe he has Lee worn down enough yet to buy him out at a reasonable price."

Evidence showed that after the Union commenced financing Parish *The News* did expand its attempts to injure *The Herald,* but their efforts resulted in accelerated losses.

In February, 1951, Bryce and Scheyer met with the ITU executive council in Indianapolis. What occurred there seemed sufficient to establish a conspiracy in violation of antitrust laws. Bryce couldn't recall what had occurred at the meeting, although he did not deny it took place.

Scheyer, however, had no difficulty remembering that there was a general discussion about advertising lineage, rates and the prospect of ultimately eliminating *The Herald.* As a direct result of this meeting the ITU furnished additional funds to *The News* and continued granting money over the years.

Then, too, there were the letters from Bryce and Parish to the ITU, an abundance of them, like the one Bryce wrote in April, 1951, which said, "We know the mechanical problems of our staff. We are always telling them that there is plenty of newspaper equipment right on the ground when we take over the field."

Parish testified that he had dreamed of ultimately controlling the morning and evening fields. The letters of Parish and Bryce were entered as evidence of a conspiracy and were referred to by Jonson in his final arguments.

The Herald's attorneys felt the most damaging arguments against the defendants was the secretive way in which they conducted their business. They stressed in their summation that if it had been a legitimate business operation *The News* and the ITU would not have kept their business association a secret. But because it was a conspiracy, the Union kept its involvement from the public and, above all, from *The Herald.*

By virtue of the devious methods used to keep their secret, they purposely failed to record documents in the county; they caused the wrong names of ownership to appear in the masthead of *The News;* they handled funds in a circuitous method, routing the money through Parish and Seattle banks rather than directly to the newspaper; they used a sly method to carry on their correspondence—to Bryce and Parish in Seattle rather than directly to the newspaper plant; and, finally, the conspirators told the few who knew of the association to keep quiet. An example of this was when Jim Reed, a Union 831 member, after talking to Glenn in early 1955, went back and talked to Marvick and Parish and asked them if it was true the Union was financing *The News.* They told him, "Absolutely not!"

Parish stubbornly denied there was any Unitypo financing even to his national advertising representatives. He also withheld the information from the Audit Bureau of Circulation. Even after the ABC made an investigation, Parish withheld the facts and bragged about it in a letter to the ITU. The letter was offered in evidence.

In the Fall of 1954, Bryce denied the Union involvement in a conversation with Glenn in the White Henry Stuart Building in Seattle. After Glenn had contacted the sons of the late John X. Johnson to try to get to the truth, Parish quickly cut off this source of information by talking to the Johnson brothers and warned them to say nothing. It was necessary to start a law suit to get the facts.

The list of evidence and illustrations droned on endlessly. Methods used to keep advertisers from *The Herald* with special rates if they would advertise exclusively were documented. These rates were below those listed on the rate card. Furthermore, it was brought out *The News* gave its paper away; that a substantial number of residents in Tri-Cities got it free while other subscribers received reduced rates.

Defense attorneys based their arguments on the assumption *The Herald* followed the same procedures and thus the fight between the two newspapers was good, clean competition. Attorney Dickstein referred to it as a "knock-down drag-out newspaper fight." Attorney Barto quoted the famous statement of Justice Holmes that it was not the purpose of the Sherman Act to prevent competition but to encourage it. He quoted another statement: "If one competitor has been successful, we cannot then turn on the unsuccessful competitor."

To make his point, Dickstein referred to a case of the United States against Harte-Hanks Newspapers. In that case, there were two newspapers within a small town in Greenville, Texas, with a population of about 16,000. The court found that the two papers fought and competed bitterly and each lost more than $1,000,000.

One group could stand the pressure better because it had more money to lose. Finally the other group, having been driven to the wall, sold out for $300,000. The government then made a charge of monopoly, claiming the winning paper had successfully monopolized and therefore violated Section 2 of the Sherman Act.

However, Dickstein continued, when the case was appealed the court said, "No, not at all. There is no room for competition here. We cannot protect the entrenched business against a competitor, and if we say the successful competitor had been violating the antitrust laws, we have destroyed competition. This is a field in which there is no room for the anti-trust laws to apply."

That, said Dickstein, was applicable to the Tri-Cities and *The News* and *The Herald*.

The two newspapers competed in an upright fashion, he said. He skirted the secrecy issue.

The trial ended in November. Then came the wait for the decision. The weeks went by, and as time passed Glenn and Bob were sure that the delay meant the decision would be in favor of the defendants.

It was in February that the call came from Carl Jonson with the news. Judge Murray had released his decision — and it was against *The Herald!*

251

The decision was lengthy and failed to find any violations of Sections 1 and 2 of the Sherman Act.

"This was not to drive the *Tri-City Herald* out and form a monopoly," Judge Murray wrote, "but to take advantage of the opportunity in the area with a bonafide attempt to establish a competing business enterprise."

Judge Murray found that the communication between Parish, Bryce and Unitypo and ITU were merely in an effort to keep the money coming. The publisher also welcomed the assistance to help them build circulation.

The judge also found that *The News* and ITU did not violate the Robinson-Patmann Act and Section 3 of the Clayton Act. He held that some of the remarks like "driving Lee and the Scott Publishing Co. to the wall," "forcing a merger," "beating Lee," were also merely communications on the part of Parish in a "nature of a sales pitch in an effort to keep the money coming."

"Further indications of the lack of intent and purpose of Parish to destroy the *Tri-City Herald* and create a monopoly lies in the method of the way the money was expended," Judge Murray wrote. "Even if $1,178,000 had been spent by Unitypo, it was spent over a period of nine years. Otherwise, success would be more likely to be achieved by spending the money in a relatively short time to cut subscription rates and circulation to such a point that the *Tri-City Herald* would have been unable to compete."

The judge said he was not moved by evidence that when Parish was unsuccessful in buying *The Herald* for his price, he declared he would establish a paper in the area, force Philip and Lee to the wall and buy out their interest for five cents on the dollar.

When the judge's decision was announced, Glenn immediately summoned all the staff to the backshop. He climbed on a "turtle"—the four-legged stand on which page type is assembled—and announced Judge Murray's verdict.

"Sure, I'm disappointed," he said, "just as I know you are. But I'm not depressed and don't anyone in this plant be. The *Tri-City Herald* is coming out. We've taken the worst those bastards can throw at us and still we grow. We will continue to forge ahead, fighting off all unfair opposition. We're *going to win!*"

He thanked everyone for their loyalty. If he had to do it over again, he told them, nothing would be changed.

The verdict was a body blow to Glenn, although he successfully concealed his disappointment. It had to be a stunning personal loss after all those years of striving, of effort, and determination, to bring the case so far and then lose it. Always a tough competitor, it would take a major adjustment for him to reconcile his feelings.

The next step was to appeal to the U.S. Ninth Circuit Court of Appeals in San Francisco. That took another year of preparation, including printing entire transcript of the trial and briefs.

Some of the points made in the appeal were that direct evidence established that the defendants did attempt to force a monopoly; that there was a finding of a conspiracy; that unsound inferences were drawn by the trial court; that the cooperation found by the trial court did violate Section 1 of the Sherman Act. The appeal argued the defendants did violate the Robinson-Patmann Act and that the defendants did not have immunity from the anti-trust laws.

We thought we had an ironclad case, but in the decision the U.S. Court of Appeals upheld Judge Murray. The case was then appealed to the United States Supreme Court in the October, 1961, term but the Supreme Court refused to hear it.

As it turned out, the Union won a major battle but lost the war. *The Herald* surged ahead from that setback with new public confidence and greater acceptance. As for *The News*, it became more defensive, more restricted, and started to run down. It never recovered from Judge Murray's verdict. Within three years it expired.

15   *The Steam Plant*

SEPTEMBER, 1962 . . .

Glenn burst through the doors of the House of Representatives Press Gallery in Washington, D.C., and raced down the line of telephone booths in the press room until he found Don.

"We did it! We did it!" he yelled, and jerked open the loor, neglecting to note that Don was leaning against it.

Don toppled over backwards and sprawled on the floor, grabbing frantically for the phone.

"We won!" Glenn shouted. "We won! It's all over!"

There was a moment of silence and in that moment Don could hear Bill Bequette's voice on the phone yelling, "What the hell's going on? Don, are you there? Hey, we've got a deadline!"

Don seized the phone and told Bill to hold on. Grabbing Glenn's hands, they danced a little jig around the room.

While Glenn rustled through his notes of final minutes of the House vote, Don turned back to Bequette.

"Where was I?" Don asked.

"You were talking about Westland (Congressman Jack Westland of Everett) and his comment . . ."

Don interrupted him. "Here's Westland now. Hold on again."

Gleeful members of the Washington delegation to Congress started coming through the door. Rep. Catherine May of *The Herald's* congressional fourth district had reason to be overjoyed. So did Rep. Julia Butler

Hanson. She was a freshman in Congress, but her experience in the Washington State Legislature had shown itself in the efforts to authorize the Hanford electrical generating steam plant.

Many things *The Herald* had done before and would do in the future would attract attention to the newspaper. None, though, would match the recognition and credit *The Herald* would receive for its work in winning the fight in Congress to build the controversial Hanford nuclear facility.

Surprisingly, this also happened to be one of *The Herald's* shortest campaigns. It lasted only 90 days. True, the newspaper had campaigned for years for construction of the dual purpose reactor at Hanford. The period from early July to September 14, however, told the story. It was a case of do or die, and the project won.

The Herald's press rolled late that September day, but few minded. The screaming headlines told the story everybody wanted to hear. This doesn't seem possible in the environment of the 1970s when nuclear power is under attack. Yet, in 1962 the success of Hanford's nuclear power plant was one of the big items on the *Associated Press* budget. It was the banner headline in almost all the newspapers in the state.

The nuclear reactor—Hanford's ninth—had been under construction since 1958. But this reactor was different from the others. It had been designed to produce both plutonium and power. The tremendous heat from the nuclear process and the necessity for huge quantities of cooling water created great vapors of steam that were a nuisance and a waste with the early reactors. The new one was designed to capture the steam and convert it into electricity; enough electricity to almost equal the electrical output of two Bonneville dams.

To insure that the reactor would do this, features were built into it to put the steam into giant turbines, but a snag developed. The problem wasn't technology; it was politics.

"We don't want the Atomic Energy Commission in the

power business," an opponent cried. In a way, AEC would have been. The commission had worked out an arrangement with the Bonneville Power Administration to market the power. But AEC would produce the power and the negative reaction to that couldn't be overcome.

Despite the fact Congress had voted to authorize spending between $25,000,000 and $46,000,000 to give the reactor convertibility features to become the Free World's first dual purpose reactor, Congress would not permit these abilities to be used.

Three times in 1961 the issue was debated in the House of Representatives, and three times it was voted down decisively. The last time, 235 to 164.

The long way back proved treacherous. The steam plant project—a completely different legislative creature in 1962 because government funds were not involved—had to survive three more votes in the House, the first of which, on July 17, 1962, it again lost. Small wonder its opponents smirked at the project, and even its staunchest supporters began to think they had enough.

Thus the complete reversal on September 14 proved a stunning victory as well as a surprising one. Among other things, it gave the administration of President John F. Kennedy a tremendous psychological lift. He had accumulated a poor legislative batting average. Whereas Democrats controlled the House and the Senate, the White House couldn't control the Democrats. The Hanford steam plant campaign illustrated this point. Kennedy favored the legislation but his endorsement couldn't override sectional bias and special interests.

Rep. Chet Holified of California, ranking Democrat on the Joint Committee on Atomic Energy and its chairman, wrote to Don on July 26, following the first 1962 defeat for the Hanford proposition:

"I only regret that we were not successful in saving this national resource of steam for the benefit of the people of the Northwest and the Nation. It was impossible for us to overcome this combined opposition of the private utilities and the coal interests. The merit of our position was never really considered. It was one of the most ruthless power plays of self interest groups that I have ever witnessed."

Glenn and Don worked chiefly with House Republicans. Altogether in five trips to Washington, D.C. — three by Don and two by Glenn — they met singly or together with a total of 40 Republican Congressmen and won support from 38 of them. It had to be the turning point. In addition, many of these men pulled other votes along with them. By this process they were able to neutralize what had been negative votes.

Even now, one sometimes wonders how in the world the Hanford steam plant legislation won. The opposition against it was formidable and it packed both economic and political clout.

First, there were the giant private power utilities massed under the banner of the Edison Electric Institute, their lobbying arm. They had been spurred to action by Pacific Northwest private utilities who fought Hanford from ambush. They insisted they were "neutral" and declared they would not take a stand either for or against the steam plant. What they said publicly and what they did privately was quite different.

There would be no federal funds in the 1962 Hanford proposition but there would be public power funds. Private utilities feared the prospect of a public-power combine contracting with a federal agency. They had turned down the chance to build the steam plant themselves. Now they adopted a dog in the manger attitude.

Then there were the coal states, especially Pennsylvania and West Virginia. These were bad times for coal. Under no circumstance did they intend to assist in the development of nuclear fuels, least of all, nuclear power.

And finally, there were the railroads who drew in with them the U.S. Chamber of Commerce and the National Association of Manufacturers. The Northern Pacific Railway, now a part of the merger that formed the Burlington

Northern, owned a coal mine at Roslyn, Washington, that had at one time employed as many as 500 people. Its employment in 1962 was down to 150 and the Northern Pacific wanted markets for coal or, better yet, to sell the mine.

Glenn and Don discovered the interlocking system of directorships that had coal mine owners on the board of directors of railroads or private utilities, and railroad officials on the boards of private utilities and coal mines.

"We are definitely and emphatically opposed to this (Hanford) proposal," Robert MacFarlane, president of the Northern Pacific, wrote in May, 1962, to Congressman Ben Jensen of Iowa, a member of the House Appropriations Committee. "We urgently ask that you do everything in your power to prevent approval of this proposal."

MacFarlane was also a director of the giant Northern States Power Company. He had double strength for Rep. Jensen, who did yeoman work in fighting Hanford.

The strength of the coal states was massive. For example, Washington, Oregon and Idaho combined had 13 congressmen. Pennsylvania alone had 30, and 28 of them opposed Hanford. It was no mystery why Hanford's steam plant went down in 1961 from blockbusters like that.

Its only hope in 1962 was to gather converts from other states.

A wave of dismay swept the Tri-Cities when Hanford lost in 1961, chiefly because no one figured it would lose. The Tri-Cities was unprepared for what had happened. Often proposals for Hanford had been in trouble, but then, somehow, Senator Henry M. Jackson, a member of the Joint Committee on Atomic Energy, and Senator Warren G. Magnuson always pulled a rabbit from their hats.

It was different this time because Hanford lost in the House where neither Magnuson nor Jackson could help it. Without exception, Hanford won each time in the Senate in 1961 and 1962.

The Tri-Cities weren't ready to surrender. The first voice with an idea was that of Earl Coe, State Director of Conservation and a close friend of Don and Glenn. Coe suggested state involvement with AEC and the Bonneville Power Administration. A former state senator and Secretary of State, Coe knew his proposal had some real problems. Public and private power battles in the state legislature had in recent years sometimes split the majority Democratic party. Even the support of Governor Albert Rosellini could not guarantee unified action by the Democratic majority.

A far better alternative arose from the Washington Public Power Supply System (WPPSS), a joint operating agency which represented 16 county Public Utility Districts. WPPSS had been studying the possibility of building the steam plant. On October 20, 1961, its executive committee, under managing director Owen Hurd, authorized construction of the Hanford generator.

Hurd had proposed that WPPSS should finance, build and operate the power facilities; that the AEC would make available the waste steam from the new reactor, and that Bonneville would be the marketing agent, wheeling the power over its grid of transmission lines.

The proposal received enthusiastic reception and for a while it appeared that WPPSS would have clear sailing. With the sanction of the Kennedy Administration, Bonneville and AEC started making arrangements with WPPSS early in 1962. After a while, however, things came to an abrupt halt. In checking with the U.S. Comptroller General to insure that AEC was authorized to enter into the agreement, it was discovered that this could not be done with existing legislation. It would be necessary to go back to the same Congress which had turned Hanford down.

What private power would do was uppermost in many minds. There was no love lost between private utilities and WPPSS. For one thing, they were fighting bitterly over which would build dams on the Middle Snake River. For another thing, WPPSS was just beginning to take its first steps. Private power would never wish to be accused of having helped it to walk.

The Tri-Cities had been a public power area with a public utility district in each county. *The Herald*, however, had supported private power, and Glenn was well acquainted with executives of the private utilities. He quickly telephoned Kinsey Robinson, president of Washington Water Power Company in Spokane and a tower of strength and influence in the power field.

"Kinsey, I'm calling from Kennewick and I want to ask you some questions about the Hanford dual purpose reactor," Glenn said.

"What about it?" Kinsey said.

"We like the proposition that Owen Hurd and his agency are working on and I was . . ."

Glenn never got to finish.

"That is the craziest thing I've heard of," Robinson said. "We studied that plant and turned it down. The costs are fantastic and it is wet, low-pressure steam."

"Kinsey, Owen's group is willing and ready to go ahead. They have studied it and I haven't. What I want to know from you is will private power take a stand against them?"

There was a pause.

"Glenn," said Robinson, "we're not going to oppose Hanford. We're not going to support it, either. I can't speak for the other utilities. I think they share the view, though, that we should remain neutral."

Glenn had hoped for something better. Yet while he wasn't pleased with what he had been told, he wasn't unhappy if it meant "hands off" of Hanford on the part of private power.

There was optimism that this time Hanford would pass. And why not? There would be no need for government funds. Congress would obtain its dual purpose reactor without having to put up the money itself.

The first battle would be in the Joint Committee on Atomic Energy. Here the proposal would encounter the opposition from Rep. James Van Zandt of Pennsylvania. On the other side would be Rep. Holifield and Senator Jackson.

Glenn and Don were on the telephone constantly trying to keep up-to-date on what was happening. Interest in the Tri-Cities was high and this was especially true for Glenn and Don who were so close to the situation.

260

Little by little, the picture began to unfold. Owen Hurd was already in Washington, D.C. He told Don that Rep. May's office had received word Pacific Power and Light Company, one of the large private power firms, would oppose the proposal. Hurd also wondered if Governors Mark Hatfield of Oregon and Albert Rosellini of Washington could intercede with Democrats and Republicans not to oppose the WPPSS proposal.

Glenn immediately went to work attempting to line up the support of the two governors. Charles Luce, the Bonneville administrator, had left for Washington, D.C. Before he left, he had talked to Donald McClung, president of Pacific Power and Light.

"McClung said he's not for it but he hasn't made up his mind whether to oppose it publicly or not," Don was told by Russ Holt, Luce's administrative assistant. "When Chuck talked to McClung he got the feeling McClung was talking for the private power industry in the Northwest because he kept saying 'we'," Holt added.

Glenn and Don compared notes.

"Pug, you'd better go back," Glenn said.

The Joint Committee meeting was scheduled for 11 a.m. on Tuesday, July 10. Don's plane landed at Friendship Airport in Baltimore that morning and he scrambled to get to the hearing. Owen Hurd had reserved hotel space but it wasn't ready. So Don left his bag in Hurd's room, grabbed a taxi and was in the Joint Committee hearing an hour after the meeting started. The fireworks were still going on. The proposal before the committee was to permit the Atomic Energy Commission to contract with WPPSS for power facilities to be built into the new Hanford reactor. Senator Bourke Hickenlooper of Iowa demanded that the committee delay action for further study.

"You'll study this thing to death," Chairman Holified told him. "I intend that this committee authorize the AEC to enter into the contract."

Hickenlooper countered that WPPSS be required to pay for all facilities in the reactor to permit its conversion for power production.

"If it wasn't for this they wouldn't be in here today seeking authorization," he declared. "We have to take a realistic approach on a cost basis."

Holified replied: "Those features are built in there and it's impossible to take them out. They were authorized by Congress and are in there whether we sell the steam for one dollar or a million dollars. This payoff schedule proposed by the Power Supply System will reimburse the government for the money it has expended. How can we get a better deal than that?"

Senator Henry Jackson pounded his hand on the table in disgust.

"If this project has some form of Body Odor that is disturbing the private utilities, I think we ought to know about it, and I wish they would come in here. It is obvious they are opposed to it, and I would like them to come in and say what their objection is."

Jackson asked Owen Hurd, who was sitting before the committee:

"Suppose there is a provision that not less than half of the power output at Hanford would be available to the private utilities upon their request on a long-term basis. How would you feel about that?"

Hurd answered: "I personally, without any consultation or discussions with my board, would feel that there would be no serious objections to such an arrangement."

When the hearing adjourned, Don asked Jackson why he had suggested permitting private utilities to share in the power.

"It was right off the top of my head," Jackson answered. "I wanted to do something that might shake them loose. I also think that private power is going to be handicapped by fighting a project when they will share in its benefits."

Jackson's proposal met some disapproval from public power supporters who disliked having to ram through a proposition over private power objections and yet end up dividing the power. From a tactical standpoint the maneuver was to prove a big selling point in getting the steam-plant approved.

But what about private power? Was it really opposing Hanford as much as some claimed? Don decided to find out. He had heard that Kinsey Robinson was in Washington, D.C., but he couldn't locate him. He finally contacted John Burke, president of the Pacific Northwest Power Company, a combine of five private power companies seeking to build High Mountain Sheep Dam on the Snake River. Washington Water Power Company was one of the five companies.

"How do you feel about the Hanford proposition being placed before Congress?" Don asked Burke.

"I really don't know that much about it," Burke replied.

"Well," said Don, "I've been looking for Kinsey Robinson. I'm told he's back here. Do you know where he is?"

"No," Burke said. "I haven't heard from him."

"If he's back here, do you know where he stays?" Don asked.

"No," Burke said.

Later, Don met Ken Billington, manager of the Washington State PUD Association, and they discussed private power and its opposition to Hanford.

"I've heard Kinsey Robinson is back here but I can't confirm it," Don told him.

"Oh, he's back here," Billington said. "I was on the plane with him. He flew back with John Burke."

"Are you sure?"

"Yes, of course. Why do you ask?"

Don explained what Burke had told him and that Burke didn't know where Robinson was staying.

Billington laughed. "Kinsey is probably at the Mayflower Hotel," he said. "That's his hangout."

Sure enough, Robinson was at the Mayflower but Don couldn't make contact with him and he didn't return Don's calls. Before long Burke also couldn't be reached.

Although he didn't get to talk to them, Don eventually found where they were and what they were doing. They had visited Rep. May, Jack Westland, Craig Hosmer, and gradually the pattern formed.

"They are here to gut this project," Jackson said. "They

haven't called on me because they know my views, but they are busy with their dirty work."

Private utilities descended on Hosmer because he had carried the fight against Hanford in 1961. Now they found the young and influential California Republican on the other side.

Hosmer wrote a personal letter to each House Republican voicing his concern.

"I write because I'm worried about how our Party is going to look with so many Republicans voting against the new 1962 Hanford Project.

"The old 1961 Hanford public power deal was a mess . . . But except for the coal state people, voting against the new 1962 Hanford project is hard to justify.

"The new Hanford simply sells by-product heat from the plutonium reactor which otherwise would go to waste. Local interests put up all the money—there's not a cent more federal money going into it . . .

"All in all, there is a real good chance of picking up $50 million for the U.S. Treasury and very few risks involved. I don't see how blowing $50 million into the air instead of funneling it to the U.S. Treasury can be explained . . ."

The issue was to come before the House of Representatives on Tuesday, July 17. Don was telegraphing two articles a day back to *The Herald*, one in the morning on the latest information—the three-hour difference in time zones worked in *The Herald's* favor—and one in the late afternoon, an "overnighter" in newspaper parlance. In between times, he was working closely with Rep. May in her attempts to coordinate efforts to sway House Republicans.

Rep. May wrote a letter urging support for the Hanford proposal and giving her reasons why. Then she proved the mainstay in rallying signatures for it from all members of the Washington, Idaho and Oregon delegations, Democrats and Republicans alike. The letter went to all members of the House. In addition to Rep. May, those who signed it were Walt Horan, Rep. Hanson, Don Magnuson, Thomas

264

Pelly, Thor Tollefson and Westland, all of Washington; Edwin Durno, Edith Green, Walter Norblad and Al Ullman of Oregon, and Ralph Hardin and Gracie Pfost of Idaho.

Among other things, the letter listed these advantages that a favorable vote would mean:

1. Give the government its only opportunity to recoup the $25 million it had spent on convertibility features in the reactor.

2. Permit the use of a resource (steam) that would otherwise be wasted.

3. Fill a critical need for power in the region.

4. Make maximum use of reactor-defense facilities for peaceful purposes.

The letter stressed testimony given in the Joint Committee hearings that over a 24-year period the federal government would receive payments totaling $125 million for steam that would be otherwise wasted.

Now new support started flowing in. Oregon Governor Hatfield, a Republican, sent a telegram endorsing Hanford to Van Zandt and urged the Pennsylvanian to support it. Others in the Pacific Northwest delegation also wrote letters urging support. Don's exclusive articles noted Senator Jackson's growing optimism. The proposal sped through the Senate. Jackson felt that since the change had been made to include private power, the objections to the steam plant would be overcome. A banner headline topping one of Don's stories read: "Jackson Predicts OK Of Hanford Proposal."

But then the full effect of what the opponents were doing started to come through.

Urged on by Pacific Northwest utilities, other private power firms talked to their state delegations. Worse yet, prominent in the opposition was the alliance of the United Mineworkers Union and the coal-mine operators. Together, and with private power, they talked down Hanford on the basis that it would "put the government in the power business."

On the Sunday afternoon prior to the vote, Don and Owen Hurd drove to the home of Alex Radin, managing director of the American Public Power Association. An old hand at legislative battles, Radin shattered any optimistic illusions they harbored.

"The real problem is education," he said. "I don't think the point has gotten across to the majority of Congressmen. They haven't heard enough yet to make them change their minds. We're sold on the proposition. They aren't. I don't think they're listening."

Don now found Jackson quite concerned as the showdown approached. The senator said he had only one vote he could count on from Pennsylvania, West Virginia and Kentucky. Loss of the heavy Democratic support from those states would hurt.

'My problem is that I'm limited in what I can do," Jackson said. "I'm a senator and House members are proud of their prerogatives. If they get the impression a senator is trying to throw his weight around in the House, look out."

By a strange turn of events, Rep. May and Don had lunch with Rep. Jensen, the tall, fiercely anti-public power congressman from Iowa. Don knew Jensen would be one of the leaders of the opposition, but how rough was he going to be? The conversation was guarded and, at times, somewhat awkward as Rep. May and Don cautiously tried to get some of their points across. As the luncheon broke up, Jensen told them, "I'm opposed and I'm not going to change, but I won't speak against Hanford."

They thanked him.

But when the debate on the project raged on July 17 in the House Chambers, Jensen rose and called the Hanford proposal a "subterfuge" and a device to trick Bonneville Power Administration into paying for the project. "One of the disturbing aspects of this Hanford issue is the confusion that is being created by the supporters of the project," he declared.

As Jensen spoke, Don looked down at Rep. May, and she

looked up at him and shrugged in dismay. By now, nothing surprised Don.

Van Zandt led the attack. He proposed an amendment to the Hanford legislation that would prohibit the Atomic Energy Commission from entering into "any arrangement" for the production of electric power from the new reactor.

Said Rep. John Dent of Pennsylvania: "We who want to see our coal and railroad industries revived are not so naive as to believe that Hanford power would not eventually move into markets now served by solid fuel. Thus Hanford would not only deprive coal miners in the State of Washington from the jobs they need; it would also come east and snatch employment opportunities from states east of the Mississippi River."

When the votes were counted, House Republicans had voted against Hanford 132 to 29 while 100 Democrats had voted against it, 62 of them from the South. It was all over by 5 p.m. At midnight, Don was on his way home. It had been a long day but he wasn't tired, just terribly dejected. He sat up during the flight writing an editorial and a story for Wednesday's *Herald*. His editorial read:

"Shortly after yesterday's vote which defeated the Hanford steam plant proposal, a lobbyist for the Coal Producer's Association was overheard being asked, 'Do you fellows have enough money to cover your commitments?'

"It would be over-simplification to say that what happened yesterday was entirely due to the campaign fund pledges from the coal and private utility companies.

"Nevertheless, when it came to voting it was apparent that a large segment of the House was motivated by something other than logic or the facts.

"Trying to spot the exact reasons for the steam-plant rejection is difficult because many factors indicated their presence.

"One fact evidenced bears no comfort to the Pacific Northwest. It is fear of our great power potential and low power rates on the part of the Middle West, East and South.

They fear our great asset will leave them poorer because it will induce industry to locate here rather than in their regions.

"The day is over when they feel we are a bunch of country cousins whom they should help.

"Also disturbing yesterday was the lethargy and indifference of some Congressmen. Many weren't interested in determining the facts. They voted sectional or personal bias. The incredible thing is that they voted to waste a resource— steam—and also to forbid the Federal Government to recover the millions that they had authorized for just that purpose . . .

"And finally the attitude of this Congress—heavily Democratic—towards the Kennedy Administration again displayed itself. The President had urged support of the project.

"In the face of that, 100 Democrats ignored him and voted for the Van Zandt Amendment which killed the project.

"The project should have won, and would have won—31 votes would have turned the trick—but for the stand of the Northwest private utilities . . . they weren't out for power— they wanted blood and the public be damned . . .

"They won their point, and residents of this region can only hope it gives them complete inner satisfaction . . ."

The pangs of defeat, however, were not just *The Herald's.* Across the Pacific Northwest, newspapers editorialized angrily.

Said the *Portland Oregonian:* "The *Oregonian* is fed up with hypocrisy in the electric-utility power struggle. Private utilities of the Northwest . . . should have been fighting in Congress for Hanford power . . ."

The Lewiston, Idaho, *Tribune* wrote: "The house vote seriously raises again the question whether the House really can legislate intelligently and responsibly. It also raises the incidental question whether there can be any compromise or quarter at all any more in the battle between private and public power . . ."

Glenn, Don and Mrs. Catherine May beam shortly after House approved the controversial Hanford Steam Plant legislation, September, 1962.

Some headlines announcing the victory of the "Steam Plant Fight."

Gathered for Stokes Award ceremony in Congressional Hotel, Washington D.C., 1963, from left, Rep. Chet Holifield, D-Calif., leader of House floor fight for the Hanford Steam Plant; Rep. Catherine May; Ellis Baker, president of American Newspaper Guild and president of Stokes Award; Don Pugnetti, Dr. Glenn Seaborg, Chairman, Atomic Energy Commission; Senator Jackson, Glenn Lee.

Platform dignitaries for Hanford Steam Plant ground-breaking, September 6, 1963. President Kennedy autographed this picture for Glenn Lee. From left, back row: Charles Luce, Bonneville Power Administrator; John Conway, executive director, Joint Committee on Atomic Energy (partially hidden behind Gerald Tape, AEC commissioner); Lars Nelson, president, Washington State Grange; Glenn Walkley, president, WPPSS; Earl Coe, State Director of Conservation, (partially hidden behind Kennedy). Others are, at left, Senator Frank Moss, Utah; Senator Henry M. Jackson, Wash.; the President; Glenn Lee and Stewart Udall, Secretary of the Interior, at right. Governor Albert Rosellini behind Glenn and next to him, head turned, Senator Warren G. Magnuson, Wash.

The *Spokesman-Review* termed the power waste "unconscionable" and said, "The history of this area makes it clear that taxpayer investment in resource development has been a profitable use of public funds. The same principle applies with respect to electricity production from the Hanford reactor. Private investors can not do the job of salvaging this now wasted power resource . . . The opposition seems to be both selfish and theoretical."

The *Wenatchee World* noted: "The *Seattle Times* this week came out editorially in favor of the plan to generate electricity from waste heat at Hanford. That makes it unanimous. Now every newspaper of note in the Northwest has backed the Hanford conversion plan. This unanimity is significant because seldom do all papers see alike editorially.

"Finding the *Yakima Republic* in agreement with the *Lewiston Tribune* editorially, say, is about the same as finding Representative Julia Butler Hanson and Representative Catherine May on the same side of the fence. Yet both have happened in this case . . ."

There was no letup in *The Herald's* campaign. The newspaper seemed never to be without news stories and editorials on Hanford and the telephone lines between Kennewick and Washington, D.C., were always busy. Don was on a speaking circuit of business and professional clubs throughout the region. Excerpts of his speeches were picked up by the *Associated Press* and *United Press* and appeared in other newspapers where they drew additional editorial comment.

Under intense criticism for their lobbying actions, Northwest private utilities circulated the story that they had remained neutral in regards to Hanford; that they were in Washington, D.C., on other business and had never discussed Hanford.

Armed with copies of the *Congressional Record*, Don quoted from the transcript to illustrate the falsity of their story. This received tremendous publicity.

Meanwhile, Glenn carried on a running battle with the U.S. Chamber of Commerce. He asked John J. Meehan, assistant manager, for copies of all printed information and mailings which were sent out from the U.S. Chamber's office in reference to the steam plant. He complained of not hearing further after the Chamber had informed him they would let him know after studying the proposition.

Glenn telephoned and then followed up his call with a letter to Walter B. Garver, manager, Agriculture and National research department of the Chamber, pointing out his previous request to Meehan, which had been ignored.

In his letter, he said, "On a decision by the U.S. Chamber, as important as this one, I assume that you have either notes or minutes of meetings of your committee that rendered a negative report against this project, which resulted in the publication of the Chamber's opposition.

"I would like to have substantiation of all this material, from all sources available to you at the time of arriving at such a decision so I may see from where the opposition stemmed.

"I would also like to know whether or not you or your committee ever talked personally and conferred about this matter with Mr. Charles Luce, the Bonneville Power Administrator? Or Mr. Owen Hurd, secretary-manager of the PUD group that proposed to sell the bonds to build and operate this reactor? Or, did you make inquiry of Portland, or Richland, or Yakima, or Walla Walla, or Spokane or Seattle?"

Glenn ended his letter by stating he had been a supporter of the U.S. Chamber and private power for a number of years. But in view of the forthcoming shortage of power in the Pacific Northwest, and in the face of the private power attitude on this particular subject, he considered a serious mistake had been made which could go down in history and would haunt the U.S. Chamber and private power for a long time.

The correspondence continued to go back and forth, each letter being a little more caustic than the previous one.

On July 22, *The Herald* sent a telegram to Senator Jackson:

"We strongly urge you to go all the way and do everything possible to keep alive the Hanford Reactor Proposition. We went to Portland and had a long conference with Chuck Luce Friday. Had a long talk with Kinsey Robinson and he disclaimed any part in opposing the reactor but we believe that private power is on the war path generally and the Hanford reactor right now is just one of the battles, and High Mountain Sheep is what has them stirred up. We asked them to consider and accept your offer of 50 percent of Hanford Power and they want no part of it. PUDs gathered in session Friday and Saturday at Wenatchee passed resolution asking for investigation of private power lobbying against reactor proposal.

"Even though odds are against you we strongly urge you to go all the way for the record. — *Tri-City Herald.* Don Pugnetti and Glenn Lee."

Jackson carried the ball from there. On August 2, the Senate unanimously voted to revive the plan for power production at Hanford, using waste steam from the new reactor. The issue would now go to the Senate-House conference. This meant that both Houses of Congress would select conferees who would meet and work out compromise legislation.

Thus the battle would be whether the House would instruct — in other words, limit — their conferees as to what they could agree to. Proponents of Hanford would have to see that the conferees were uninstructed.

The strategy of Glenn and Don was to see if they could somehow neutralize Northwest utilities and the U.S. Chamber. Glenn asked for and, after much persuasion, received invitations to appear before the directors of the Portland, Seattle and Spokane Chambers of Commerce. Fact sheets in hand, he and Don flew to Portland for the first of the three sessions.

"Time is of the essence," Glenn told a crowded luncheon room. "We are on the verge of scuttling the output of two Bonneville Dams. You can't sit by and watch this done.

You're more than interested spectators. You have a big stake in this issue."

The meetings were held in the different cities, but each proved a rerun of the others. Community leaders were present. They were friendly, polite, attentive. When Glenn finished, they applauded and asked questions. Finally, they assured him they realized there were only a few days before the matter was to be debated in Congress. They would immediately "study" the proposition, they said.

Except for letters thanking Glenn and Don for their appearance, that was the end of it. Although the lack of action certainly displayed the influence of anti-Hanford groups, many Chamber members acted individually or through their business organization to help as best they could.

Glenn and Don also appealed to Governors Albert Rosellini and Mark Hatfield to go to Washington, D.C., and work for Hanford. Hatfield, in a re-election campaign, expressed his regrets. Rosellini agreed and Hatfield authorized the Washington governor to speak for him. Hatfield sent a telegram to House Republicans:

"Both parties have a moral obligation to prevent the waste of our national resources. This is a basic issue involved in the Hanford proposal. It is not a question of public vs. private power, but of power or no power. It therefore becomes a moral issue of utilizing or wasting a resource. Favorable action would assure full public and private benefits, conserve wasted energy, and enhance an important fishery resource.

"As a fellow Republican I respectfully urge your support of the Hanford proposal. Mark O. Hatfield, Governor of Oregon."

Governor Rosellini, his press secretary, Cal Johnson, and Glenn and Don took the "hoot owl" United Airlines flight from Seattle-Tacoma Airport at midnight—3 a.m. Washington, D.C., time—and the governor got little sleep.

Instead, the four of them sat up all night reviewing the Hanford situation.

Rosellini started a whirlwind pace that he kept up during the three days he was in Washington. He attended receptions, breakfasts and spent several hours in the lobby of the House meeting members. When talking to Republicans he reminded them he was speaking for Hatfield. Smiling and affable, Rosellini proved a good spokesman. But he also knew when to lash out. Interviewed by some of the capital press corps, Rosellini unleashed a stinging attack on Hanford foes calling their opposition "incredibly shortsighted and a blatant disregard of the public interest."

Other times he continually expressed optimism that the project would win "once the facts are known."

Glenn and Don began to make the rounds of the offices of Congressmen to convince them personally of the project's importance. Rep. May's office coordinated their work by setting up appointments for them. Sometimes Glenn and Don went separately, each taking a list of men they were to see. On other occasions they made the calls together.

Rep. May also prepared a "tip" sheet on the Congressmen which enabled Glenn and Don to vary their emphasis. To some Congressmen, they came down hard on the tremendous waste involved in spending millions on convertibility features and then not using them; and of the payment of millions into the federal treasury for steam that would be otherwise wasted. To others, they emphasized the defense aspects, the fact this would be the only dual purpose reactor in the Free World, whereas Russia already had *seven*. To still others, they stressed that private utilities would get one-half of the power. All of these arguments, however, were woven into each presentation.

There is a saying that it is a long road that has no turning. The besieged Hanford supporters badly needed a break, and now they got it.

Two things were on the House agenda. One was Hanford. The other was one of President Kennedy's key pieces of legislation, a $900-million Accelerated Public Works Bill, an anti-recession measure proposed by the Administration as a boost to the economy. This measure preceded the Hanford proposal before the House.

The Democrats very badly wanted passage of the Public Works Bill, particularly with the Congressional elections of 1962 coming up. Republican leadership, however, was just as vehemently opposed. Minority leader Charles Halleck felt keenly on this matter. He labeled the bill a "political slush fund for Democrats." He wanted the Kennedy bill defeated and he used all the means at his disposal to keep Republicans in line.

However, those favoring the bill were astute in winning for their side Republicans in states like Pennsylanvia, where the economy needed bolstering and where Congressmen of both parties could see the immediate benefit of Public Works programs for their districts.

When the vote came, none other than Van Zandt voted against Halleck and he carried other Pennsylvania Republicans with him. Republican opposition failed. The Public Works Bill was passed.

Halleck was furious with Van Zandt's defection. Halleck, of course, had formerly opposed the steam plant legislation but it was not as important to him as the Public Works Bill. As he pondered Van Zandt's refusal to vote as instructed, Halleck passed the word to Republicans that they were free to vote as they wished on the forthcoming Van Zandt motion to instruct the House conferees on the Hanford Bill.

Glenn and Don met with the Republican leader in an anteroom of the House. As Glenn began his plea for support, Halleck cut him short with a sly grin and the statement: "I have just circulated the word that we have no position on Hanford. My colleagues may vote as they wish."

It was a completely unexpected stroke of luck and so momentous that it took Glenn and Don a while to fully grasp the significance of what Halleck was saying. They were soon to see what it meant, however.

The floor of the House was packed as debate opened on the Hanford Bill. Holifield was floor leader and Hosmer gave him strong support. When the chair recognized Van Zandt, the Pennsylvanian was a model of self-confidence. He struck fiercely at the Bill, reminding his colleagues they had already turned it down four times. "It is no better than the last one and you must act again," he shouted.

Rep. Westland struck a telling blow when he sarcastically reminded the House of President Kennedy's inaugural statement, "Ask not what your country can do for you but what you can do for your country." And then he added, "We in the Northwest just want to spend our own money to help ourselves."

It became apparent the blows by Hanford supporters were sharper and more telling. But doubtless no one was prepared for the vote. Hanford, for the first time, was overwhelmingly supported, 246 to 148.

"It was a triumph of education," said Rep. May later. "We finally got our point across."

"Sectionalism disappeared today," added Julia Butler Hanson.

Whatever it was, 181 Democrats and 65 Republicans voted for Hanford. In July, 100 Democrats and 132 Republicans had voted against Hanford. In August, 47 Democrats and 37 Republicans had changed sides.

There was little time to savor the victory. The final vote would be September 14. Furthermore, Senator Jackson was worried that a letdown might take place. Although pleased by the House action, Jackson said it had been technically a procedural matter.

"The vote was a setback for the opposition, so you can be sure they will be working harder than ever to defeat the plan the next time around," the senator said.

There were 10 members of the conference committee, five each from the Senate and House. House members were Holifield, Hosmer, Westland, Van Zandt and Melvin Price, the Illinois Democrat. Senate members were John Pastore of

Rhode Island; Albert Gore, Tennessee; George Aiken, Vermont; Jackson and Hickenlooper, who had now become a Hanford supporter.

Glenn and Don returned home but they soon went back and began making their rounds again of House Republicans. They met many stalwarts. One was Ancher Nelson of Minnesota who had been REA Administrator under President Eisenhower. On power matters, the way he voted not only pulled Congressmen from his state, but from North and South Dakota as well. He was a natural leader and fortunately he, Glenn and Don hit it off immediately. Nelson nicknamed Glenn and Don the "Rover Boys." Other Congressmen picked up the tag.

Nelson had no particular love for public power, but he could not see the logic of the "against" forces. In the final debate, he took the floor in support of Hanford. Ancher Nelson also proved a great help to the Hanford cause.

One day, he asked Glenn how things were going. Glenn shook his head.

"Sometimes," Glenn told him, "I don't think anyone knows I'm here or what I'm doing."

Nelson smiled. "Oh, yes," he said. "Someone knows you're here and what you're doing. There's a vice president of the Northern States Power Company dogging your footsteps to put out the fires you're starting. I just had a long visit with him."

Another helpful Congressman was Clifford McIntire of Maine. McIntire had listened patiently to the presentation and was impressed. His questions were discerning, but he was puzzled why private utilities opposed the project.

"I wish you'd find out and let me know," Glenn said.

The next morning, as Glenn and Don walked to Rep. May's office, they met McIntire. He told them he had called a friend who headed a large private utility in his district to ask why private utilities would oppose Hanford. The friend didn't know, but said he knew someone in New York who could tell him. The friend then called Kinsey Robinson, who told him that private power should stand firm against Hanford. McIntire relayed this information to Rep. May. He was perturbed to hear her say that Robinson favored the steam plant in 1961 when it was a federal project. McIntire told Glenn and Don:

"They want us to take a stand that they won't take. If free enterprise ever loses in this country, all the blame can't be laid on the doorstep of the legislators."

It was a significant statement. It was also quite a piece of information. The question of what had happened to Robinson hadn't been answered. He couldn't be found in Washington, D.C., but his name kept coming up. He was somewhere and now they knew. He was pulling the strings from New York. Northwest private utilities apparently were going to die hard on the issue, if they died at all.

The first victory in five attempts gave supporters of the steam plant a tremendous psychological lift. However, it had also surprised and alarmed the project's opponents. In the two weeks before the final vote, they came alive with a vengeance. The full fury of the opposition was then revealed. The coal, private power and finally the railroad lobbies went to work in force.

Proponents of the steam plant were far outmanned, but they had one major point riding with them — defeat of Hanford was not in the national interest. To authorize the wasting of this resource would have been unthinkable.

The merits of the proposed legislation also worked against them. Private power would receive one-half of the project's benefits at Bonneville rates on a 30-year contract. Jackson's proposition had spiked them. In the final showdown, they could not adequately support their position.

When the conferees met on September 11, Van Zandt was the only member to oppose the AEC-Supply System contract. He spent only an hour with the committee, then breezed out to attend other business. Don was sitting outside the conference door and stopped Van Zandt as he left. "Has the compromise proposal lessened your opposition?" Don wanted to know.

"I heard absolutely nothing that would make me change my mind," Van Zandt said. "This is public power. We coal people are fighting for our lives. This is bread and butter for us. The whole thing is public power and a national-power grid. I will fight it as public versus private power."

Van Zandt was the only dissenter among the 10 conferees.

The *Washington Post* and the *New York Times* editorial-ized several times in favor of Hanford and now with the vote almost due *The Post* had another fine editorial. Rep. May read it and commented, "I wish it was in *The Star*, that's the paper Republicans are most influenced by."

Glenn and Don looked at each other and then hurried out, flagged a taxi and rode to the *Washington Evening Star* building. It was in mid-morning when they met with John Cline, editor of *The Star's* editorial page. Cline listened with great interest as Glenn and Don told him their story. It was Wednesday and the Hanford legislation was scheduled for debate. A Thursday editorial the next day would be too late and the press was already running on that day's edition.

Angry at themselves for not having thought of it sooner, Don and Glenn thanked Cline for his time and left. However, when they reached Rep. May's office they were told that Cline had called and left the message: "Be sure and look at our today's editorial page."

Cline had hurried and written an editorial, stopped the presses and substituted it on that day's editorial page. Titled "Last Chance in the House," the editorial read:

"The House is scheduled to vote tomorrow on a confer-ence report on the 1962 'Hanford project.' Every considera-tion of common sense dictates that the report should be approved and we hope that the House will act favorably.

"The purpose is to generate electricity with steam from the Hanford reactor—steam which otherwise would be totally wasted. The conference report contains language which meets every objection that has been raised in the

280

past. This will not be a Federal power project and it will not cost the Federal Government a dime. All risks are assumed by local groups in the area. The financial return to the Government will run from $50 million to $125 million — a break for the taxpayers. So we urge the House members to let themselves be governed by the actual language of the conference report — not by special pleaders for selfish interests."

Glenn immediately arranged to purchase 150 copies of *The Star*. The editorial page was torn out, marked, and Rep. May sent a copy by messenger to each Republican member of the House.

On September 14, a Friday, Hanford carried the House of Representatives, 186 to 150.

Everything seemed to happen to Glenn and Don that Friday. At the very moment the votes were being counted, a drama was taking place in Pasco which meant a double victory for *The Herald*. The *Columbia Basin News* announced it was going out of business.

Glenn and Don were in their hotel room rejoicing and packing for the flight home that night when I reached them by telephone with the news. Don must have asked me to repeat the message at least a hundred times. Then he put Glenn on the phone and told me to tell him. Glenn said, "Break out the champagne, we're coming home."

Tri-City civic leaders gathered at the Pasco Airport to give Glenn and Don a big welcome. The Columbians Drum and Bugle Corps with full color guard was there, too, to serenade them.

Coffee and donuts were served at the reception in the lounge, and Glenn and Don each gave a brief talk on their experiences and an assessment of what the victory meant to the area.

The honors paid to Glenn and Don did not end at the airport. In the Spring of 1963, Don was named winner of the Thomas L. Stokes Memorial Award for his articles and editorials concerning the steam plant fight. Stokes was a nationally syndicated columnist respected for his writing on the development, use and conservation of natural resources.

The contest judges wrote in part: "In his vigorous, imaginative and persistent pursuit of the public interest against long odds and entrenched opposition, Pugnetti acted in the best tradition of Tom Stokes . . . so, too, did his paper and its publisher, Glenn C. Lee, and we commend them for it."

In April, Elaine and Glenn, Don and I flew to Washington for the presentation at the Congressional Hotel. The certificate and $500 check was presented at a luncheon by J. R. Wiggins, editor of the *Washington Post* and chairman of the award committee.

In his acceptance speech Don stated: "This is a great honor and I am deeply grateful to the judges who selected me and to the Thomas L. Stokes trustees who have made this award possible on a continuing basis.

"You have paid me a tremendous tribute by this recognition of what I wrote. I feel, and I know you feel, that you have paid this tribute to the paper that I am privileged to represent, and to my publisher, Mr. Glenn C. Lee, who has earned every bit and more of the consideration that you have shown to me.

"The facts that I portrayed in my stories on the Hanford steam plant situation speak for themselves. But in order for them to speak they required a newspaper that had the integrity to print them. This, my stories had.

"We are, as has been pointed out, a small daily newspaper. But on the basis of the scope of the project that we sought to win and the makeup of the opposition which sought to kill it, I think we have again supplied proof that no voice in this land of ours is too small when raised for a righteous cause."

In September of 1963, President John F. Kennedy waved a "nuclear wand," lifting the first shovel of dirt to start construction on the Hanford steam plant.

It was a beautiful, clear, sunny September day at Hanford. The reservation was opened to the public for the first time in history and approximately 40,000 persons were on hand.

Eldon Smith flew to Montana to join the press group, traveling west with the Presidential party. His job was to see that a special edition of *The Herald* with a color photo of the President under a huge banner reading, "Welcome Mr. President," was on board Air Force One which landed at Ephrata. The Presidential party traveled the rest of the way by helicopter.

Eastern newsmen looked down on miles of arid terrain with amazement. As they crossed the Columbia River they suddenly saw the thousands of people gathered below. One newsman exclaimed, "My God! Where did they all come from!"

It was the largest turnout the President had had on his Western trip. Glenn was master of ceremonies.

President Kennedy called Hanford "a great national asset" and promised that he planned to return to Hanford when the steam plant was dedicated.

It was never to be. Two months later, he was dead.

16   *Diversification of Hanford*

THERE was joy in the Tri-Cities over the Hanford steam plant victory. There was also apprehension. For in the midst of winning it was learned that Hanford had a shaky life expectancy of 10 years or less.

From many of the contacts that Don and Glenn had made in Washington, D.C., during the steam plant campaign, information had been gleaned that America's stockpile of plutonium was growing so large, Hanford's reactors would be shut down.

This confirmed rumors that Hanford employes had been receiving from their friends in AEC headquarters.

The question was raised as to what would happen to Hanford when this occurred? No answers were forthcoming, not so much as a hint of what the time schedule might be.

Washington Public Power Supply System, however, forced the time schedule from the Atomic Energy Commission in ascertaining the cost of estimates of operating the Nuclear Reactor. The WPPSS steam plant would use waste steam from the Nuclear Reactor. When AEC no longer had use for the reactor, WPPSS would operate it just to produce steam. WPPSS needed to know how long it would be a dual purpose reactor.

Once the Washington Public Power Supply System took over the operation of the reactor as a single-purpose reactor, WPPSS would have to absorb the entire cost of operating it for steam only. To keep the cost of the power down, WPPSS would have to get as much time as possible out of its operation as a dual purpose reactor using the "waste" steam, a by-product of the fusion process.

The magic date was 1972.

You didn't have to be a nuclear expert to know what that date meant. Hanford was operating eight reactors producing plutonium. The N Reactor would be No. 9. Being the newest, it would be the last to be shut down. Between 1962 and 1972, the other eight were going to be closed, the first three in 1965. Unless something was done to diversify Hanford, there would be nothing left in 1972 but atomic relics.

One significant victory achieved in the legislation to build the steam plant was the resulting rip in the "Plutonium Curtain." The first non-federal money would be spent on the giant reservation and the first non-federal agency would have jurisdiction over an operating facility there. It wouldn't be easy. Some AEC bureaucrats would clutch frantically to preserve their little fiefdoms. The visit of President Kennedy to Hanford in 1963 to break ground for the steam plant also would be another omen. The gates of Hanford opened wide for the first time. Never again would they be so tightly closed.

So the walls of Hanford were penetrated even though AEC didn't realize what had happened. But the Tri-Cities saw the changes coming and was encouraged.

The worry over what would happen to the three cities if Hanford were shut down, was not a new one. Richland became a municipality in 1958 when, by an Act of Congress, the homes, business locations and all vacant real estate were put up for sale. Except for underlying subsidy support from AEC to the city and school district to run until 1968, the community was turned over to the people.

Any attempts to make changes at Hanford, however, had been futile. In 1961, when the possibility of a cutback seemed imminent—one of the many scares the community faced—a group of leaders, led by Bob and Sam Volpentest, approached AEC with an idea to diversify Hanford and to try and get new industry into the plant. They drew up articles of incorporation for their new venture, which they called Exo-Met Inc., short for exotic metals.

Their proposal was to lease some metal fabrication shops being phased out by AEC and operate as private enterprise. Bob was secretary-treasurer, and two former General Electric Company executives, H. A. Carlberg and W. K. MacCready, were president and chairman of the board, respectively. Volpentest, who like Bob was to have his name linked with Hanford and diversification, was vice president. Herbert Davis, Benton County prosecuting attorney, was corporate counsel.

Viewed now with the experience gained from years of the trials and tribulations of diversification, it was an ambitious but premature undertaking. The proposal was rejected by AEC, but it was a prelude of things to come.

Significantly, before Exo-Met became merely a dusty file, Sam and Bob had gone about the state on a fund-raising campaign. They contacted business executives and pointed out that nowhere else in the nation could metals of this kind be handled as they were at Hanford. They managed to gain pledges of $800,000. They proposed to lease or buy the shops, do the work for the government on a contract basis and sell the capability of special metal fabrication to food-processing plants, breweries, oil refineries and other industries requiring high-tolerance metals.

The ultimate long-range thought was that as the nuclear industry grew, there would be a mounting demand for the production of various types of metals for piping in industries and from the nuclear industry.

AEC's reception of the proposal contained all the warmth of an ice berg. AEC had only one mission at Hanford, it told Exo-Met, and that was manufacturing plutonium for the Department of Defense. In no way would they permit anything to interfere with this, or would they allow anyone from the "outside" to come in.

The proposal would have been precedent-making and a perturbed Bob wrote to Senator Jackson that if this was to remain the AEC attitude, "the opportunity to do anything to diversify or broaden the economic base at Hanford will be virtually impossible." Bob made it clear that he would not give up.

While this deliberation was going on, Glenn proposed in a speech to the Prosser Rotary Club that AEC sell Hanford. His idea raised some eyebrows but his suggestion and the attempts by Exo-Met planted the seeds from which has sprung the Hanford of today.

Selling Hanford would be no revolutionary development, Glenn said. DuPont manufactures gunpowder, Remington makes rifles, Boeing makes bombers and missiles.

"Why should not plutonium be produced by private enterprise for the federal government?" he asked. "Plutonium is the explosive in nuclear weapons.

"Twenty years have passed since we split the atom. Our same national interests of defense, security and industrial advancement in scientific fields that forced us to build the plant in the first place, places a burden upon us as a nation to open up the plant to greater use for our nation's benefit. Plutonium manufacture is no longer a one-nation secret."

Another advantage to private operation would be faster relay of scientific information learned at Hanford, to American industry. Glenn cited a statement by an AEC director who said that although Hanford was the world's greater producer of scientific information, it would take 10 years for that information to seep out to industry.

Glenn's comments moved over the *Associated Press*. They provoked considerable discussion. In a January, 1962, editorial titled "Take A New Look At Hanford," Don wrote:

"At first glance, the proposal made by Publisher Glenn C. Lee to put Hanford up for sale or lease appears to be a radical approach to the objective of diversification.

"Placed in proper perspective, however, it grows in logic.

"We have never agreed with the oft-repeated remark that only the Federal government could have pioneered the nuclear field.

"Uncle Sam went into the atomic business with a crash

program dictated by wartime conditions. It was a case of national survival.

"Naturally private enterprise couldn't have undertaken such a venture. It took billions of dollars, hundreds of thousands of people; huge chunks of land . . . brainpower, determination and frantic efforts of speed mustered together for the common defense and survival.

"America didn't move into the atomic age. It plunged headlong into it.

"But although the atomic situation has made revolutionary changes since the first chain reaction was achieved 20 years ago, our approach to Hanford has remained virtually unchanged.

"We no longer have sole possession of the atomic processes. Russia, France, and perhaps soon Red China, have nuclear capacity. The importance of atomic weapons and nuclear production and research does not need to be underscored here. That is clearly recognized.

"What isn't answered is whether a necessity continues for maintaining rigid government control of Hanford in the same manner as since the project was started . . .

"The atomic field is expanding but Hanford is standing still, anchored to aims set nearly two decades ago. So long as the plant remains under the control of the AEC with General Electric constantly in fear of a 'conflict of interest' we see no hope for diversification of Hanford.

"Without diversification of Hanford, with new industry utilizing the skills and knowledge unfolding there, we are doomed to see—incredible though it may appear—the atomic age pass Hanford by."

Whether real, imagined or merely a convenient device for doing its own thing, General Electric gave and used "conflict of interest" as an excuse for turning its back on local development. As prime contractor for the AEC at Hanford, GE officials explained they were unable to attempt any sideline to the nuclear field. At least, in the Tri-Cities.

However, GE had located an extensive operation at Vallecitos, California, where it had set up its own nuclear

288

facilities for peacetime application of what it was learning, chiefly at Hanford. From this vantage point they could "milk" Hanford of top research personnel and knowledge. Their opinion of the Hanford operation was that it was merely a production plant for the AEC. The Joint Chiefs of Staff would make a determination of how much plutonium was needed for weapons and GE at Hanford would produce it.

However, the attitude of others towards Hanford was changing. In the 1950's, such a radical suggestion as Exo-Met would never have been proposed. Neither would the idea that Hanford should be sold. Now with the hard information that Hanford could start closing up, starting in 1965, the push for diversification was intensified.

Senator Jackson had been selected as chairman of the influential Senate Interior Committee, as well as being a long-time member of the Joint Committee on Atomic Energy. Tri-City leaders had some vital questions for him to put to AEC. Some were: What will happen to Richland when the subsidy runs out or if the Hanford plant is shut or partially shut down and there is no tax base or private industry? What will the people do? What will the government do? Since Richland was no longer a company town, would it be a case of the government having "unloaded" a dead horse on the people?

The questions bothered the AEC. Prodded by Exo-Met's proposal, AEC sent out a study team headed by William Slaton of their Washington, D.C., staff. They eventually published a report—commonly referred to as the "Slaton Report"—of the one-industry town. This report promised that AEC would cooperate in local community efforts to change and diversify the area. But the community must supply the leadership.

The Slaton Report was somewhat broadly written. It may have been, in 1962, that the AEC thought it could not be pinned down on specific things as it later was to be. In its foreword, the report stated:

"It is AEC policy to extend reasonable cooperation to the

economic development efforts of communities in which AEC activities constitute the major force. In the interest of efficient performance of its programs, AEC will cooperate in broadly supported community activities directed toward the maintenance of a reasonably stable and healthful economic environment in the community. Such cooperation will not substitute for community leadership and initiative nor intrude in the management of local affairs by the elected representatives of the people."

Earlier, in a foreword, A. R. Luedcke, then general manager of AEC, emphasized the community initiative. He said:

"Industrial development of communities is not a statutory objective of AEC, but appropriate cooperation in many public affairs has been normal activities at cities where major AEC installations are located. This report, however, reflects an effort to identify specific ways in which AEC may cooperate in the industrial development of these communities . . . It is important to note that the responsibility for economic growth remains with the community. Where it can, AEC will assist, it will not take the lead."

How broadly AEC expected its wording to be interpreted no one will know. For the most part, the Slaton Report was a disappointment. Somehow, in a mere 17 pages, the Slaton Committee summed up what it considered to be the assets and the role of the AEC. It was a report not noted for specifics. Tri-City leaders had hoped for more. When they saw the results of the study they had so keenly anticipated, their spirits were low.

Probably nothing reflected this better than a letter written on November 28, 1962, by Glenn to Senator Jackson. He wrote, in part:

"We were hopeful the study and the report . . . would bear some encouragement on a possible diversification of the Hanford plant.

"It offers no encouragement to us, and I am glad that you agree on the outlook, that something must be done to get greater benefits to the area, from the nation's and our tremendous investment . . .

"I have talked long distance to some of the businessmen in Oak Ridge, Tennessee, and they have the same attitude that we have concerning this Slaton Report. It is not helpful, not encouraging, and not workable from the standpoint of the community. How can the community as such, a group of laymen, take leadership in this respect? It's impossible.

"If you can 'champion our cause' I think it will have far reaching effects. As you suggested, if the Joint Committee (on Atomic Energy) can dig into it with the Atomic Energy Commission, it will be most helpful. If you could have an independent industrial study team created to come out here, and pay a visit to the project, spend some time here, and then come up with some independent recommendations, perhaps we could make some progress.

"We sold the town of Richland to the people who live here, and perhaps we could put the entire plant up for sale for a bid by a leading American industry. They could manage plutonium for the government and then do other things for their private purposes at the plant for both production and research and development for industry.

"Now it seems like the Atomic Energy Commission is the landlord and General Electric Company is the tenant in a sort of 'captive situation,' where, if any new ideas are generated here at the plant by General Electric, they send their men with these ideas . . . down to California and develop the ideas there. Our region suffers accordingly.

"I think we need to shake up this whole situation. In your knowledge of the Atomic field, your position on the Joint Committee, and with the leadership that you have always expressed for the Hanford Project, I think you can do great and lasting good, if you will dig into this one with your usual analysis and vigor . . ."

The problem was clear enough, but how to attack it on the local level was the next hurdle the Tri-Cities had to face. The men who took up the challenge had no scientists on their team, no access to AEC files, and no permit to visit or inspect the plant. These men had lived next to Hanford for 16 years and all they really knew about it was that it produced the ingredients for Nuclear weapons.

In December of 1962, Glenn and Don happened to be in Seattle for the State PUD association convention. Wilfred Woods, publisher of the *Wenatchee Daily World*, and Don were on a panel discussing community relations, and Woods explained how the Wenatchee Industrial Council was formed to try and attract industry.

Glenn asked Woods about the financing for the organization and learned that the Chelan County PUD and the port district were included in its membership. As a non-profit organization performing services for them, these municipalities could contribute money to the council. It was a valuable piece of information Glenn filed away.

In January, 1963, Glenn made an appointment with William Allen, president of the Boeing Company, to ask if he would lend the Tri-Cities a scientist or an engineer for six months to make a study of Hanford and see how a change might be made in its operation. Allen listened, said he would think about it, and eventually declined.

"We are not interested in diversifying. We are busy making planes and profits," he said.

Glenn then went to the University of Washington with the same request. He received another negative reply, this time from Dr. Joseph McCarthy, Dean of the Graduate school.

Blocked at each turn, Glenn and Bob had many discussions as to how they could make an assessment of what facilities were behind the Hanford barricade and how they could be used to attract new industry. It was a helpless feeling, for the area's economy was largely dependent upon Hanford. Any disruption of the plant would have disastrous results, and time was running out.

There were also many conversations with Senator Jackson. He was aware of the lack of interest expressed by Boeing and the University of Washington. In casting about,

Jackson told them of a good Eastern nuclear consulting firm named Pickard, Warren and Lowe. One member of the firm, William W. Lowe, had been at Hanford as chief of the Nuclear Energy Section, from 1950 to 1954. The firm was immediately contacted and Lowe flew to the Tri-Cities, where he conferred with Bob, Glenn and Volpentest, and agreed to undertake the study. His services, however, would be $20,000.

That was too rich for the *Tri-City Herald*, which had been underwriting the expense of the steam plant fight and other efforts up to this point. Since this would be for the community, it was decided that the community should share in the cost. That was the easy decision. Trying to determine how organizations could undertake so expensive a study was more difficult. It was at this point that Glenn returned to the idea that had proven successful for Wenatchee, a non-profit corporation which would involve municipalities with a big stake in the community, access to financing, but which needed a means to involve themselves.

The Tri-City Nuclear Industrial Council grew out of this as the vehicle behind which the community could undertake the diversification of Hanford.

Formation of the Nuclear Council—nicknamed "TCNIC" in print, and "tric-nic" phonetically—was announced on the front page of *The Herald* on February 5, 1963.

Bob was elected president, and Glenn, secretary. Joe Stricker, manager of the Richland branch of Seattle-First National Bank, was treasurer; Volpentest, who would again prove himself as a tireless community worker and astute fund raiser, was made vice president.

The board of directors was a cross section of the community that rallied around the new organization. It typified the Nuclear Council's claim that it could properly speak for the community.

Directors were Mickey Cochrane, owner-manager of Huico Co., an exotic welding firm located at the Pasco Industrial Park. (Huico later was to play a major part in the welding of zirconium tubes for the steam plant); Robert Allen, manager, Old National Bank in the Tri-Cities; Larry King, representing the AFL-CIO Local Unions; Harold Kinney, Port of Benton; Ed Ray, owner of Dunning-Ray Insurance Co., Pasco; Cal Dorough, manager of Chevron Chemical at Finley; Harry Hudlow, manager, Franklin County PUD; Thomas Black, manager, Benton County PUD; Del Isaacson, manager, Port of Pasco; Lyle Beavers, manager, National Bank of Commerce; John Neuman, manager, Port of Kennewick; Mayor Joyce Kelly, City of Richland; Herbert Davis, Benton County Prosecutor, and Ralph Ecker, owner of Empire Electric Co., Pasco.

Volpentest worked full time, week after week, signing up prospects. Eventually 85 members were signed and $40,000 raised for the first year. In 1964, Volpentest went out and resold these commitments.

There were no paid employes for the Nuclear Council and there would not be any until 1970 when Volpentest retired from his banking position in Richland. He was then persuaded to work for the organization full time as a paid executive vice president. Before that time, Volpentest spent about 80 percent of his time as a volunteer for the Council.

A native of Seattle, Volpentest had spent 22 years in the wholesale grocery business before moving to Richland in 1949 with plans to open a super-market. When these plans fell through he went into the tavern business and ultimately became the owner of seven taverns throughout the area. He later sold all but one.

In 1963, he was one of the organizers of the Bank of Richland, which later merged with the Old National Bank of Spokane, with Volpentest as vice president.

Community activity was nothing new to him. He served a two-year term as president of the Richland Chamber of Commerce and his big contribution was the Federal Office Building which he was able to obtain with the push of his long-time friend, Senator Magnuson. The efforts to get the nine-story steel and concrete structure represented quite a feat.

In the beginning, however, the Nuclear Council was an awkward organization, showing all the signs of power and potential, although stepping gingerly as it took its first steps.

By the time the Council finally achieved many of its aims, it became nationally known and Hanford was secure. Then came the highest form of flattery as other communities borrowed its ideas. In 1973, the community of Idaho Falls formed a Nuclear Council and asked the Tri-City organization for its articles of incorporation.

Oak Ridge, Tennessee, also asked for the articles of incorporation.

Success, however, was far away in 1963, when the Nuclear Council began groping about, picking its way uncertainly. The money spent for Pickard, Warren and Lowe's assessment of Hanford proved to have value. A tentative list of 10 major objectives they proposed in the exploration of diversification was instrumental in aiding Senator Jackson to induce key members of the AEC to visit Hanford in March, 1963.

This group, headed by Dr. Glenn Seaborg, chairman of the AEC, set up the rules and machinery by which the local group could work with officials at Hanford. Others in the group included James Ramey, AEC Commissioner; General Luedecke, general manager of AEC; Ed Bloch, his assistant, and Lyman Fink, a vice president of General Electric Company.

The meeting proved somewhat historic, for it resulted in the establishment of three "task forces" to help study Hanford and seek to change it. A top man from AEC, Paul Holsted, and a top man from General Electric, Dr. Fred Albaugh, were assigned to work directly with TCNIC and were authorized direct communication to Washington, D.C.

For the first time in the history of Hanford, a group of local citizens had direct connections with Washington, D.C.

The Nuclear Council also was granted its request to be able to personally meet with every group of visitors that came to Hanford. This proved decisive. Before long, the major companies in America would inspect and study Hanford with a view of taking over some phase of its operation. But each successful applicant for Hanford would also have to pledge to establish a separate installation to employ local technical labor.

In the past, when representatives of a company interested in Hanford visited, citizens of the Tri-Cities had no way of knowing they were even there. Two examples were Aerojet-General and the Boeing Company. Each was interested in the tremendous expanse of land at Hanford. They were told by AEC, with little ceremony, that Hanford was a plutonium production plant and outsiders were not welcome. Having sampled that type of attitude the firms went elsewhere. One can only suspect that William Allen remembered this when he wouldn't send one of his technical men to study Hanford diversification.

An example of how overly protective and provincial Hanford AEC could be was shown over the use of the term "nuclear." James Travis, manager of Hanford operations, suggested when the Tri-City Nuclear Industrial Council was organized that it not use the term "nuclear." Travis strongly implied that an industrial council with the word "nuclear" might be infringing on the prerogatives of the Atomic Energy Commission. The matter was debated briefly but Glenn was adamant on retention of "nuclear" to identify the Tri-City organization.

The deeper TCNIC members became involved in the diversification, the more clearly they saw that if Hanford were not changed, the thin economic ice that held up the Tri-Cities would dissolve.

The first visitors were other government agencies. They came from the Defense Department, National Aeronautics and Space Administration, General Services Administration and so forth. Their purpose was to see if there was anything Hanford could do for them. Nothing monumental resulted.

After them, however, came the big companies. Their interest was more keen and their examination more intense and discerning. Among these were Dow Chemical, United

Nuclear, Westinghouse, Battelle Memorial Institute, Illinois Technical Institute, Allis-Chalmers, Martin Marietta Corp., Minnesota Mining and Montana Sulfur and Chemical.

It was not an unusual week for more than a hundred representatives of leading companies to come and investigate Hanford. Hanford proved a tremendous lure for these companies wanting to get into the nuclear industry. They wanted contracts in the program. By a mere stroke of a pen, companies that had been outside of the nuclear field could enter it full blown. So they flocked to Hanford like bees to honey.

The problem, however, was what would they do for the Tri-Cities? It had been emphasized that merely taking over a portion of Hanford wasn't enough. What they were bidding on was their ability to bring some type of facility separate and distinct from Hanford that would put our citizens to work.

Some firms like Kaiser Engineers, made extensive surveys of the Horse Heaven Hills to see if they could bring in new farmland and processing plants. Many times representatives asked Bob and Glenn: "What can we do here?"

Finding an answer proved a real problem. The Tri-Cities was rich in climate, land and water. But putting in a major diversification costing millions was a tough hurdle. Also, some of the companies were in competition with General Electric and they were concerned because GE was the prime contractor. They would be under GE supervision. These companies were hesitant to say much or to reveal much because they felt it would give too much of an insight into their operations.

General Electric was aware of this. The company had also received much criticism for failure to make any lasting contribution to the Tri-Cities. So GE took a decisive step when on January 24, 1964, it announced that it was giving up its position as sole contractor at Hanford and leaving the area.

The Herald saluted the company with a front-page

editorial titled "GE Steps Aside For Tri-Cities Benefit." It called the move an "act of statesmanship." The editorial went on:

"To diversify Hanford, to make greater use of its facilities, to build and expand the project rather than let it die by inches and by years, General Electric steps out so others may step in," the editorial glowed . . . "It will be like a 'shot of adrenalin.' An infusion of new industries will bring new ideas, new energy, new enthusiasm, and new payrolls . . ."

Behind the scenes, people wondered whether the decision was based on GE's wish to serve the community by clearing the way for new industry, or because it did not want other companies looking over its shoulder and acquiring some of its technical knowledge.

Whatever the real motive, GE's move was beneficial to the area.

The idea of having other companies locate at Hanford grew out of a meeting in Ritzville one January day in 1963 between Senator Jackson and Bob, Glenn and Sam. Jackson was on a political swing through the state and the group arranged to have breakfast with him.

They drove icy highways to Ritzville, but it was well worth the ordeal. The result of the meeting was a formula that each new company should make a tangible contribution as a price for taking over part of Hanford. Hanford would be segmented into five or six separate pieces.

United States Testing was the first company to win a contract. Battelle Memorial Institute was the second, arriving shortly after the withdrawal of General Electric. It established a separate company for Hanford, Battelle Northwest. The third company was Douglas United Nuclear, a combination of Douglas Aircraft and United Nuclear.

All three of these companies proved sincere in their efforts to follow the diversification formula. U.S. Testing took over the film badge monitoring system and other similar laboratory work. As its contribution to diversification it brought soil-testing work and employed 20 people.

To Glenn Lee
With best wishes and deep appreciation
for your loyal and continued support,

September 26, 1971

Richard Nixon

Glenn shakes hands with President Nixon when the president came to Hanford September, 1971. Governor Evans in the background, Sam Volpentest is at Glenn's left.

Battelle Northwest took over AEC's research and development work, which included biology, weather data and environmental studies. Besides taking over the laboratories formerly operated by GE, Battelle built its own laboratories. The company estimated their laboratories when completed would cost $10,000,000. They exceeded this figure by almost that amount and on January 15, 1973, announced another $6,000,000 expansion that would employ an additional 200 people.

In addition, Battelle had "spinoff" companies. Among them were a subsidiary called "Nortec" which manufactures instruments; and Automata Corp., a small electronic manufacturer. Battelle also constructed an Oceanographic Laboratory at Sequim, Washington, an office in Seattle, and a "think factory" called Battelle Research, also located in Seattle.

Douglas United Nuclear became the reactor and fuel fabrication operator. It brought to the Tri-Cities the Donald W. Douglas Laboratories and Sandvik Special Metals Co., in Kennewick. The plant manufactures zirconium tubing used in nuclear reactors.

Computer Sciences Company took over operation of all Hanford computers and also established its own Pacific Northwest computer operation.

But there were other aspects of diversification that were not for the best. Whereas companies like Battelle, Douglas United Nuclear, U.S. Testing and Computer Science lived up to their commitments without any nudging, others like International Telephone and Telegraph, required repeated prodding before they carried out their promises.

Another company, Isochem, which grew out of the combination of United States Rubber and Martin Marietta Company, took over the chemical separations plant and waste storage. The company had its contract abruptly terminated by AEC because it didn't follow through on its promise. Isochem won out over other bidders by stating it would construct a multi-million dollar isotope and encapsulation plant. The company was the only one that did not live up to its agreement. It made excuses for the continuous delays by explaining that the encapsulation plant was too many years ahead of its time and the company would not "break even" if it built such a facility.

Finally, Glenn and Volpentest met in Seattle with Senator Jackson and AEC officials to determine what was going to be done with the company. They listed their repeated attempts to hold the company to its commitment.

"What are you going to do about it?" Volpentest asked.

"We're going to kick them out," said Robert Hollingsworth, general manager for AEC.

Glenn looked at Volpentest as if to verify what he had heard.

"Do you really mean it?" Volpentest asked.

"Wait and see then," Hollingsworth answered.

They didn't have to wait long. The Commission soon showed it meant business. The action had a beneficial affect on companies like ITT, which realized it had made a very tangible commitment and that it must perform.

This giant company had bid on a contract with the Air Force to manufacture electric generators for Vietnam. A location was found in a warehouse at Big Pasco, a World War II reconsignment point operated by the Port of Pasco. The ITT attempted to make out that this represented their diversification effort. They were unsuccessful because it was a separate contract and had nothing to do with Hanford or their contract to handle support services.

It was necessary to repeatedly prod ITT. When the corporation eventually did fulfill their commitment, it was not done in the spirit of diversification, rather just to tide things over. They erected a steel prefabricated building in North Richland, one which could be amortized rapidly. They transferred an electric switch-assembly operation into it. They were not serious about doing something of a permanent nature for the Tri-Cities economy. This was underscored when their contract expired. ITT transferred the assembly operation, locked the building, and moved out.

Isochem was succeeded by Atlantic Richfield Hanford Company, which made a sizeable investment in the Tri-Cities. The company purchased the old Desert Inn hotel, tore it down and built the Hanford House in its place. The Hanford House is a resort motel that has proved a great asset. The company also established a large cattle feed lot at Pasco, and constructed a meat-packing plant at Wallula, about 10 miles southeast of Pasco. Atlantic Richfield also made contributions to the Graduate Center at Richland, enabling it to bring in a distinguished list of speakers. Like the other companies, it also has been active in community affairs.

The contractors had many problems, too. Most of them stemmed from the attitude of the Atomic Energy Commission. The diversification program started to show tangible results in 1965, but then AEC began shutting down reactors.

It always seemed that between Christmas and New Years, Hanford would face a crisis. Word would trickle down to TCNIC, and especially to Glenn and Sam, that another one or two reactors would be shut down.

"The holiday season is supposed to be a happy time," Volpentest said. "I'm getting so I dread it."

One Christmas season Glenn put through a frantic telephone call to Senator Magnuson. He reached the senator at home and Mrs. Magnuson, recognizing Glenn's voice, put the senator on the phone. But Magnuson hadn't caught the name of his caller.

"Who is this?" he asked.

"It's Glenn Lee, senator."

"Oh, good Lord," groaned Magnuson. "Not another crisis!"

Knowing the shock wave that a reactor shutdown would have, Glenn, Volpentest and Bob would try to gain time in attempts to ease the blow. Citizens knew that one day all the reactors would be closed, but TCNIC leaders believed bureaucrats in Washington, D.C., would like to get the job done quickly. The Nuclear Council harbored the fear that the game was to shut down Hanford to insure that other AEC installations could keep operating.

There were stronger loyalties, it was felt, among AEC people at headquarters toward other installations. It was estimated that 80 percent of the staff had been employed at other AEC locations, but not at Hanford.

So, from the standpoint of its position geographically and its lack of a prominent spokesman inside the AEC bureaucracy, Hanford was low man on the totem pole.

Typical of the problems and how they were faced by the Nuclear Council, was a meeting December 29, 1966, in Seattle. An unusual group had assembled in the Olympic Hotel. They were not happy over leaving home during the holidays. Present were John Conway, executive director of the Joint Committee on Atomic Energy; Ed Bloch, assistant director of AEC; Don Cole of Senator Magnuson's office; AEC Commissioner James Ramey, and Senator Jackson.

The Nuclear Council had asked Jackson for the meeting. He had delivered. When Jackson gave the "word" it was a command performance and prominent people flew to Seattle.

Glenn started the meeting by pointing out that two more reactors were due to be closed. Five reactors out of nine in a two-year period was radical surgery. He was angry.

"Not only has Richland been sold to the people, but new contractors have spent some substantial time and money to come to Hanford," Glenn said. "The great asset at Hanford is its collection of people, brain power and facilities. If diversification does not go forward, or if more reactors are shut down, the entire picture will be disrupted and the brain power previously concentrated at Hanford will be disbursed gradually."

Volpentest said it was common knowledge that former Hanford employes of GE could go back to the company and receive all the benefits they had formerly enjoyed.

"If people lose faith in Hanford, our top people will leave," he said.

Glenn drew attention to another problem.

"If diversification does not go forward, and if more reactors are closed, it will irrevocably shake the confidence of businessmen in the stability of the area, and inflict psychological damage that can never be repaired," he said.

Next came the Hanford contractors. They minced no words.

Dr. Sherwood Fawcett, managing director of Battelle Northwest, said that the laboratories Battelle was building might just as well be in Seattle or Columbus, Ohio, "if we can't tap into the pool of brain power at Hanford."

Battelle had started trying in April to get AEC to understand "in principal" some of the problems, but nothing had been done in spite of the fact Battelle went ahead in June with its construction.

Because of the AEC attitude, Battelle was withholding further construction, Fawcett said.

"The general attitude seems to be that the top people understand what diversification means. But the rank and file of the AEC's staff at Richland and at headquarters haven't found out yet," he said. "Either the Atomic Energy Commission, at all levels, must understand what diversification means, or please put us out of our misery."

Dr. Charles Harrington, head of Douglas United Nuclear, said that he was very anxious for diversification to succeed since that was the heart of Hanford's continued existence as a nuclear center. He was concerned by the morale problem. He had recently talked to 40 people who were operating the N Reactor. They had but a single thought: What will happen on June 30, 1967? Should they stay and work for Douglas United Nuclear at the reactor, or, should they transfer back to General Electric?

Harrington estimated it would take five years to get momentum going via diversification. Rumors and unrest could be disastrous for morale. The truly good technical people would go, and the poor ones would stay. Large numbers of people would displace themselves under the wrong conditions. Diversification would be a complete failure.

Douglas Laboratories was used as another example of AEC Bureaucratic hamstringing. It required a year for Douglas to use the AEC Laboratory. When Douglas finally did get permission, there were strings attached to it.

"My people were not permitted to take notes of the material they were reading, and, every time they used the library, they had to be monitored," said Dr. Willard Matheson, director of Douglas Laboratories. "Obviously, they couldn't do anything so extreme as checking out materials from the library. Douglas was given the impression we could use all of the facilities at Hanford and thus it was an attractive proposition for us to come to Hanford and to invest in our own laboratory."

Douglas wanted to get some of their people oriented and to get them involved early. They wanted to transfer programs to Hanford, have access to the nuclear area, and to put two chemists to work.

"The answer was 'no,' " he said. "We were told we would have to relinquish all patent rights, and about all we would be getting was some floor space and some janitorial services!"

The problem, as Dr. Matheson described it, was that he couldn't get any action out of AEC.

Arthur Speckhard, manager of Computer Science Corporation, said, "AEC's attitude is wrong. The experiment at Hanford took a lot of courage by the contractors and by the commission's top level people. But this spirit of diversification has been lost by the Atomic Energy Commission. The whole situation is running out of gas."

Senator Jackson was concerned. "It would be an absolute tragedy and a terrible indictment if diversification at Hanford is not a success," he said. "You must make a top level policy directive that this situation must be worked out. Diversification must work and no part of the mission can be aborted."

The comments fell on fertile ground. Commissioner Ramey agreed there must be a long-range definitive policy concerning the general outlook for diversification. He agreed that the policy must be more concrete, and that the message must get down to the rank and file.

He suggested regular meetings every six months to check signals.

Conway agreed the government must meet its commitments. He recognized there were problems of communications between headquarters and Hanford, and promised the Joint Committee would watch the program more closely.

Jackson had asked for figures on the total number of workers on reactors. These showed there were 1,800 people on five reactors. But a reduction in one reactor would touch off other reductions along the line. He estimated there would be a loss of 350 people for every reactor closed.

What worried him, he emphasized, was that the good people would leave first. They would probably transfer back to GE. The poor ones would stay.

The problem was that diversification had to work. It was Hanford's only hope. Glenn pointed this out again in 1969 in another unusual meeting in Washington, D.C., before the full Commission and all top AEC administration. The Tri-Cities presentation was made by Glenn and Volpentest. Don kept notes of what each participant had to say and what the conclusions were as he saw them.

At stake was the C reactor and the equivalent of one K reactor. There were two K reactors at Hanford. The proposal was to operate each K half time. The schedule for closing the C reactor would mean that some 250 to 300 jobs would be eliminated. But because of TCNIC, another 200 to 300 Hanford jobs were saved.

Hanford's first reactor had gone down in December, 1964; the second in May, 1965; the third in June, 1965; the fourth in June, 1967; and the fifth in January, 1968.

The end for Hanford as a production plant was near and the Nuclear Council was desperately trying to buy time to give diversification a chance to work.

On that February day in 1969 when Glenn and Sam faced the AEC, however, things were grim.

"The commission has spent many thousands of dollars preparing studies, making reports, sending other government agencies to Hanford to see what could be done with diversification; but when it is all added up, not very much has occurred," Glenn said.

"The reports are gathering dust and they all seem to have reached the same conclusion, that Hanford has no raw materials, is isolated, has high labor costs and management problems. Hanford has received wonderful publicity in Seattle, Portland, Spokane, *The Wall Street Journal, Business Week, Nucleonic's Week, Nuclear Industry* and many other publications and on national television. Hanford has been held up as a model of achievement and success. But where do we go from here?"

"You are a very eloquent spokesman for Hanford," said Dr. Glenn Seaborg, commission chairman. "I do not think the situation is so grim, however. I think many positive things have resulted, and I feel more will occur."

"If you examine it more closely," Glenn Lee said, "it isn't too healthy. When you shut down two more reactors, sooner or later corporations responsible for Hanford contracts are going to take a second look. The possibility exists that they will either pull out of Hanford when their contracts are up, or, they will not build and expand. So, we may well end up with one operator at Hanford in a few years, except instead of General Electric, it would be Battelle."

Glenn and Sam called on Rep. May, Senator Magnuson, Rep. Chet Holifield, and Don had a long discussion with Craig Hosmer, now ranking Republican on the Joint Committee.

Jackson was strong with the White House, for President Nixon had asked him to be Secretary of Defense. He had been to the White House, Bureau of Budget and the AEC and he was the one to announce the continuance of the K reactors. Only the C would be shut down.

The cheers of 1969 were short-lived. In 1970, the fight was on again. The time that TCNIC had purchased with its efforts was gone too soon. Word was being circulated that both K reactors would be closed.

Late in February, Glenn, who appealed to Governor Evans for help, met the governor at Seattle-Tacoma Airport and they flew to Washington. Glenn briefed the governor and, once on the ground, their schedule was jammed.

Two key meetings were with Robert P. Mayo, director of the Bureau of Budget, and John Erlichman, director of Domestic Affairs for the President. Governor Evans and Glenn urged that no more reactors be closed until new programs could be instituted, either by AEC or in the private sector, to create new employment and thus prevent economic disaster in the community.

There had been rumors that both K reactors would shut down. As a result of their trip, only one K went down. By June, all of the reactor staff had been laid off.

That left only one K and the N reactor operating as 1971 approached. Reactors, of course, were only part of the picture. As they went down, the supporting services began to dry up. At stake, therefore, would be thousands of jobs and the future of Hanford.

The Tri-Cities seemed to get one psychological jolt after another. The jolts were more frequent, yet the area was gaining both strength and momentum. Diversification was taking root.

No one, however, was prepared for the greatest jolt of all —the announcement in January, 1971, that not only the last K but also the N reactor would be closed!

There hadn't been a suspicion, not a hint, that the N reactor would be shut down.

"They can't do that, we have a contract," Owen Hurd exclaimed when he heard the news.

Contract or not, the order was out. The N reactor was to go down.

It doesn't seem possible there could be a love affair between a community and a nuclear reactor! Yet the awesome mass of concrete, lead and steel far out in the desert held a special place in the hearts of Tri-City people. They had followed the successful campaign in Congress to make it a dual purpose reactor.

But that was in 1962. Now it was 1971, and the Tri-Cities had to go to those in Washington, D.C., and fight for it again.

The three cities pulled together for their common goal. Everyone was involved; granges, clubs, lodges, civic organizations, municipalities, schools—school children flooded the White House with letters—labor unions, and individuals.

The Herald published the AEC's formal closure announcement on January 29, 1971, and blood pressures went even higher:

"The Atomic Energy Commission will immediately shut down and place in standby the two remaining plutonium reactors at its Hanford plant near Richland. The decision to shut down these reactors was made following an examination of requirements for reactor products," AEC announced.

"Some associated facilities at the plant also will be closed and about 1200 Hanford contractor employees will be terminated by June 30, 1971.

"The three heavy water production reactors remaining in operation at the AEC's Savannah River plant are more versatile than graphite moderated reactors at Richland for the production of the various military and non-military reactor products for which requirements have been defined.

"The production capacity of these three reactors is sufficient to meet established requirements. Consequently, no funds have been provided for operation of the 'KE' and 'N' reactors in the fiscal year beginning July 1, 1971."

One puzzling question was why, since the reactor would be taken over by WPPSS, would AEC seek to close it? The reason, it was learned, was that AEC hadn't made the ruling to close the reactor. It was made by the Bureau of Budget, a department under the Nixon Administration.

The question also arose of what would happen to the

steam plant? Without a power source it seemed destined to become like a giant dinosaur, alone in the desert.

Some changes had taken place in the nine years since the steam plant campaign. The steam plant was producing 800,000 kilowatts of badly needed power, of which private power firms received half. This time, private power lined up with public power to battle *for* the reactor.

The three cities urged everyone to write to the President. A community-wide committee, headed by G. E. Bauer, was organized to send 50,000 letters. A huge facsimile of a letter to the President was put together and got as far as the White House before it was intercepted.

The State Legislature was in session and it passed resolutions condemning the closure. But despite the public outcry, the N reactor was closed before the end of the month.

Governor Evans formed what he called the Governor's Task Force and went to Washington.

The Nuclear Council was represented by Ray Dickeman, general manager of Exxon Nuclear and former Hanford manager for GE. Others on the Task Force were:

State Senator Dan Jolly and Representative Stewart Bledsoe, who represented the Legislature; Richard W. Shaffer, Kennewick, representing International Brotherhood of Electrical Workers, Local 77, and the State Labor Council; Ralph Davis, president, Puget Sound Power and Light Company, representing private power companies; Owen Hurd, representing WPPSS; Dr. Oswald Greager, former Hanford scientist and chairman of the State Thermal Power Plant Site Evaluation Council; Dan Ward, director of the State Department of Commerce and Economic Development; John McCurry, deputy director of the State Office of Program Planning and Fiscal Management; H. Dwayne Kreaker, economist and former director of the State Department of Commerce and Economic Development, and Ken Billington, managing director of the State PUD Association.

The Task Force operated in two ways. One, as a unit, meeting together with White House officials. The other, spreading out, to individually make calls to gather support. Governor Evans spent 40 minutes in closed session with President Nixon. "With that much time with the President, I had an excellent opportunity to express our concern about the closure as well as explain the details of our proposal," he said.

The proposal that the governor mentioned was a proposition to pay up to $15,000,000 a year for steam from the N reactor in return for an agreement that AEC would operate it as a dual-purpose reactor. The money would come from WPPSS.

Governor Evans was successful. The N reactor was soon back on the line.

As a reward for their efforts in regards to Hanford and nuclear energy, the founders of the Nuclear Council had the satisfaction in November, 1972, of receiving the Allied-Gulf Nuclear Services award for "significant contributions to public understanding of nuclear energy."

The citation commended TCNIC "for its pioneering efforts in encouraging public acceptance of nuclear power both in the Tri-Cities and abroad.

"Through its widely diverse programs it has informed its own area, the nation and the world about the benefits of peaceful uses of nuclear energy."

The presentation was made jointly to Bob and Sam Volpentest in Washington, D.C., at a meeting of the Atomic Industrial Forum, a non-profit association of business, professional, education, labor and government organizations concerned with peaceful uses of nuclear energy.

"There could, in my judgment, be no more deserving recipient of the Forum Award than the Tri-City Nuclear Industrial Council," Senator Jackson said.

Bob told the crowd present: "The most important ingredient that made this (award) possible, was the community cooperation and the acceptance of our objectives.

"Our membership, representing business, labor, financial institutions, public and private utilities and professional organizations, was a complete cross-section of our area and played a major role.

"This citation is the culmination of 10 years of effort, representing close cooperation and understanding by our elected leaders in state and federal government and the Atomic Energy Commission."

At present, TCNIC has over 130 members, including small businesses, corporations and labor unions. Its promotional activities don't conflict with those of other agencies.

Its activities have ranged from encouraging the Washington Public Power Supply System to build nuclear plants at Hanford, where environmentalists and the general public would approve, to support of warm water irrigation studies and a bill by Senator Magnuson to create a one-stop siting agency for federal nuclear-siting approval. This agency would be similar to the nuclear siting committee originated by TCNIC and passed by the State Legislature.

Other activities include: participation in nuclear trade fairs; planning a Hanford nuclear park; providing testimony before government agencies and commissions, and working with civic groups.

The Nuclear Council celebrated its tenth anniversary on April 19, 1973, with a widely attended dinner at the Hanford House. The theme was, "Miracle in the Desert 1963-73." The four guests of honor—to whom credit for much of the Council's success is due—were Senators Magnuson and Jackson, Governor Evans and Commissioner Ramey.

The driving force behind the Tri-City Nuclear Industrial Council has been the management of the *Tri-City Herald* and Sam Volpentest. Without *The Herald*, the council may not have survived, or, as a matter of fact, it might not have begun.

On the other hand, even with *The Herald's* active

participation, it would not have been a success without the community support. This support has been constant.

Because of the Nuclear Council's success, the economic growth of the Tri-Cities is assured and the *Tri-City Herald* has become the successful newspaper it is today. The two go hand in hand.

President Kennedy said it so well, that sunny September day in 1963, at Hanford:

"A rising tide lifts all the boats."

17   *Good Roads For The Tri-Cities*

DON WAS "all ears" as Glenn described his proposed route from the Tri-Cities to Seattle on a piece of copy paper.

Little by little, the route unfolded. By a mixture of county roads and secondary state highways, Glenn's route inched up the paper towards four crossed lines labeled, "Othello."

"Right here. This is where it is," Glenn said, tapping the paper with his pencil.

Horizontally across the paper, to another set of cross lines labeled, "Vantage," was a heavy straight line.

"That's the highway," Glenn said. "Straight as an arrow."

Don's brow furrowed. "Are you sure? Are you *really* sure?" he asked.

"Hell, yes," Glenn exclaimed. "The guy from the Highway Department just came over it. He told me all about it."

Don looked at me. "What do you think, honey?" he asked. "Should we try it?"

I sensed I really had no choice, not if I intended to reach Seattle in the family car. I was looking forward to a visit in Seattle, but not to the trip. It was August, 1955, and the temperature was a hundred degrees. That was before air conditioners became standard equipment in most Tri-City cars.

"We'll take some extra ice water and I'll put in an extra five gallons of gas," Don said.

Strangely though, whenever I think back on that trip I

can't recall the heat or the dust, only the great thrill we experienced as we breezed along, all alone, over a brand new highway.

It is listed as Highway 26 on state road maps, and it is the main route from the Puget Sound country to the Columbia Basin and to Washington State University. But in 1955, it was to be a farm-to-market highway for Columbia Basin agriculture and its designation was concealed because the bridge over the main irrigation canal at Othello was not completed.

I carefully kept a log on that first trip, noting the mileage (10 miles between bends in the road) and the driving time. We described it to Glenn with great enthusiasm, and he wrote an equally enthusiastic front page report in his column, "The Way I See It." The column stirred much interest in the Tri-Cities. It also received a reaction—an angry one—in Yakima. In their eyes, Glenn had done a treasonable thing. He had encouraged motorists to bypass their town. The *Yakima Daily Republic* printed an editorial on August 12, 1955, titled "Glenn Lee, Pioneer." Glenn framed it and it still hangs proudly from his office wall. The words read:

"The intrepid Glenn Lee, publisher of the *Tri-City Herald*, having braved the blistering sun and having survived a trek by auto along the back roads north and west of Eltopia to Vantage, advises his readers to do likewise when they travel between the Tri-Cities and Seattle. He says the route is longer than the route through the Yakima Valley and the road markers are few, but suggests that someday it will be "THE" route for his people.

" 'You can miss the traffic in the lower Yakima Valley, miss the Ellensburg Canyon, and save a half hour's driving time,' he writes. But he also suggests that if you take his favorite route you can also miss your way, unless you stop at Mesa to ask questions and unless you have a good sense of direction.

" 'Now, when a person gets into Yakima,' he says, 'it takes a long time and a good deal of careful driving to get through Yakima. On this new route you eliminate Yakima altogether.'

"We suspect that is his real goal—the elimination of Yakima. Yakima, however, is here to stay. It is not hard to drive through and will be easier when the state builds its freeway—a project which must irk Lee almost as much as the Wahluke Slope road, which soon will give Yakima access to the lower Columbia Basin which Lee seeks to pioneer for Pasco, Richland and Kennewick. Mr. Lee is also pioneering the so-called North-South highway, which will shoot Basin people right into the Tri-Cities. This is a worthwhile project which should be built as the Basin grows, but it will not be the only highway serving the Basin folks.

"There isn't much traffic on Eltopia-Mesa-Vantage desert route, and of course, no trucks, and it may be that one can save a half-hour. But there are good reasons why there isn't any traffic, the main one being that no one wants to go that way.

"Just the same, Yakima people should be aware of what our friend in the Tri-Cities is saying about us. It should spur us to get the Yakima Valley route widened sooner than is now projected and to stay at the job of smoothing the traffic flow through out city."

Yakima's furor only made the *Tri-City Herald* more enthusiastic in promoting the new route. The next step for Glenn was to escort a delegation of officials from the three cities over it. On that trip, Don and Dick Galbraith carried a step ladder in a station wagon. At convenient intervals, they stopped to post direction markers. The signs were printed in *The Herald* commercial shop and read, "To Ellensburg." They carried an arrow, below which was printed in smaller type, "Compliments of the *Tri-City Herald.*"

Don and Dick used the step ladder to make sure the signs were nailed high enough so they could not be torn down by employes of the rival *Columbia Basin News.*

Occasionally this was accomplished by *The News,* which

had dubbed the route the "Glenn Lee Highway." On one trip, I noted, just south of Othello, one of *The Herald* signs lying in the dirt. Beside it, on a post, was a rural newspaper box belonging to *The News*. In anger, I reciprocated by pushing it over.

Eventually, the signs were either torn down by *Columbia Basin News* staffers or others, or they deteriorated in the weather. By this time, the route was well traveled by motorists from the Tri-Cities and Walla Walla going to Seattle. Road improvements further increased the flow of traffic on the "Glenn Lee Highway."

From the time of its inception *The Herald* has campaigned for highway projects and good roads. The first state writing award that Don received was for an editorial decrying the inadequacy of the Old Pasco-Kennewick bridge, at that time the only link between the two communities and a nightmare to travel. That was in 1948, before *The Herald* had celebrated its first birthday.

The problem with highways in the Tri-Cities was that there really weren't any. The main traffic artery was old Highway 410, which rambled leisurely from Yakima through the Yakima Valley, through the Tri-Cities to Walla Walla. The highway had been adequate before World War II because there weren't many people around to drive it. With the post-war population surge, the old highway bulged and the accident rate grew. Traffic became so heavy that at least 30 minutes had to be allowed to drive from Pasco to the Richland Y—the turnoff at which you departed Highway 410 for Richland. Today, a few minutes is adequate.

A drive between the Tri-Cities and Seattle in the old days was tiresome and required six hours. There was only one route and it was a heavily traveled two-lane highway with an abundance of trucks and trailers.

When Don and I first arrived from Seattle we had to drive a long, circuitous route from Ellensburg through the Ellensburg Canyon; through the Yakima Valley; down the main streets of no less than seven communities, before we broke over the last hill and saw Richland, Kennewick and Pasco spread out before us.

As time passed, a highway, dubbed the "Track Route"— because it paralleled the Northern Pacific Railway tracks— was improved. It was the straightest highway from Yakima to Prosser, and the fastest. It was also two lanes, however, and cluttered with trucks.

So, highway travel was a frustration to Tri-City residents. Highways were either woefully inadequate or nonexistent.

The *Yakima Republic* editorial that chided Glenn contained more truth than perhaps the writer realized. Yakima would have an Interstate freeway that would bypass the city; Yakima was going to get an east-west road into the Columbia Basin project; the North-South Highway from Pasco into the Basin was a long ways in the future; and, the Wahluke Slope, which peered into the Hanford plant and was contiguous to the Tri-Cities, would be connected to Yakima many years before the Tri-Cities would have access to it.

In brief, Yakima was organized and its leaders had a talent for getting things done. Of course, Yakima was an established community. The Tri-Cities were three small towns working independently of each other.

Time and again, Don would mutter, "We lack muscle" as he watched highway dollars slipping away to other cities. The Tri-Cities were not unified. They couldn't compete with other regions when the State Highway Department was deciding what projects should get top priority.

Pasco realtor Wendell Brown and J. C. Pratt, Benton County Assessor, were the "roads men" for the Tri-Cities. They represented Franklin and Benton Counties, but Brown had little influence on the Benton County side of the river, and Pratt likewise on the Franklin County side. Brown served as president of the Washington State Good Roads Association in 1957. In the Legislature, he worked with Representative O. H. (Ole) Olson of Pasco. Olson was a power in the Legislature, but was not on any highway committee. However, he was able to trade favors, and tried to get a share in the highway priorities.

This ended in 1956, when Olson died of cancer. Don has always felt that Olson made some deals on highways for the Tri-Cities which, after his death, were not honored. The area was left with little representation. Its roads progress continued to lag.

The turning point really came in November, 1962, just prior to the 1963 Legislative Session. State Senator Mike McCormack of Richland, called a meeting of Tri-City leaders. Its purpose was to decide road priorities for Benton and Franklin Counties for the state budget.

Don carefully studied those who attended. He knew them all, but he was bothered by the atmosphere of distrust that surrounded the meeting. Each community was sure one of the others was trying to get a larger slice of the "pie" at its expense.

"I'm reasonably sure I can get us one good highway project," McCormack said. "What shall it be? Can we agree on one?"

"What have you got in mind for it, Mike?" Wendell Brown asked.

"I haven't anything in mind," McCormack replied. "I want this group to decide and then tell me."

"Why not each city establish its priority, and you take three to Olympia? Mayor Joyce Kelly of Richland asked.

"I don't want three. I just want one," McCormack answered. "I could pick three myself."

"Oh," said Brown. "Have you already decided on them, Mike? What about Pasco? Where did you put us?"

"I didn't place you anywhere," McCormack answered angrily. "That's why we're here. I want the three cities to decide."

And so it went, like an unfriendly poker game, with each player sure either the dealer was crooked or the cards were stacked. Then Don noticed that the community representatives were seated together. Richland was with Richland, Kennewick with Kennewick, and so on.

Worse yet, they couldn't decide on a project. They named three, one for each community. Then they argued over how they would be listed for fear the one at the top might get the highest priority.

When Don told Glenn about the meeting, he said, "We've got to have something better than that. We've got to come up with some vehicle that can speak for all three communities."

"What have you got in mind?" Glenn asked.

"I'm not sure, myself. Some type of organization that represents both counties. Something with enough muscle to spell out a program and make it stick."

"Yakima has one that has a representative from each chamber of commerce from Ellensburg to Goldendale," Glenn said.

"That may work up there, but it won't work down here," Don said. "You should have been there today and felt the tension. I knew things were bad, but I never dreamed they were that bad."

There was another highway battle raging in the Tri-Cities during 1962. It concerned Interstate Highway 82. At long last, there was a chance the area might get a four-laned highway to Puget Sound.

The proposed interstate ran from Ellensburg to Pendleton, Oregon. Its purpose was to link up two other interstate highways, I-90 from Seattle to Spokane, and I-80 from Portland to Pendleton. But Interstate 82 missed the Tri-Cities and went far to the west, beyond Prosser to the Columbia River. Then, to add insult to injury, it followed the river east in southern Benton County.

The Tri-Cities was furious over a much needed highway being 25 miles away, in a remote part of their counties. Another study was ordered and a hearing held in Prosser to try and change the interstate. The idea was for the interstate to come as far as Kennewick and then veer south to Umatilla, Oregon.

The state tried to compromise and succeeded in making nobody happy. It brought the interestate almost to Prosser, then routed it over the Horse Heaven Hills to Umatilla. It was closer than before but now the wheat farmers were mad.

"We couldn't come any closer to the Tri-Cities because we didn't have enough interstate mileage," said Ernest L. Cowell, chairman of the highway commission.

The Federal Government funds 90 percent of interstate highways, so it has a say in how many miles are set aside for each project. Cowell was correct. Only 125 miles had been allocated to Interstate 82. It couldn't reach the Tri-Cities!

Formation of the Tri-City Nuclear Industrial Council gave a major impetus to the Roads Association that Don was formulating. For the first time, segments of the three communities were welded together. Each city is fiercely independent. But when there is a challenge from the outside, they immediately band together. The Hanford Steam Plant campaign broke the ice and helped unite them. The threat to Hanford really pulled them together.

Now came the Benton-Franklin Counties Good Roads Association.

It was an awkward sounding name, but the title also told the story. Don's idea was so simple he wondered why it had taken him so long to figure it out. There would be 16 members. Each City Council and each Chamber of Commerce would have a representative. Each board of County Commissioners would have a representative, and the Tri-City Nuclear Industrial Council would have one.

Benton County cities would be Prosser, Benton City, Richland and Kennewick. Each would have two representatives. Franklin County cities included Connell, Mesa and Pasco, but there were only five representatives because little Mesa didn't have a Chamber of Commerce.

Immediately, there was a stir in Pasco. Franklin County

would be outnumbered. A Pasco delegation went to Don's office. They wanted more representation.

"Numbers aren't important," Don told them. "What we need is a good program and unity. One guy could do it by himself, if everybody was behind him."

It wasn't that easy. Franklin County feared that larger Benton County would get all or most of the Tri-City road funds.

"Look at it this way," Don finally said. "You talk about losing road projects. What projects? We don't have any, and we don't because Yakima plays one city against another or one county against another. If you want to see highways, go to Yakima. What do you have to lose by this roads association? We haven't been getting anything but bare bones anyway."

The first few meetings of the Roads Association were almost a replay of McCormack's meeting. There were suspicious glances, and each proposal was carefully scrutinized to insure it didn't have some hidden meaning tucked away.

Delegates were to vote on an executive board, with three members from each county. It was suggested that each county caucus and they did, but in opposite corners of the room with voices lowered. Then, all delegates voted on a president. Don was the unanimous choice.

"Sometimes I feel like a lion tamer going into a cage," Don said. "I almost feel undressed without a whip and a pistol."

Initial suspicions quickly began to subside as the Roads Association began appearing before Legislative Committees, the State Highway Department and the Highway Commission. Slowly, recognition that the area needed to fight for a good roads program sunk in.

Regular meetings also helped. Members soon were on a first-name basis. They became acquainted with the highway needs of the two counties.

The greatest unifying force, however, was Interstate 82.

The political clout of Washington Senator Warren G. Magnuson repeatedly demonstrated itself as the senator assisted efforts of the region to place itself on an Interstate Highway.

President Kennedy addressing crowd gathered for the ground-breaking of nuclear steam plant, September, 1963. 40,000 attended.

Yakima fanned the flames by vigorously rejecting any suggestion for another study to determine if I-82 couldn't be turned to the Tri-Cities.

"It has been decided," said Howard Peterson, president of South Central Washington Roads Association. "You are just going to delay it or to lose it altogether."

Then Don learned Yakima had met secretly with Pendleton and discussed strategy to keep the interstate from the Tri-Cities. This further inflamed the Tri-Cities.

At the height of the controversy, Glenn, Don and Sam Volpentest flew to Washington, D.C., to consult with Senator Magnuson. Volpentest was the Nuclear Council's representative to the Roads Association. He was also its treasurer.

A memo Glenn made of the meeting, dated July 27, 1964, gives a good account of what transpired:

"Upon arriving in Washington, D.C., Sam, Don and I met with Fred Lordan (Magnuson's administrative assistant) concerning the Interstate Highway situation. Fred made an appointment with Clarence D. Martin, Jr., Under-Secretary of Commerce for Transportation, and we went to see him immediately.

"A few minutes after we arrived Mr. Bridwell and Mr. Zwick of the Bureau of Public Roads came into the office.

"We explained the situation concerning the request of the Tri-Cities to have the Interstate route go through this area and that we had expressed our views to the Washington State Highway Commission. We also told Mr. Martin it was our understanding that the Washington State Highway Commission had made a request to the Bureau of Public Roads that the Tri-City route be approved.

"Mr. Bridwell and Mr. Zwick stated that the Commission had not recommended anything; they had just made a preliminary request for additional information. They have appraised the Bureau of Public Roads that the Washington Highway Department does not wish to do any additional

325

work or spend any additional money unless this change of route would be accepted.

"An additional 20 miles would have to be added, and they stated that the extra miles are not available."

The Bureau's decision remained unchanged. Don, Glenn and Sam returned to Senator Magnuson and carefully went over the entire situation with him again. They penciled the route, plus some alternate proposals, on a Washington State highway map and left it with the senator.

The memo went on to say:

"On arrival home, Don called Ernie Cowell (Highway Commission Chairman). Cowell informed him that a letter had been received from the Bureau of Public Roads, denying extra mileage for the change through the Tri-Cities and the story was scheduled to be released on Monday, July 27.

"Don called Fred Lordan in Washington, D.C., on Saturday night, July 25. Lordan authorized Don to make another call to Cowell and tell him that Senator Magnuson had intervened in this matter; that no story on this matter was to be released on July 27."

So, as he had done so many times in the past, Senator Magnuson again assisted the Tri-Cities. As chairman of the powerful Senate Commerce Committee which controls the Department of Commerce, which in turn controls the U.S. Department of Transportation, Magnuson was able to arrange for an independent firm to make a survey to determine the validity of the Tri-Cities proposal.

The firm was Transportation Consultants, Inc., based in Washington, D.C. Its representatives traveled to the region and surveyed the problem. Their recommendation contained the following:

"Efforts should be directed towards attempting to gain approval from the Bureau of Public Roads to locate Interstate 82 from Prosser to the Tri-City area to Wallula to Pendleton. If Interstate 82 is constructed across the Horse Heaven Hills as planned, the State of Washington must undertake its maintenance upon completion and, in addition, must undertake the construction and maintenance of a similar facility from Prosser to the Tri-City area into Walla Walla.

"Therefore, the state's interest lies in using I-82 to serve the Tri-City-Walla Walla area to the extent possible and a net reduction in the state's maintenance costs by not having to maintain an expensive facility across a sparsely populated Horse Heaven Hills."

Senator Magnuson had stressed that he didn't want the three communities to quarrel among themselves over just where the Interstate would pass through the Tri-Cities. They assured him the area would abide by the engineer's decision.

Now a second study was made, this time sponsored by Oregon and Washington, to see if the interstate could be justified by more exhaustive studies.

Two separate firms were given the job. They did it jointly and the next year, the Gray-Osborne-Lochner Report was made public. One firm, Gray and Osborne, was based in Washington State. The other, H. W. Lochner, was from Chicago.

They recommended bringing the interstate from Prosser to the Tri-Cities, crossing the Columbia River in the vicinity of Richland, going north and east of Pasco and, entering Oregon by way of Van Sycle Canyon, joining Interstate 80 just west of Pendleton.

Washington Director of Highways Charles Prahl announced with elation the findings in October, 1966. "I am hopeful construction can be started within two years," Prahl said. Such was not to be, however. As it turned out, no work was done on the interstate until 1972, when ground was broken on the Oregon Street Interchange near Pasco.

Although Interstate 82 soaked up most of the spare time of the Roads Association and made many demands on the organization's energies, there were other highway projects to be built. Unified, the Tri-Cities began making tremendous strides in getting them done.

The bypass highway—U.S. Highway 12—around Pasco was four-laned, and overpasses and interchanges constructed at Sylvester Street, Court Street, Chase Street and Fourth Avenue.

Highway 14 from Kennewick across the Horse Heaven Hills to the Umatilla Bridge was realigned and rebuilt.

The Association helped break the deadlock between the Bureau of Reclamation and the Corps of Engineers on a wasteway that was holding up construction of an overpass at Mesa. As a result, the overpass and a bypass of Mesa was constructed, eliminating a railroad crossing that had killed eight persons in five years.

The Highway 260 overpass and bypass of Connell was constructed, and Highway 260 in the vicinity of Kahlo'us was realigned and improved.

Another project was the linking of Highway 240 from Horn Rapids to Richland.

There were numerous other projects the Roads Association was able to have built. Two giant interchanges under construction when Don and I moved to Tacoma in 1973, were those at Oregon Street in Pasco—the intersection of Highway 395 and U.S. 12—and at Benton City on U.S. 12.

Both projects will be a part of the interstate after it is built. Altogether, more than $30,000,000 was spent on highway projects in Benton and Franklin Counties during the Roads Association's first nine years.

One of Don's pet expressions is, "It's a long road that has no turning," and it is quite appropriate when applied to highways. In the case of Interstate 82, there were times when he wondered if it would ever be built.

After years of battling Yakima and Pendleton over where it would go, in 1970 the new National Environmental Protection Act came up with some new foes, many of them in the Tri-Cities.

Some of these "environmentalists" owned property that

was either in the path of the Interstate or near it. Others owned property that wasn't near the Interstate, so they wanted the highway closer to their property.

It would be incorrect to claim all opponents were motivated by selfish financial interest. Many opposed the highway because they were against further accommodation of the automobile.

The Interstate route through the Yakima Valley and across the Columbia and Snake Rivers in the Tri-Cities has remained under attack. The environmental group joined with Oregon in opposing the Interstate going into Oregon by way of Wallula.

Now leadership supplied by the *Tri-City Herald*, the Nuclear Council and the Roads Association is waging the interstate campaign.

One truly unfortunate thing has occurred because of the delays. Don and I experienced it when we left the Tri-Cities for Tacoma. More than 25 years had passed since we drove the two-lane highway through the Yakima Valley to reach the Tri-Cities. That was in 1947.

For sentimental reasons, we drove through the Yakima Valley and realized we were driving on the same old two-lane highway.

That just doesn't make good sense.

18   *160 Acres*

L AND, SUN and water. Those are the great assets of the Tri-Cities. But late in 1969, word trickled into Glenn's office that the U.S. Department of Interior would permit a farmer to pump only the amount of water necessary to irrigate 160 acres! That decision, if permitted to stand, would have ended private irrigation development.

The years 1969 and 1970, were not vintage years for the Tri-Cities, though they should have been. First of all, Columbia Center, the huge shopping area between Kenne- wick and Richland, opened its doors that Summer and Fall. It meant new accounts and new advertising lineage for *The Herald*. But it also capsized many smaller "mom and dad" stores that operated on a marginal basis in the three cities.

Columbia Center also displaced the retail shopping areas of the Tri-Cities, particularly Pasco and Kennewick. Main- stays, like J. C. Penney stores, for example, operated a store in each community. Now the company had merged them into one giant store in the new shopping area.

So there were both bright and dull spots, the latter caused chiefly by the abrupt displacement of business houses when the new shopping area opened.

Many good things were on the horizon for Hanford, although at the time, there appeared to be as much activity as one would expect to find at a swamp. The busi- ness atmosphere was smudged and sluggish. Less than a year after Columbia Center opened, Glenn appeared before its store managers, to explain what a really terrific area it was for retail business.

That may sound strange, but giving pep talks about the Tri-Cities has been Glenn's stock-in-trade ever since he arrived. It has been that kind of an area. "Maybe things aren't any better when I'm finished, but they feel better," Glenn says. And they do. He dotes on statistics and he backs up his facts with charts and graphs that visually lay out the Tri-City picture.

"We wear a mustard seed," said Don, referring to the pins Glenn handed out to some of his cohorts during the worst days of the strike, "but Glenn must be eating them."

"We are what we think," says Eldon Smith, who is now Glenn's assistant. And Glenn's theory is, "You can't argue with success."

There is much to reassure a listener when Glenn makes one of his speeches on the state of the Tri-City economy and its future. Glenn and Bob Philip bet on the Tri-Cities in 1947 and won big. They have both put a large share of their time in serving the region. And their newspaper operation is a hard-hitting, trim and business-like organization. Even if Glenn didn't have much to say, he has a way of saying it that would hold attention. However, there never has been a time that Glenn didn't have a lot to say.

There was one big, shining ray of hope for the Tri-Cities in the late 1960's and that was the beginning of private irrigation developments along the Columbia and Snake Rivers.

Ever since the white man reached the region he knew the land would be productive if he could get enough water on it. The water was there. But the economics of earlier developments were so shaky that the landscape was dotted with the mounds of old irrigation canals leading to nowhere, now, blown full of sand and grown over.

The big hope was Federal development, and the Columbia Basin Project, constructed after World War II, speaks to the success of that. But Federal reclamation languished in the 1960's and has continued to do so.

In the late 1960's, private interest in developing huge chunks of land began to appear. Wheat farmers, who had depended upon rain to nourish their dryland crop, began to diversify their crop by going to automatic circle sprinkler irrigation. The Universal Land Company entered the area and purchased land on the south side of the Snake River, east of Burbank, in the vicinity of Ice Harbor Dam. They built a pumping plant on the river, then leveled, planted and began irrigating thousands of acres of formerly arid land.

Throughout the region of Southeastern Washington and Northeastern Oregon there were other thousands of acres waiting for water, growing only bunch grass and sagebrush. The ability to pipe water for long distances and to pump it up to higher altitudes now existed. The whole region was ripe for development.

And now came the big blow—the Department of Interior issued an administrative order that the National Reclamation Act applied to private irrigation projects if they pumped from a Federal reservoir—no more than 160 acres per single ownership.

It was an incredible decision, but from Senator Scoop Jackson's office came a word of warning when Glenn began checking on where the decision came from, and why: "It might not be a wise thing to start to fight the opinion at this stage, as it might harden the position of the Interior Department; or, inject it into Congress and really mess it up, while the opinion could still be in a stage to be molded."

"How in the hell do you reverse it, if you sit on your hands and keep your mouth shut?" Glenn demanded.

At the same time, he appreciated Jackson's warning. Thus far it was an "opinion" issued after the Bureau of Management and Budget had asked why it was that irrigators were taking water from Federal reservoirs and not paying for it. The matter had arisen in the Upper Missouri River Basin where South Dakota irrigators had a Corps of Engineers easement to cross Federal land to reach the river for their pumping operation. When they sought to have it renewed, the Corps told them that the National Reclamation Act of 160 acres would apply. That, of course, ended the development.

A *Herald* editorial of October 20, 1969, by Bill Bequette, titled "Killing Irrigation," did an excellent job of summing up the picture:

"The dog-in-the-manger attitude towards Western reclamation that the Bureau of Reclamation is expounding must be overcome if there is to be any development at all.

"We can sympathize with the Bureau's dilemma. It has a file drawer full of feasible irrigation projects but no funds to put them into action. Furthermore, funds for reclamation have been in a steep decline for some years.

"It has been established it would take 40 years for the Bureau to catch up if the deadlock on reclamation funds was broken. But there is little likelihood it will be. Rep. Wayne Aspinall, D-Colo., chairman of the House Interior Committee, said in Spokane last week that reclamation is faring worse now than it was during his 25 years in Congress.

"But whereas we can sympathize with the Bureau's problem, for it truly is our problem also, we cannot sympathize with this dog-in-the-manger policy it seeks to enunciate.

"There are hundreds of thousands of acres within easy reach of the Columbia and Snake Rivers that can be developed by private irrigation. We are witnessing a move in this direction in the Mid-Columbia region.

"Large tracts of land have been developed along the Snake River, for example, at witness the K2H farms and Universal Land.

"In the K2H development, three longtime wheat farmers put up their land and U & I Sugar Company put up the money. Their first crop is being harvested this year.

"The Universal Land organization came here from California where urban sprawl and a lowering water table was pricing their land out of the farming market.

"A subsidiary of the Shell Oil Company is planning a multi-thousand acre irrigation development in the Boardman area of Oregon. It will pump from the Columbia River.

"Undeveloped land and abundance of water are the attractions. They estimate their cost when the land is ready to seed runs about $500 an acre. So a 10,000-acre development costs the farmer about $5 million.

"Alarmed because its funds from Washington, D.C., are drying up because of the emphasis private development is taking, the Bureau has countered by saying irrigation water pumped from waters impounded by federal dams comes under the National Reclamation Act. This would limit the individual ownership to 160 acres, which would be the death knell for private development.

"Senator Henry M. Jackson says the issue is a complex one. But not so complex, we believe, that a sensible solution cannot be worked out. The bureau's position doesn't make sense."

The threat to the region was obvious and the effects of the administrative order would have been lasting. Doubtless, the Tri-City region never could reach its full potential if this ruling wasn't rolled back.

As with so many of the things Glenn and the newspaper tackled, the portion that leaked through to the public was like the tip of an iceberg—the 10 percent that showed. Most of the effort, the planning, the devices, the writing, the talking, the telephoning and the traveling never reach the eyes or ears of the public.

News stories and editorials tried to keep the reader informed in the conventional newspaper sense. But the means by which *The Herald* organization caused changes to come about and obtained the facts for its stories was hardly by conventional journalism.

It is this extra dimension, this extra effort, that makes *The Herald* different from other newspapers. It doesn't merely write about momentous events that effect its community, it attempts to turn or shape the event to the advantage of the region. The 160-acre campaign is an example of this, just as was the Hanford Steam Plant campaign and the formation of the Tri-City Nuclear Industrial Council.

As so often happens, the average person isn't usually aware of the significance of orders, requests and rulings that swirl about him, even when these are spelled out in the news columns of his local paper. One of the frustrating things about newspapering is to cover a subject thoroughly and then later, when the full impact of the event strikes home, to have readers say, "Where was the newspaper on this? Why wasn't this explained to us?"

So it is essential that a newspaperman must be well informed on his community and able to react quickly to the things that effect it, regardless of how remote they may be. This isn't an easy rule to follow, but it reflects the vitality of the newspaper and the public awareness of its management.

Other newspapers in the Pacific Northwest carried stories on the 160-acre limitation and some carried editorials. Only *The Herald* involved itself in attempting to get the matter corrected.

One thing that helped is that Glenn established communications with Publisher R. B. Hipple of the *Daily Capital Journal* in Pierre, South Dakota. It was in Hipple's area that the limitation opinion first struck. Between them, they were able to coordinate efforts between two regions of the United States concerned with the same problem.

But the last thing the Tri-Cities needed at that time was stoppage of the one bright development in its economic picture. And private irrigation development plans had come to an instant stop when the 160-acre limitation was threatened. There was no means to arrange for financing, either for pumps and pipe or land acquisition or machinery and equipment. Nothing would move until the acreage limitation was cleared up.

Glenn's telephone line was hot. His calls jangled in the offices of Senators Magnuson and Jackson and Rep. Catherine May. He was in repeated contact with Governor Evans. When Evans was not available, Glenn worked closely with the governor's aides.

James R. Smith, Assistant Secretary of the Interior for Water and Power Development, was a key man. So was President Nixon's director of domestic affairs, John Ehrlichman, at the White House.

The story Glenn pumped to these people was the same— Hanford was being shut down, we were a long ways from market, we had no raw materials like iron and copper, we had high labor costs. All we wanted was to utilize our water, land and sunshine. We could pull ourselves up by the boot straps if we could borrow money and develop our land and use the water from our rivers.

The acreage limitation becomes a fascinating story when one reads the arguments made by the Pacific Northwest states against such a restriction. Water is vital to the West. Blood was shed time and again in the Old West over water holes. The water rights of individuals and states as well as Uncle Sam are imbedded in the law.

Don summed up *The Herald's* position in a November 18, 1969, editorial titled, "Let's Develop Our Own Assets." He wrote, in part:

"Assuming the so-called federal reservoirs created behind the dams do give Uncle Sam some rights on the water stored, the question must be answered as to what rights the states have.

"A Federal dam may create a reservoir, but God created the river. The states and the water were there long before the dams. Impounded or not, the basic water flow of the river continues to exist. Doesn't any of that flowage belong to the states?"

Said the director of the Washington State Department of Water Resources: "The position of the state is that there has been a historic flow in the rivers and we grant rights to withdraw water from this historic flow."

Glenn's activities were not confined to letters and the telephone. His trips took him to Olympia to see Governor Dan Evans, to Washington, D.C., for personal meetings with Department of Interior people and Ehrlichman, as well as congressional leaders. And he met in Oregon with Governor Tom McCall's chief aides.

"L. B. Day, who was regional coordinator for the Department of Interior under Jim Smith, was a key man," Glenn recalls. "I also had a meeting in Portland at which I prevailed upon Oregon Representatives Stafford Hansell and Irwin Mann to go with me because they knew L. B. Day personally."

Hansell, veteran member of the Oregon Legislature and chairman of its powerful Ways and Means Committee, was from Hermiston. Mann, another tower of strength in the legislature, later resigned to accept an appointment as Oregon Director of Agriculture.

Day was formerly with the Teamsters Union in Oregon. He ran for the legislature as a Democrat, but later switched over to the Republican side.

Hansell and Mann emphasized to him that all irrigation development in Northeast Oregon had stopped since the 160-acre limitation cloud was raised. Glenn described the situation in Southeastern Washington.

Day listened intently and after a long session in which the matter was fully explored, he promised to take it up with Assistant Secretary James Smith as soon as possible.

In a personal memorandum on the March, 1970, meeting, Glenn wrote:

"He promised he would give us an answer one way or the other on whether or not he thought something could be done.

"We urged that this situation not get into legislation,

that it not break out into the open, that it should be handled as a directive or an internal memorandum in the Department . . ."

The bite of all these meetings, telephone conversations, personal confrontations and the pounding of news stories and editorials, took their toll. But along with it, the Federal government took a position that infuriated the states and made them battle all the more intensely. This really broke into the open at a February 13 meeting in Portland when Oregon, Washington and Idaho officials met with J. Lane Morthland, associate solicitor from Washington, D.C., who handled Interior's presentation.

However, Morthland wasn't alone. Many Federal agencies—the Corps of Engineers, Bureau of Reclamation, to name two—were also present. The government's position, said Morthland, was this:

1. There is no natural flow in the river. All water is managed and controlled and stored.

2. Water stored behind a Corps of Engineers dam is Federal water and anyone who pumps such water is subject to the Reclamation Act, which limits irrigators to 160 acres.

That was a shocker for the Pacific Northwest. The position of the states shows how far apart the two sides were. Idaho, Oregon and Washington said:

1. There is a natural flow in the rivers. The rivers may be managed and controlled but the natural flow remains.

2. There is no "stored" water within the concept stated by Interior. The dams were constructed as power dams, not storage dams, and the reservoirs they created were not designed for irrigation but to insure a head of water for power production.

John Day Dam, on the lower stem of the Columbia River, was used as an example. It was debated before the dam was constructed whether or not it would be a storage dam. The decision was that it would not be for storage.

The meeting broke up with government officials appearing smug and state officials walking away, their heads shaking in disbelief. Don, who had sat in on the meeting and who wrote the story of the meeting in *The Herald*, was shaking his head, too.

The conclusion of his editorial, "Who Owns Our Rivers?" appeared February 16, and explained the problem as *The Herald* saw it:

"There were so many questions provoked, questions rooted deep in the traditions, the law and the history of the West. It is a deep, emotional subject—for nowhere but in the arid, parched lands of the West is water so treasured.

"Should only Uncle Sam develop the land? If the government's position is sustained, that will be the result. The government's legal representatives say they are obeying the law and that this is the will of Congress.

"Is this really what Congress means and intends? It appears that Congress should begin looking into this situation itself, for what is occurring has cast a suspicion over every major water right in the West."

The threat was great. Had the government's position not been relaxed most of the development that has come to the Mid-Columbia region of the Tri-Cities and Northeast Oregon would not now exist. *The Herald* truly was battling for the future.

However, not all readers were in accord with its strong editorial position and its intense coverage of the subject. One militant farm group, the National Farmer's Organization, was particularly incensed.

"We've already got an over supply of agricultural products, yet repeated attempts are being made to increase farmland and farm production," said Vance Combs, a Columbia Basin farmer and head of special commodities for the NFO in the six Western states.

In the vast Columbia Basin project, the farmers were limited to 160 acres. But even the Bureau of Reclamation had recognized that this was too severe a restriction. So a farmer and his wife could each own 160 acres. Many farmers worked other deals, either by leasing additional land or by developing added acreage for somebody else. This had its drawbacks, too. Often the pieces of land he was farming were not contiguous and farm equipment had to be hauled from one farm to another.

The farmers were also discovering it difficult to find a middle ground—a place in the farm economy where they could make a living without having to be too big, yet not so small that they couldn't amortize their investment in land, crop and equipment. Consequently, their lives proved to be a continual gamble and even some of the Columbia Basin's better farmers were sucked under by the quicksand of costs.

It is understandable why there should have been no love for the larger farm developers who started to enter the picture. Other farmers had visions of the newcomers absorbing the available market for farm products and, worse yet, providing a glut for it. Some didn't want more farmland developed.

As the situation turned out, the large farmers who developed their land in great tracts did not prove to be the threat that others had envisioned. They opened more processing plants, more markets and actually provided better markets for the smaller farmers. But in 1969 and 1970, when the bitter fighting over the 160-acre limitation proposal was being waged, farmers were hard-pressed to make ends meet. They wanted no more land put into production.

"The water is available to these people in the large developments because the taxpayers, through the Bureau of Reclamation, have raised the water level, stabalized the flow of the river and made it feasible for the large, independent land development companies to get to the water," the National Farm Organization claimed. "If the Columbia was still a free flowing stream it would not be feasible to pump from it because of fluctuation, the excessive life, and the silting situation."

It was a complicated and intense subject that lent itself to much generalization and overstatement. It was also easy to get away from the question of whether only the government could produce more farmland. A 160-acre restriction would rule out private development and leave the field open only to an agency like the Bureau of Reclamation, when even its concepts in farmland development are being subjected to review.

There was also the matter of the water rights of the states and the secondary uses of the water for such things as nuclear power plants or sewage treatment. And, finally, there was the overriding fear that somehow the Southwest states of America had manipulated the Department of Interior's thinking to delay any development in the Pacific Northwest until the 10-year moratorium established by Senator Jackson had expired.

The moratorium was placed into effect in 1968 to stop any plans for diversion of Columbia River water to other regions, until the Northwest could determine its own needs.

This was a rather remote possibility, however. The real reason the Interior Department developed such a memorandum decision on acreage limitation remains unknown.

The tremendous outpouring of protest and pressure generated by their action caused the Federal agency to back away. On April 28, 1970, Assistant Secretary of Interior Smith announced:

"It has been determined that the provisions of Federal reclamation law do not apply to a private irrigator when the water to be diverted is covered by a valid natural-flow water right under state law, and whose water supply is not dependent at any time during the irrigation season upon the existence or operation of Federal project facilities."

The Herald happily announced the story and quickly followed this with an editorial praising Smith for his action. Glenn had followed the situation so avidly and worked so hard on it that he got quite a surprise on May 1 from Publisher Hipple, in South Dakota. Hipple wrote to him:

"Thanks very much for your good letter and the copy of your news story of Monday. Incidentally, congratulations on scooping all the rest of the newspapers, including our own, which did not get the story until it was moved by the wire services on Wednesday.

"All of us in the Missouri Basin, of course, are greatly pleased that Secretary Smith has agreed with the position we have taken ever since it was first suggested that private irrigation operations might be subject to the Reclamation Law.

"It was surely of enormous help to have that position supported by your own people in the Columbia Basin. I am sure that you must take the same sense of personal satisfaction with the result of your personal effort that I do with respect to my own."

Glenn's satisfaction flowed chiefly from the feeling of relief in knowing that a great threat to private irrigation had been averted. Thousands of acres of arid land lying alongside two of the nation's mightiest rivers were just begging for water. Now they would get it.

19   *Epilogue*

THE YEARS went by so quickly. Our supposed brief stay in the Tri-Cities passed the 25-year mark. The children grew and, all too soon, began to move away, one by one. There is both sadness and satisfaction to that.

On its 25th birthday, *The Herald* didn't resemble that first issue which now, neatly framed and like a prized baby picture, hangs on our recreation room wall with other mementoes of those trying, but wonderful, years.

Some big newspaper lessons had been learned, and often relearned. Experience can be profitable and *The Herald* gained much from its harsh lessons. Now, strong and confident, it has acquired stature and is a major factor in its region. On Thanksgiving Day in 1947, it was understandable that someone might ask Don, "What is the *Tri-City Herald?*" No one asks that question anymore. *The Herald* is established and its reputation and influence reaches beyond its circulation boundaries.

Not only has the influence of its newspaper spread far out, but so, too, has the influence of the Tri-Cities. They are large, stable and growing. *The Herald* is home delivered many miles away in Columbia Basin communities like Othello and Warden; in Oregon, to Hermiston, Umatilla and Boardman; and, in the Yakima Valley.

It has three bureaus—in Hermiston, Sunnyside, and Othello—and three daily editions. In 1955, *The Herald* purchased a press from the *Minneapolis Star and Tribune*. It is now a larger press, for two additional units have been added to increase its capacity and three color units, plus paper reels and tensions. *#1

Everything about *The Herald* is bigger. It started with 25 people. Now the payroll is 150, with 40 in the editorial department alone. This department expanded in 1966 to a large news room with glassed-in offices, upstairs over the composing room. The room seemed huge then. Six years later, when the 25th November 13 for *The Herald* came around, the room was already snug. This is true with the rest of the plant.

Glenn enjoys saying "We're doing business in a barn,

*#1/The Scott Press, purchased in 1955 from the Minneapolis *Star Tribune* originally consisted of five units four plates wide, a double folder, one unit reversible and one color cylinder. It was possible to run a page of advertising in black and three colors.

Additional equipment has since been purchased. A black unit (16 pages of capacity) was obtained from Rockford, Illinois, plus another color cylinder. This unit and a color cylinder added, gave the press tremendous capacity of up to 64 pages and full color, plus 14 other positions available in one press.

Later another color cylinder was purchased from Santa Rosa, California, and other spare parts and press equipment were obtained from Rochester, Minnesota. When the *Wall Street Journal* plant at Riverside, California, changed to offset, reels and tensions for handling newsprint underneath *The Herald's* press were obtained. Newsprint roll changes now are made automatically. The press never stops, saving substantial time with each press.

Additional press cylinders and folder equipment were also obtained from the *Press-Enterprise* at Riverside, giving a plentiful supply of parts and equipment.

Another color cylinder has been erected and another black unit "reversed." So *The Herald* has a great maximum capacity for color work, full pages and three colors, double trucks and three colors, up to 80-page capacity in any given press run. *The Herald* publishes over two million lines of color annually.

On an average, the press runs are "double plated" three days a week and single plated three days a week. In the Spring of 1975 all stereotype equipment was purchased from the *Everett Herald*. As other newspapers have changed from the conventional hot metal system to offset, other equipment has been purchased for *The Herald's* plant to give it a maximum high-speed production, and adequate backup in case of emergencies. This is true throughout the composing room, the stereotype and casting department, and in the mail room. *The Herald* is one of the best equipped "hot-metal" newspapers in the country in its circulation bracket.

Glenn's theory is to produce a well-printed newspaper, on time, and have the mechanical capacity to make over a page each day for the Oregon edition, the Yakima Valley edition, and the Tri-Cities, plus making over the stock page, 500 New York stocks, high and low closing quotes at 1 p.m., New York time, and again at 3 p.m., to give *Herald* readers the latest and best news possible.

Immediately next door to the original Kennewick plant, additional warehousing and land has been purchased to store newsprint, spare press parts and other general supplies. For future parking, and/or future expansion, an additional square block of land has been bought by *The Herald*. Immediately across the street from *The Herald* the purchase of the Twin City Creamery building and property on Cascade Street was completed in 1973. This building will be used by larger engraving facilities and will be the future location of the circulation department and accounting office. It will take care of growth and expansion which is on the drawing boards and in construction stages in *The Herald's* circulation territory.

down by the railroad tracks." *The Herald* plant, however, is no longer the barn-like facility that it was in October, 1948, when the paper began publishing in Kennewick. Every corner of the building is being utilized and it has been expanded several times.

The Herald's most satisfying circulation moves were the ones it made into Hermiston and the Yakima Valley. It had head-to-head confrontations with long established newspapers in those areas. Yet *The Herald* quickly added circulation.

The lesson it learned was to never take your traditional areas for granted. Never lose contact or appear unresponsive to them. *The Herald* went into both areas with five-year programs. It expected hard sledding in its efforts to take a part of the market.

A sign of things to come was indicated during one of Don's first trips into Hermiston. He was given a tour by one of the city's leaders. "In Pendleton," the man said sarcastically, "they think there are only two things—Jesus Christ and the Roundup."

Three years later, when *Herald* representatives moved into Sunnyside, people shook hands with them, clapped them on the back and said, "We're glad you're here. Maybe this will wake up Yakima."

The important point, of course, is not whether the Yakima Valley and Hermiston areas were neglected by the newspapers that had been serving them. It is that many of the people in those areas felt they had second-class status. Resentment usually builds towards the largest city in the county. The task of working to ease such feelings is a continual one. To neglect it, is to encourage it.

When it was decided to go into Oregon, Glenn asked the department heads to predict how many subscribers *The Herald* would gain in three years. Each man put down a number. The figures ran from 500 to 1,500.

Glenn predicted 1,000. He was delighted eventually to find he had been conservative. The figure was 2,000 and after three years is still growing.

New subscribers did not come easily. It meant hard work, intense promotion and good news coverage. *The Herald's* subscription campaigns always received strong backup from the news staff.

"Getting the paper into the home is one thing," Eldon Smith reminded everyone. "Keeping it there is something else."

So *The Herald* urgently endeavored to give the best coverage and service. As a result, once it got into the home, it usually stayed.

There was a difference though, in its early efforts to spread from the Tri-Cities into the surrounding areas of Benton and Franklin Counties.

During the fierce days of the strike, attempts to reach out with circulation resulted in many union-inspired problems. The ITU stepped up harassment activities to prevent people from taking the paper or newspaper carriers from delivering it. Newspaper bundles that went north into Franklin County were sent by railroad to Eltopia and Connell.

The railroad unions, of course, were sympathetic to the ITU. In addition, there was that residue of bitterness toward *The Herald* that existed in Pasco—where most of the railroaders lived—because it had moved to Kennewick. Time and again, as the Northern Pacific train sped into the county, *Herald* bundles would "accidentally" fall under the train's wheels, and shredded bits of paper would scatter across the countryside.

Circulation workers were continually being rushed out to replace lost newspapers. The trip by rail became so costly and frustrating that it was abandoned and the bundles were shipped by truck.

In those days, it seemed we always talked about the farms in the Columbia Basin, but the farms didn't develop rapidly. The work of the Federal Bureau of Reclamation came first. There appeared to be quite a gap in time before farmers began settling the land.

Glenn and Clarence Gossen, mechanical superintendent,
view an additional unit for the Scott press, purchased from
the Minneapolis Star Tribune in 1955. This unit arrived in
1965.

Glenn holds up his gift to departing Sports Editor, Charles Van Sickel at a luncheon, 1968. Van Sickel started his own logging operation in Montana.

Herald employees gathered (1965) for the joint birthday celebration of Jack Gillis, advertising manager, and Mrs. Hill (Ursula) Williams, society editor. From left are: Don, Virginia Tully, Jack Gillis, Catherine Kelso, Opal Graber, Donna Malstrom, Esther Knowles, Claudine Kimble, Sue Butner, Roy Stapleton, partially hidden behind Grace Updike, Ann McColley, Tiny Wright, Gordon Moen, and Charlene Davis. Gertrude Arnold, Glenn's secretary, is beside Ursula.

One of the wise things *The Herald* did, however, was to send the paper into the Columbia Basin areas of Franklin County long before it was economically feasible to deliver there. Such circulation was expensive, but Glenn adopted the long-range view. He foresaw the day when all the farm units would be settled.

It was a slow process, but as the farm areas began to fill with people, the demand persisted for *The Herald* to penetrate even deeper into the county. Residents, especially many members of the Mormon Church, offered to get their own motor route drivers to insure delivery of the paper. One Mormon leader, Bill Rigby, was active in this group. The circulation in the Basin, in northern Franklin County, began with 25 subscribers. Today, it numbers over 2,500.

The community that proved most difficult for *The Herald* to penetrate was Prosser, seat of Benton County and the most likely place for the county's only daily newspaper to circulate.

Several things contributed to the resistance. Perhaps, in a way, *The Herald* encountered a reverse psychology from that which helped it years later during its drives into the Yakima Valley and Oregon.

Prosser was the largest community in the county before World War II. In 1955, when *The Herald* commenced its circulation effort there, Prosser was among the county's small cities. Richland and Kennewick had completely outdistanced it.

Sitting off by itself, at one end of the county, Prosser was also nervous about the courthouse, which is one of its economic mainstays. Rumors continually flew that an attempt would be made to move the county seat to the more populous Tri-Cities. Ex-Kennewick *Courier-Reporter* publisher Ralph Reed was a leader in an unsuccessful move to do just that. So Prosser was suspicious of the controversial *Tri-City Herald*.

Prosser is also located at one end of the Yakima Valley, just a stone's throw from Grandview and Sunnyside. It enjoyed close relationships with Yakima County communities. It also depended upon the Yakima newspapers for the daily news. For local news it had the weekly Prosser *Record-Bulletin*. In 1955 Prosser related more to Yakima than to the Tri-Cities.

The *Herald's* first efforts to circulate in Prosser almost failed. It took much hard sell and several years before *Herald* circulation began to match its Yakima competition. Reading habits are difficult to change and in the middle 1950's there wasn't much about the Tri-Cities to entice Prosser readers.

Mrs. Cormac (Inez) Thompson was hired in 1957 to represent the paper. A longtime resident of Prosser, her husband is an architect and was a member of the city council. Inez proved a hard worker and a good promoter. She recruited carriers, supervised circulation and worked tirelessly on her news stories. Little by little The Herald began to progress.

Glenn has always credited *The Herald's* success to people. Machines are important and necessary, he says, but all newspapers have these. It is the staff, their dedication, loyalty and overall competence that makes the difference.

Through all of its travail in finding workers. *The Herald* was always fortunate in having a strong basic organization that remained unshakeable. Over the years there has been a turnover in people. Yet surprisingly, the smallest turnover occurred during the years when the paper suffered its hardest times. Perhaps it was that people felt their need and responded. Undoubtedly, too, their constancy during these times was motivated by pride and respect in the stance their paper was taking.

I can't mention all of those who have come and gone, but a few of the staffers most remembered, other than those already noted, are: Ellen Turner, photo technician; Ralph Smith and Ralph Worsham, photographers; Charles Van Sickel, Don Becker, Gil Gilmore and Tom Burnside, all sports writers and sports editors; Wally Knief and Hill

Williams, Richland reporters; Charles Lamb, feature writer and columnist; reporters Malcolm MacNey, Matt Miletich; Jim Grant and Barrie Hartman, now managing editor of the Eugene, Ore., *Register-Guard.* Ragnar Nowakowski, who like Hill Williams, became an expert on Hanford, returned to the staff in 1973 after several years with the Atomic Energy Commission and as a Congressional press secretary. Also Harold Carr, sports writer.

Mrs. Jerry Dunwoody and Mrs. Esther Knowles retired after many years as woman's page writers. Helen Jones Wheeler also wrote woman's page copy during the early years. Cathy Kelso came to *The Herald* as a photo lab technician in 1957 to begin a long period of service.

Two who were to play key roles in the success of the paper were Bill Klink, now managing editor, and Jack Briggs, associate editor and columnist. Jack came in December, 1960, and Bill arrived in August, 1961. Some of the other "class of the 1960's" were Pat Bushey, political writer and now managing editor of the Klamath Falls, Ore., *News-Herald;* Bob Wherry, special writer and former regional editor; Carroll Clark, editorial writer and Terence Day, farm writer.

Throughout the rest of the plant, the number of employes is too numerous to list. I will mention the old timers such as Stanley Sojka and Kivas Tully, who were with the original group to replace the strikers in 1950. Kivas' wife, Virginia, worked in the business office and became business manager in 1959.

Others on the mechanical side who have been with *The Herald* are: Larry Benjamin, former mechanical superintendent; Chuck Carey, printer, 1953; Clarence Gossen, who started as a machinist in 1952 and became mechanical superintendent in 1969 when Robert Yeiter left. Gossen's assistant, Jerry Tinker, 1957; and Carl Poole, commercial plant superintendent from 1952 to May, 1970, when he retired. He was replaced by Art Claxton.

Getting away from the mechanical end, other old timers are Opal Graber, advertising, who arrived in 1957, and

351

Ann McColley, Sue Butner, Grace Updyke, circulation, 1952; Tiny Wright, advertising, 1952; Glenn's secretary, Gertrude Arnold, 1960; Kip Tenley, advertising, 1962; Charlene Davis, 1960; Donna Malstrom, 1960; Claudine Kimble, 1952, and Minta DePue, all business office. In the advertising department, mainstays have been Gordon Moen and James Reid, now advertising director.

It is satisfying to watch the progress of the younger staff members. Jim Philip, Bob's son, began as an intern while an undergraduate at the University of Washington. He is now political writer. Jim began as a regular reporter in December, 1967. *The Herald* also provided him with a wife, the former Kristi Henderson, a product of the U of W who joined the news staff from college.

In 1967, Eldon Smith moved into advertising from circulation when Jack Gillis retired. Eldon was replaced by Larry Thomas, who started in the circulation department while at Pasco High.

This brings us to 1975. And what of the future for *Tri-City Herald* and the communities it serves?

Glenn feels that irrigated farming will continue to develop and its impact on the growth of the region will be very substantial. He also sees Hanford as a nuclear energy center, especially if it should be the site of a fuels enrichment plant. These should double *The Herald's* circulation in the next 15 years. In the next 25, he predicts a total of 75,000 subscribers.

New food processing and cold storage plants will further boost the region's population and bring additional retail stores.

"We were just laying the foundation during the first 25 years," Glenn says. "The next quarter century will be twice as spectacular. I hope I'll be around to see it."

The future does indeed look bright. Somehow though, it will be difficult for the years ahead to ever overshadow the colorful past. As Don said in 1947, "Anybody can work for a daily newspaper, but how many guys get to start one?"